THE GOSPEL OF LUKE

Explorations in Christian Scripture

ED GALLAGHER

HERITAGE
CHRISTIAN UNIVERSITY
PRESS

The Gospel of Luke: Explorations in Christian Scripture

Copyright © 2022 by Ed Gallagher

Cataloging-in-Publication Data

Gallagher, Ed (Edmon Louis), 1979-

The Gospel of Luke: explorations in Christian Scripture / Ed Gallagher

Cypress Bible Study series

p. cm.

ISBN 978-1-956811-08-7 (pbk) 978-1-956811-09-4 (ebook)

Library of Congress Control Number: 2021923358

1. Bible. Luke—Criticism, interpretation, etc. I. Author. II. Title. III. Series.

226.406—dc20

Cover design by Brad McKinnon and Brittany Vander Maas.
For more information:

Heritage Christian University Press
PO Box HCU
3625 Helton Drive
Florence, AL 35630

www.hcu.edu/publications

For Miriam,
with much love and admiration

CONTENTS

PREFACE

The Third Gospel has never been the most popular. In the early church and probably still today, that award goes to Matthew and John, with Luke coming in at number three. (Sorry, Mark!) Luke was probably also the third Gospel written. But it does earn the top prize in the category of number of words: the Third Gospel is the longest, containing the most material about Jesus. Moreover, Luke's Gospel contains some of the favorite passages for many Christians, including probably the two most popular parables: the Good Samaritan and the Prodigal Son. It's also from Luke's Gospel that we have our only canonical story about Jesus as an adolescent, and Luke's is the only Gospel that narrates the Ascension. If you want to find what Jesus said about prayer, your best bet is to turn to Luke. If you want to get people to donate to a cause, turn to Luke, which has more teaching about money than any other Gospel. If you want to think about how Jesus reached out to sinners, you need to study Luke. I don't know whether the book you are holding will make Luke's Gospel your favorite biography of Jesus, but I hope this book will help you appreciate the Third Gospel's place in our Bibles more than you have before.

This series of studies on Luke was written for Bible class teachers. As with my previous volumes in the Cypress Bible Study Series, I wrote the following chapters for a specific set of Bible class teachers: the ones covering the adult classes at Sherrod Avenue Church of Christ (Florence, AL). These lessons were written during the winter of 2019/20. I want to thank Greg Sharp, Paul Newton, Rick Hamm, and Dusty Wear for teaching this material in its first incarnation.

When I quote the Bible in this book, I usually use the NRSV, sometimes the KJV or other translations. But whenever I include a quotation of the Old Testament (in whatever translation), you'll see the word YHWH instead of "the LORD" (which is used in every major English translation). I've made this substitution mostly to remind you that when you see "the LORD" in your Bibles, that phrase corresponds to a name in the Hebrew Bible, and that name is spelled with the consonants YHWH, probably to be pronounced Yahweh. Translating God's name with "the Lord" instead of using the actual name is a practice that goes back a long way, all the way back to the first translation of the Hebrew Bible, the Greek Septuagint, which was translated before the birth of Jesus. The use of "Lord" in Greek (the Greek word is κύριος, *kurios*) for the name of God probably has implications for the identity of Jesus, who is called *kurios* in the New Testament. I have explored these issues elsewhere.[1] But this topic also relates to Luke's Gospel in a special way, since this Third Gospel—more than the other three—refers to Jesus as "Lord" (*kurios*). Nevertheless, as I said, you'll see YHWH in the Old Testament quotations in this book.

One difference between this book and previous volumes in this series is the inclusion of a discussion guide. I've always included discussion questions, but here I have also provided a guide for thinking about those questions. This guide is not

---

[1] Ed Gallagher, *The Book of Exodus: Explorations in Christian Theology*, Cypress Bible Study Series (Florence, AL: HCU Press, 2019), ch. 2.

supposed to provide the right answers, but is simply supposed to help you see how I think about these questions. You will often probably come up with better ways of thinking about them.

I offer my appreciation to Jamie Cox, Brad McKinnon, and Brittany Vander Maas for their help bringing this book to print. Once again, they have done excellent work in a remarkably brief time. It is my pleasure to work with them.

My wonderful wife, Jodi, has put up with me now for nearly 22 years, and she manages to make life incredibly enjoyable. If for no other reason, having her in my life assures me that God will require much from me (Luke 12:48). My children—Miriam, Evelyn, Josiah, Jasmine, Marvin, and Elizabeth—add great happiness and fun to our lives. As she nears high school graduation and contemplates her college choice, my oldest child, Miriam, is especially in my thoughts. She will soon leave our home. It has been a unique blessing to be her father and admire up close her growth as a human being, as a young woman, as an imitator of Jesus. I have no doubt that she will live a life in service to God, though I don't yet know what form that will take. It is my pleasure to dedicate this book to her.

Bible Abbreviations

Old Testament

Gen	Genesis
Exod	Exodus
Lev	Leviticus
Num	Numbers
Deut	Deuteronomy
Josh	Joshua
Judg	Judges
Ruth	Ruth
1–2 Sam	1–2 Samuel
1–2 Kgs	1–2 Kings
1–2 Chr	1–2 Chronicles
Ezra	Ezra
Neh	Nehemiah
Esth	Esther
Job	Job
Ps	Psalms
Prov	Proverbs

Eccl	Ecclesiastes
Song	Song of Solomon
Isa	Isaiah
Jer	Jeremiah
Lam	Lamentations
Ezek	Ezekiel
Dan	Daniel
Hos	Hosea
Joel	Joel
Amos	Amos
Obad	Obadiah
Jonah	Jonah
Mic	Micah
Nah	Nahum
Hab	Habakkuk
Zeph	Zephaniah
Hag	Haggai
Zech	Zechariah
Mal	Malachi

New Testament

Matt	Matthew
Mark	Mark
Luke	Luke
John	John
Acts	Acts
Rom	Romans
1–2 Cor	1–2 Corinthians
Gal	Galatians
Eph	Ephesians
Phil	Philippians

Col	Colossians
1–2 Thess	1–2 Thessalonians
1–2 Tim	1–2 Timothy
Titus	Titus
Phlm	Philemon
Heb	Hebrews
Jas	James
1–2 Pet	1–2 Peter
1–2–3 John	1–2–3 John
Jude	Jude
Rev	Revelation

THE GOSPEL OF LUKE

Introduction to Luke

None of the Gospels name their authors in the text. The traditional titles (Gospel according to Matthew; Gospel according to Mark; etc.) are known from the Greek manuscripts of the Gospels and from our earliest sources that mention them, going back to the second century. The Gospels never circulated under any other names (as far as we know); in other words, the Gospel we know as "according to Matthew" was never attributed to Thomas, or Peter, or Paul, but always Matthew. That doesn't necessarily mean that the attribution to Matthew is correct, but it is consistent. The same holds true for Mark and Luke and John. It is still possible that these attributions are simply guesses by early readers, but they are odd guesses (why would someone guess at Mark, or Luke?), and if they were simply guesses one would think that different people would propose different

4 / The Gospel of Luke

authors. The consistency (and oddness) of the attribution is a point in favor of the authenticity of the tradition.[1]

About Luke and John, there is a little more to say. The Fourth Gospel never names its author, but it does name "the Beloved Disciple" as the source of its material (John 21:24). Presumably the original audience would have known the identity of this disciple. As for the Third Gospel, the author names an addressee, Theophilus (Luke 1:3). Not only would the author have been known to Theophilus but most likely his name would have been attached to the book originally.

If the author is Luke, we still know very little about him. The name "Luke" appears in only three passages in the New Testament.

> Colossians 4:14, "Luke, the beloved physician, and Demas greet you."

> 2 Timothy 4:11, "Only Luke is with me. Get Mark and bring him with you, for he is useful in my ministry."

---

[1] For an argument that the traditional titles in the manuscripts are very early, see Martin Hengel, *The Four Gospels and the One Gospel of Jesus Christ* (Harrisburg, PA: Trinity Press International, 2000); Graham N. Stanton, *Jesus and Gospel* (Cambridge: Cambridge University Press, 2004). For more on the titles in the manuscripts, see Simon J. Gathercole, "The Titles of the Gospels in the Earliest New Testament Manuscripts," *Zeitschrift für die neutestamentliche Wissenschaft* 104 (2013): 33–76, available online: http://khazarzar.skeptik.net/books/titles.pdf.

Philemon 23–24, "Epaphras, my fellow prisoner
in Christ Jesus, sends greetings to you, and so do
Mark, Aristarchus, Demas, and Luke, my fellow
workers."

It is the passage in Colossians that suggests that Luke may
be a Gentile, since he seems to be separated from "those of the
circumcision" (Col 4:11). These passages also show that Luke was
a companion to Paul, which is consistent with the author of the
Third Gospel, who was also apparently a companion of Paul.
That last suggestion is based on two propositions: (1) the Third
Gospel and Acts were written by the same person—as almost all
scholars acknowledge, and as a comparison of Luke 1:1–4 and
Acts 1:1–2 validates; and (2) the author of Acts traveled with
Paul, as attested by the "We Passages" in Acts, that is, the
passages in which the author narrates as if he himself were a part
of the action. "When he had seen the vision, we immediately
tried to cross over to Macedonia" (Acts 16:10).[2]

At any rate, whoever the author was, I will use the
traditional name and refer to him as Luke.[3]

Counting the Gospel and Acts together, Luke was
responsible for more of the New Testament than any other

---

[2] For the "We Passages," see Acts 16:10–17; 20:5–15; 21:1–18; 27:1–28:16.

[3] For a comprehensive evaluation of the tradition of Luke as author of the
Third Gospel, see F. J. Foakes Jackson and Kirsopp Lake, eds., *The
Beginnings of Christianity*, part 1: *The Acts of the Apostles*, vol. 2:
Prolegomena II: Criticism (London: Macmillan, 1922), 207–359.

author. Luke and Acts together make up about 28% of the New Testament by word count.[4]

The Structure of the Gospel

As we will see in the next section, the Gospel of Luke—or, more properly, the Gospel (of Jesus) according to Luke—has the same basic structure as the other Gospels: from the baptism of Jesus to his death and resurrection, with teaching and miracles in between. It is now widely recognized that the way this story is told is similar to the way ancient people wrote biographies.[5] So while the Gospels may not conform to our expectations for biographies—since they concentrate on only a small slice of Jesus's life—ancient readers would have classified them as biographies.

Within that basic structure shared by all the Gospels, each Gospel has some unique elements. One obvious difference is where they all choose to begin telling their story. Mark begins with the ministry of John the Baptist, leading immediately to the baptism of Jesus, which is the start of Jesus's ministry. Matthew, instead, begins with the birth of Jesus. Luke begins with the birth

---

[4] Joel B. Green, *The Theology of the Gospel of Luke* (Cambridge: Cambridge University Press, 1995), 2n5, gives the following statistics, based on the third edition of the United Bible Societies' Greek New Testament: New Testament word count, 137,888; Luke-Acts, 37,951; thirteen canonical Pauline letters, 32,429.

[5] Richard Burridge, *What Are the Gospels? A Comparison with Graeco-Roman Biography*, 25th Anniversary Edition (Waco, TX: Baylor University Press, 2018).

of John the Baptist. And John begins before creation, identifying Jesus with the eternal Word of God.

For Luke, the big question is whether the author intended from the first to write a two-volume work (Luke and Acts) or whether the idea to write the history of the church after Jesus's resurrection came to Luke only after completing his Gospel. Most scholars these days think that Luke had the full work in mind from the beginning, so much so that scholars are in the habit of referring to the complete work as Luke-Acts to indicate its unity. An influential early scholar who argued for this position more than eighty years ago was Henry Cadbury, who wrote that Luke and Acts "are not merely two independent writings from the same pen; they are a single continuous work. Acts is neither an appendix nor an afterthought. It is probably an integral part of the author's original plan and purpose."[6] He suggested that (on analogy with other similar multi-volume ancient works) we should perhaps call the two volumes *To Theophilus I* and *To Theophilus II*, but Cadbury eventually settles on a minor tweaking of the traditional titles by just adding the hyphen, Luke-Acts.[7] If Cadbury is right and Luke did plan out his work as including Acts from the beginning, it may be that in writing his Gospel he highlighted certain themes that would come up again in Acts, or perhaps he omitted certain themes because he knew

---

[6] Henry J. Cadbury, *The Making of Luke-Acts*, 2d ed. (London: SPCK, 1958), 8–9.

[7] There has been some resistance to this way of looking at Luke and Acts; see Andrew F. Gregory and C. Kavin Rowe, eds., *Rethinking the Unity and Reception of Luke and Acts* (Columbia, SC: University of South Carolina Press, 2010).

he would address them in Acts. For instance, Luke generally (not completely) portrays the apostles more positively than does Mark or Matthew, and maybe that's because they would play such a big (and positive) role in Acts. Also, the Third Gospel contains fewer interactions between Jesus and Gentiles, and more between Jesus and Samaritans, perhaps because of the way these themes would feature in Acts.

But now limiting ourselves to Luke's Gospel, we notice a unique structure. Not quite halfway through the Gospel, there is a major transition at Luke 9:51: "When the days drew near for him to be taken up, he set his face to go to Jerusalem." Jesus actually arrives in Jerusalem (the Triumphal Entry) at the end of ch. 19, so he is on his way to Jerusalem for about ten chapters. This is Luke's Travel Narrative. A few times during the Travel Narrative, Luke reminds his readers that Jesus is still heading toward Jerusalem (13:22; 17:11). It is in this section that there appears much of the material that is unique to Luke.

So the Gospel has this basic structure.

Preface (1:1–4)
Preparation (1:5–4:13)
Ministry in Galilee (4:14–9:50), with much material paralleling Mark
Travel Narrative (9:51–19:28), with much unique material
Passion/Resurrection Narrative (19:29–24:53)

THE SYNOPTIC PROBLEM[8]

The first three Gospels are called "Synoptic Gospels" because their many parallel passages can easily be arranged in a synopsis to show the similarities and differences among their narrations of the same stories. The Gospel of John, on the other hand, is wholly different, not only in the stories it tells but in its structure (with frequent festivals providing much of the setting) and geographical emphasis (Jesus is in Judea most of the time, not Galilee). The Synoptic Gospels all have their differences, of course, but they are all structured more-or-less the same: narrating the baptism of Jesus near the beginning of the Gospel, telling about the ministry of Jesus in Galilee—including his teaching in parables, his casting out demons (neither demons nor parables appear in John), his appointment of twelve disciples as his special envoys, his preaching the immanence of the kingdom of God (another theme largely absent from John)—and then describing his journey to Jerusalem for Passover, where he would be crucified and then resurrected from the dead.

The three Synoptic Gospels tell this story so similarly that scholars have assumed that there must be some literary relationship among the three, that is, one must have used the other(s) as a source. The passage about John the Baptist provides a good illustration of the issues.[9]

---

[8] A full comparison of material in Luke with Matthew and Mark is located in Appendix C: Color-Coded Synopsis.

[9] Note that in the chart below I have rearranged vv. 4–5 of Matthew 3 in order to match Mark's arrangement.

Matthew 3	Mark 1	Luke 3
[1]In those days John the Baptist appeared in the wilderness of Judea, proclaiming, [2]"Repent, for the kingdom of heaven has come near."	[4]John the baptizer appeared in the wilderness, proclaiming a baptism of repentance for the forgiveness of sins.	[3]He went into all the region around the Jordan, proclaiming a baptism of repentance for the forgiveness of sins,
[5]Then the people of Jerusalem and all Judea were going out to him, and all the region along the Jordan, [6]and they were baptized by him in the river Jordan, confessing their sins.	[5]And people from the whole Judean countryside and all the people of Jerusalem were going out to him, and were baptized by him in the river Jordan, confessing their sins.	
[4]Now John wore clothing of camel's hair with a leather belt around his waist, and his food was locusts and wild honey.	[6]Now John was clothed with camel's hair, with a leather belt around his waist, and he ate locusts and wild honey.	

[7]But when he saw many Pharisees and Sadducees coming for baptism, he said to them, "You brood of vipers! Who warned you to flee from the wrath to come?		[7]John said to the crowds that came out to be baptized by him, "You brood of vipers! Who warned you to flee from the wrath to come?
[8]Bear fruit worthy of repentance. [9]Do not presume to say to yourselves, 'We have Abraham as our ancestor'; for I tell you, God is able from these stones to raise up children to Abraham.		[8]Bear fruits worthy of repentance. Do not begin to say to yourselves, 'We have Abraham as our ancestor'; for I tell you, God is able from these stones to raise up children to Abraham.
[10]Even now the ax is lying at the root of the trees; every tree therefore that does not bear good fruit is cut down and thrown into the fire.		[9]Even now the ax is lying at the root of the trees; every tree therefore that does not bear good fruit is cut down and thrown into the fire.

		¹⁰And the crowds asked him, "What then should we do?" ¹¹In reply he said to them, "Whoever has two coats must share with anyone who has none; and whoever has food must do likewise." ¹²Even tax collectors came to be baptized, and they asked him, "Teacher, what should we do?" ¹³He said to them, "Collect no more than the amount prescribed for you." ¹⁴Soldiers also asked him, "And we, what should we do?" He said to them, "Do not extort money from anyone by threats or false accusation, and be

		satisfied with your wages."
		¹⁵As the people were filled with expectation, and all were questioning in their hearts concerning John, whether he might be the Messiah,
¹¹"I baptize you with water for repentance, but one who is more powerful than I is coming after me; I am not worthy to carry his sandals. He will baptize you with the Holy Spirit and fire.	⁷He proclaimed, "The one who is more powerful than I is coming after me; I am not worthy to stoop down and untie the thong of his sandals. ⁸I have baptized you with water; but he will baptize you with the Holy Spirit."	¹⁶John answered all of them by saying, "I baptize you with water; but one who is more powerful than I is coming; I am not worthy to untie the thong of his sandals. He will baptize you with the Holy Spirit and fire.
¹²His winnowing fork is in his hand, and he will clear his threshing floor and will gather his wheat into the		¹⁷His winnowing fork is in his hand, to clear his threshing floor and to gather the wheat into his

granary; but the chaff he will burn with unquenchable fire.		granary; but the chaff he will burn with unquenchable fire.

Here we have some material that is shared among all three Gospels, some material that is shared by Matthew and Luke but not Mark, and some material that is unique to Luke. The only major category of material in these three Gospels that is not represented by this passage is material unique to Matthew, but if we kept reading in the immediately following verses, we would find some such material, since Matthew narrates the baptism of Jesus in a distinctive way. On the other hand, there is hardly any material unique to Mark—not just in this passage but for the entire Gospel; almost the entirety of Mark is paralleled in Matthew and/or Luke.

As I mentioned earlier, the nature of the similarities among the Synoptic Gospels suggests to most (all?) people that the later Gospel writers must have used the earlier Gospels as a source. For the past couple centuries, most (not all)[10] scholars who have studied the issue have determined that Mark was the first Gospel written, and that both Matthew and Luke used Mark as a source.[11] The reason for thinking that Mark must have come first and not the other way around is that Mark is shorter, and Mark's language is less sophisticated. It would have been odd for

---

[10] See Wikipedia, "Two-Gospel Hypothesis." This is also called the Griesbach Hypothesis.
[11] See Wikipedia, "Marcan Priority."

someone to take a longer and more polished Gospel and to cut material out and make its language less polished.

But what about the material shared by Matthew and Luke but not Mark? Did Matthew use Luke alongside Mark, or did Luke use Matthew alongside Mark? I'm not sure that anyone has ever thought that Matthew used Luke, but the idea that Luke used Matthew (and Mark) does have some adherents and seems to be gaining in popularity over the past several decades.[12] It could be relevant that Luke mentions that "many" had already undertaken to write accounts of Jesus's life before he did (Luke 1:1).

If it is not the case that Luke used Matthew, then where did they both get the same non-Marcan material? It could be that there was some other written source available to Matthew and Luke that has subsequently been lost. This is the Q-hypothesis.[13] The letter Q stands for the German word *Quelle*, meaning "source." It is hypothetical, based on guesswork, but educated guesswork. Most of the material that Matthew and Luke share that is not in Mark—that is, most of the Q material—is "sayings" material, especially sayings from Jesus. So the idea is that maybe there was an early collection of the sayings of Jesus, and maybe Matthew and Luke both had access to this collection.[14]

So just to summarize: almost everybody would say that Mark was the first Gospel, but there are some who wouldn't. Among those who do hold to Marcan Priority, there are two

---

[12] See Wikipedia, "Farrer Hypothesis."

[13] See Wikipedia, "Q Source."

[14] On the Q material in Luke, see C. F. Evans, *Saint Luke*, TPI New Testament Commentaries (Philadelphia: Trinity Press International, 1990), 21–26. He discusses various proposals for Luke using Matthew, ultimately settling on the Q hypothesis.

main ways of explaining how Matthew and Luke have so much common material that is not in Mark: most believe that Matthew and Luke used some other document consisting mostly of the sayings of Jesus (Q), but others think that Luke used Matthew (the Farrer Hypothesis). I myself do accept Marcan Priority, but I am not sure whether Q or the Farrer Hypothesis makes most sense.

Luke does not include all of Mark's material, but he does use Mark's Gospel for the basic storyline.[15] Here is a list of material in Mark omitted by Luke.

> Sections of Mark omitted in Luke
> (sections marked * also omitted in Matthew)
> *3:20–21, family thinks he's crazy
> 4:26–29, seed sprouting at night
> 4:33–34, summary about parables
> 6:45–52, walking on water
> 6:53–56, healing at Gennesaret
> 7:1–23, eating with unwashed hands (cf. Luke 11:37–40)
> 7:24–30, Syrophoenician woman
> *7:31–37, deaf man healed
> 8:1–10, feeding 4000
> *8:22–26, man healed twice
> 9:9–13, Resurrection and Elijah discussion following Transfiguration
> 9:41, cup of water
> 10:1–12, divorce

---

[15] On Luke's use of Mark, see Evans, *Saint Luke*, 17–19.

10:35–45, request from James and John

11:12–14, 20–21, cursing fig tree

11:22–24, on faith

11:25, on forgiveness

14:27–28, prediction of scattered sheep

*14:51–52, naked young man

15:16–20, soldiers mocking

15:34–35, cry of dereliction

15:36, sponge with wine

Luke's Unique Material

Aside from the material that Luke shares with Mark and/or Matthew, there is also the material unique to Luke. About half of the Gospel finds no parallel in Matthew or Mark (or John, of course), whereas about a quarter of the Gospel corresponds to material in Mark (and perhaps Matthew) and another quarter is Q material (i.e., parallel to Matthew but not Mark). The unique material includes the very beginning (Infancy Narrative) and the very end (Resurrection Narrative) of the Gospel, as well as much of the middle section (the Travel Narrative, 9:51–19:28).

Luke has many parables that have no parallel in the other Gospels.

- Good Samaritan (10:25–37)
- Friend at Midnight (11:5–8)
- Rich Fool (12:16–21)
- Unfruitful Fig Tree (13:6–9)
- Seats at the Banquet (14:7–11)
- Lost coin (15:8–10)

- Prodigal Son (15:11–32)
- Dishonest Manager (16:1–13)
- Rich Man and Lazarus (16:19–31)
- Widow and the Dishonest Judge (18:1–8)
- Pharisee and Tax Collector (18:10–14)

Luke emphasizes several themes more prominently than do other Gospels, including prayer, repentance, sinners in Jesus's ministry, wealth and poverty, and Samaritans. He talks about John the Baptist more than any other Gospel. Luke contains a genealogy very different from the one we find at the beginning of Matthew's Gospel. Luke refers to Jesus as "Lord" more than the other Gospels.[16]

It is this unique material that will serve as the basis for our study.

RECEPTION OF LUKE[17]

The earliest manuscripts we have for Luke (as for all the New Testament writings) are often quite small. A good example is the manuscript known as P^{111} (= Papyrus # 111), from the third century. It was originally a codex (= book, not scroll) of the Gospel of Luke (and maybe more?), but now it survives only as a

---

[16] Evans, *Saint Luke* 26–27, provides a full list of material unique to Luke.

[17] For a full study of the early reception, see Andrew Gregory, *The Reception of Luke and Acts in the Period before Irenaeus: Looking for Luke in the Second Century* (WUNT; Tübingen: Mohr Siebeck, 2003).

tiny fragment containing merely Luke 17:11–13 (on the front) and 17:22–23 (on the back).[18]

Figure 1. P[111] (Luke 17:11–13).
Courtesy Bodleian Library. University of Oxford.

There are some more substantial manuscripts, though, from the early centuries. The earliest copy of all four Gospels in one manuscript (along with Acts) is P[45] from the third century.

---

[18] Other tiny fragments include P[69] (3rd cent.), P[82] (4th cent.), 0171 (4th cent.).

We have no manuscripts of Luke from as early as the second century. Actually, a few manuscripts might possibly be that early, but the dating is debated, and it is probably safer to conclude that they are from the third century.

P[75] in its present form contains Luke 3:18–24:53 followed by John. It has been proposed that this papyrus codex may have contained all four Gospels. This manuscript preserves the ending of the Third Gospel and the beginning of the Fourth Gospel.

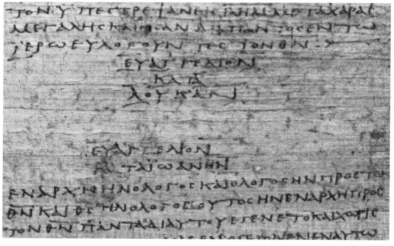

Figure 2. P[75]. Courtesy Vatican Library.

The ending of the Third Gospel here says εὐαγγέλιον κατὰ Λουκᾶν (*euangelion kata Lukan,* "gospel according to Luke") and the beginning of the Fourth Gospel says εὐαγγέλιον κατὰ Ἰωάνην (*euangelion kata Iōanēn,* "gospel according to John").

P[4], now considered part of the same manuscript known as P64 and P67, containing Matthew. The combination papyrus codex now contains material from Matthew chapters 3, 5, 26, and

Luke chapters 1–6. It is also possible that this codex originally contained all four Gospels.

There is no known manuscript in which Luke circulated either alone or with only Acts. It is always known as a companion to at least one of the other Gospels.

As for what early Christians said about Luke, there are several writers in the late second century that talk about Luke as the author of the Third Gospel.[19] Writers in the earlier part of the second century (e.g., Papias, Justin Martyr) do not mention Luke, though they may have made use of his Gospel. The earliest person to mention Luke was apparently Irenaeus, the bishop of Lyons, who wrote in about AD 180. After quoting the "We Passages" of Acts, Irenaeus says, "Since Luke had been present at all these events, he carefully wrote them down."[20] Irenaeus goes on to explain at some length Luke's credentials for writing Acts and the Gospel.

> Through him [= Luke] we have learned very
> many quite important parts of the gospel, as the

---

[19] On the early reception of the Gospels and on their collection as specifically a fourfold Gospel canon, see Edmon L. Gallagher and John D. Meade, *The Biblical Canon Lists from Early Christianity: Texts and Analysis* (Oxford: Oxford University Press, 2017), 32–39.

[20] Irenaeus, *Against Heresies* 3.14.1, quoted from Henry J. Cadbury, "The Tradition," in Foakes Jackson and Lake, *Beginnings of Christianity*, vol. 2, 209–64, at 215. See also the Anti-Marcionite Prologues and the Monarchian Prologue, available in English online here: http://www.textexcavation.com/latinprologues.html. Two other important "receivers" of Luke's Gospel in the second century are Marcion and Tatian, but both are problematic.

birth of John and the story about Zacharias, and the coming of the angel to Mary, and the cry of Elisabeth, and the coming down of the angels to the shepherds, and the things that were spoken by them, and the testimony of Anna and Simeon concerning the Christ, and how when twelve years old he was left behind in Jerusalem, and the baptism of John and at what age the Lord was baptized, and that it was in the fifteenth year of Tiberius Caesar. (*Against Heresies* 3.14.3)

Irenaeus continues pointing out the passages unique to Luke, arguing that our preaching and our knowledge about Jesus would be greatly diminished if we did not have this Gospel.

Another early testimony to Luke is the Muratorian Fragment, which is a brief introduction to the New Testament written probably in the late second or early third century.

The third book of the Gospel is that according to Luke. Luke, the well-known physician, after the ascension of Christ, when Paul had taken him with him as one zealous for the law, composed it in his own name, according to [the general] belief. Yet he himself had not seen the Lord in the flesh; and therefore, as he was able to ascertain events, so indeed he begins to tell the story from the birth of John.[21]

---

[21] For the text and translation of the Muratorian Fragment, see Gallagher and Meade, *Biblical Canon Lists*, 175–83.

From very early, then, at least late in the second century, the consensus view associates the Third Gospel with Luke and attributes to it authority alongside the other three Gospels. We also begin to have surviving manuscripts from around the same period, and manuscripts even of the four Gospels together from the third century.

I
GOOD NEWS OF GREAT JOY
LUKE 1–2

What would you do if you learned that you were going to have a baby? Some people would rejoice. Some people would panic. At this point in my life, I'm more in the latter category. I know that because not too long ago my family was presented with the opportunity to bring a baby into our home, and my first reaction was utter terror. Babies are a lot of work, and they're exhausting. Modern American society has developed a sophisticated "family planning" strategy, which often means, "how to avoid having a baby."

I admire my wife because her first reaction to the prospect of receiving a baby at the start of our fifth decade of life was not utter terror.[1] And I admire Elizabeth and Mary in Luke's opening chapter because their first reaction was not utter terror.

---

[1] That baby is now a toddler and adopted into our family. You can see who won that discussion between me and my wife. I'm glad I lost.

Neither one of them was in the prime "baby period" of their lives. Elizabeth was too old; Mary was too young. Proper family planning would not have called for either to have a baby in that season of their lives. We often find that God works against human convention, contrary to expectation.

Elizabeth and Mary submitted to, and even rejoiced in, these unusual pregnancies because they understood the significance of these babies. As Mary sang, "from now on all generations will call me blessed" (Luke 1:48), and Elizabeth, filled with the Holy Spirit, understood that Mary carried within her "my Lord" (1:43). They both knew that the births of their two babies, and especially the younger, was a moment of "good news of great joy" (2:10).

The Birth Accounts

Matthew and Luke both contain accounts of the birth of Jesus, while Luke's is the only Gospel to narrate the birth of John the Baptist. But the two accounts of Jesus's birth are very different, as this chart illustrates.[2]

---

[2] Chart based on Greg Carey, *Luke: All Flesh Shall See God's Salvation*, An Introduction and Study Guide (London: Bloomsbury, 2017), 19. For an early Christian attempt to harmonize the birth accounts, see Epiphanius, *Panarion* 51.9.9–13.

Matthew	Luke
Annunciation to Joseph (1:18–25)	Announcement of John (1:5–25)
Herod and visit of magi (2:1–12)	Annunciation to Mary (1:26–38)
Flight to Egypt (2:13–15)	Mary visits Elizabeth (1:39–56)
Slaughter of Innocents (2:16–18)	Birth of John (1:57–80)
Return from Egypt (2:19–23)	Jesus's Birth (2:1–7)
	Visit of Shepherds (2:8–20)
	Baby Jesus at the temple (2:21–38)
	Jesus's growth (2:39–52)

It is difficult to know how all the details fit together, and for the purposes of our study of Luke, we'll basically ignore Matthew.

THE HOPES OF ISRAEL

But I will say that Luke and Matthew have one major (but, perhaps, too-often overlooked) feature in common, and that is the prominence of Old Testament themes and imagery in their birth accounts.[3] Such a statement might be a little surprising in regard to Luke since there are hardly any Old Testament

---

[3] On this theme, see the article by Jewish New Testament Professor Amy-Jill Levine, "The Jewish Origins of the Christmas Story," *TheTorah.com* (2019). You'll easily be able to find it online.

quotations in the first two chapters (only at Luke 2:23-24). In fact, as Kavin Rowe has remarked, "The characters and events of the Old Testament are everywhere present and nowhere mentioned."[4] The only way to understand the significance of John and Jesus is by paying careful attention to the Old Testament, to the promises it contains, to the hopes it instills in God's people, to the prophecies about a coming salvation. Luke's language constantly looks back to the Old Testament to inform readers about what this all means.

The very beginning of Luke's story tells us about an old barren couple, and we recall—since we know Israel's scriptures well—other stories about old barren couples, specifically Abraham and Sarah. (Abraham will be explicitly named a couple times later in Luke 1, in Mary's song and Zechariah's prophecy.) There were also other stories of barren women, like Jacob's favorite wife Rachel (cf. Gen 29:31; 30:22-24), or Hannah (Samuel's mama; cf. 1 Sam 1) or Mrs. Manoah (Samson's mama; cf. Judg 13). We know how these stories work: the whole point of mentioning the barren woman is to tell a story about how her barrenness was overturned and she had a son, and not just any son, but a special son, an important son, one who would play an unusual role in God's plans.

So also this old barren woman Elizabeth with her priestly husband Zechariah will have a son. This time, as in the case of Samson (Judg 13), there's an angel who makes this announcement: the angel Gabriel, who "stands in the presence of

---

[4] C. Kavin Rowe, *Early Narrative Christology: The Lord in the Gospel of Luke* (Berlin: de Gruyter, 2006), 33.

God" (Luke 1:19). He tells Zechariah that his son should receive the name John (1:13). (God also chose Isaac's name; Gen 17:19). We are never told why his name needs to be John. The name means "The Lord is gracious" (or, better, "Yahweh is gracious").[5] This child will be special, just like Isaac and Samuel and Samson. John's birth will be an occasion for rejoicing (1:14). Again, like Isaac and Samuel and Samson, John will be a special agent from the Lord (1:15). In his case, this specialness will mean that he should abstain from alcohol—perhaps because (like Samson; Judg 13:5) he'll be a nazirite from the womb? (Num 6:3)—and instead he will be filled with the Holy Spirit (cf. Eph 5:18). What will be his mission?

> He will turn many of the people of Israel to the Lord their God. With the spirit and power of Elijah he will go before him, to turn the hearts of parents to their children, and the disobedient to the wisdom of the righteous, to make ready a people prepared for the Lord. (Luke 1:16–17)

Malachi had prophesied that the appearance of Elijah would precede the "great and terrible Day of the Lord" (Mal 4:5), and so Jews were on the lookout for him (cf. John 1:21). Still today Jews leave out a cup of wine for Elijah during their Passover Seder. John's birth signals that things are now moving toward that great and terrible day of the Lord. Elijah is finally making his re-appearance.

---

[5] Wikipedia: "John (given name)."

Next is a different kind of story, one we haven't seen before. It's another story about a woman being promised a son, but this woman is not barren; she's not even married; she's a virgin. The same Gabriel comes to her and tells her about her forthcoming son. There's also a special name for this son, Jesus (1:31), and once again Gabriel fails to explain the significance of the name. Perhaps Mary would have understood that since "Jesus" (or, in Hebrew, Yeshua) means "salvation," that this Messiah would bring deliverance.[6] The angels tell the shepherds that this baby is a savior (Luke 2:11). At any rate, the connection between the name "Jesus" and "salvation" is made explicit in Matthew's Gospel (cf. Matt 1:21).

Just like John (Luke 1:15), Jesus also will be "great" (Luke 1:32), but beyond that he will be called the Son of the Most High, and he will receive the throne of David. Gabriel explains: "He will reign over the house of Jacob forever, and of his kingdom there will be no end" (1:33).

We cannot understand the importance of this Annunciation without referring to the promises to David, promises that enflamed some first-century Jews with nationalistic fervor. A thousand years earlier, God had promised David that his descendants (his seed; 2 Sam 7:12) would reign over Israel forever. At the time that Gabriel visited Mary, no descendent of David had reigned over Israel for half a millennium. David had been Israel's greatest king, a warrior king who routinely defeated in battle Israel's enemies. Descendants of David were "adopted" by God as his special sons (cf. 1 Chron

---

[6] Wikipedia: "Yeshua."

28:6). In a sense, any human king, a descendant of David, could be called a "son of God" in this loose sense.[7] Gabriel's words to Mary announce the fulfillment of the ancient promises to David; a new king is on his way, in her womb.

The problem is, as Luke has already explained, that this particular birth is impossible because Mary is an unmarried virgin. So, while it may have been impossible for Abraham and Sarah to have a baby at their age (Gen 17:17), and the same for Zechariah and Elizabeth (whose exact age we don't know), it is even more impossible for Mary to conceive in her current situation. So, she naturally wonders how she's supposed to go about facilitating the birth of the Messiah. "How shall this be, seeing I know not a man?" (1:34 KJV, which gives a literal translation). Gabriel's answer reveals that "knowing a man" is quite irrelevant in this case.

> The Holy Spirit will come upon you, and the power of the Most High will overshadow you; therefore the child to be born will be holy; he will be called Son of God. (Luke 1:35)

As we saw earlier, the title "son of God" did refer in the Old Testament to the human king on Israel's throne, but here Gabriel makes it clear that this king to be born of Mary will be "Son of God" in another sense. He will not merely be adopted by God, but God will be his father. Mary will become pregnant through

---

[7] Adela Yarbro Collins and John J. Collins, *King and Messiah as Son of God: Divine, Human, and Angelic Messianic Figures in Biblical and Related Literature* (Grand Rapids: Eerdmans, 2008), 1–24.

an action of the Holy Spirit. It was not so unusual in the ancient Greco-Roman world to imagine a god fathering a child with a human woman; Zeus was rather famous for doing this. But clearly what Zeus did with women is not what Luke is describing at 1:35. The conception of Jesus is wholly different, instigated by completely different motives.[8]

What Luke (or Gabriel) is describing is the Incarnation of God.

That's what makes the conception of Jesus different from the conception of John. John's conception is very much parallel to the conception of every "special" child in the Old Testament, as we have seen. In such instances, there's no doubt that the child to be born will be fully human, not at all divine, not immortal. But that's where the Annunciation of Jesus is different from all the other angelic announcements of long-awaited pregnancies. First of all, Mary has not been waiting for a pregnancy. In fact, that's probably the last thing on her mind. And, second, this child will not be just like any other person except with a special mission from God. This child is the product of God's direct action within the womb of this young woman, without the contribution of a human father. That makes Jesus different from all the other biblical stories of pregnancies brought about by God. Again, one might think that the birth of Jesus is something like what we read about in Greek mythology: Hercules was the son of Zeus and a human woman. But the story associated with the conception of Hercules—Zeus disguised himself as Amphitryon, husband of Alcmene, so that he could sleep with the woman—

---

[8] Collins and Collins, *King and Messiah*, 143–45

makes the conception of the child merely a byproduct of the union between Zeus and Alcmene. The story is about Zeus' lust and deception and the on-going tension (to put it kindly) with his own wife, Hera. There is nothing of this in Luke 1:35.

One more point about this verse: the incarnation of God as described by Gabriel has affinities with certain things we read in the Old Testament, but differences, too. There are several stories in the Old Testament that depict God as embodied.[9] Think about those three visitors that ate with Abraham in Genesis 18, or the manifestation of God (again, in the context of a meal) in Exodus 24, where the text says that Moses and Aaron and others "saw the God of Israel" (v. 10). These stories about God as embodied are similar to Luke 1, which also involves the embodiment of God. But, none of those Old Testament stories describe the incarnation (or, enfleshment) of God. It's not like God became a human in Genesis 18. He temporarily manifested himself in human, physical form. In Luke 1–2, God becomes a human. God experiences growth in a woman's womb, experiences birth, experiences aging (and eventually experiences death). There are similarities with stories of God's embodiment in the Old Testament—and, indeed, many Christians throughout history have interpreted these stories as previews of the incarnation, as pre-incarnate appearances of the Christ—but the incarnation of Christ in the Gospels is unique.

---

[9] For a major academic study of this topic, see Benjamin D. Sommer, *The Bodies of God and the World of Ancient Israel* (Cambridge: Cambridge University Press, 2009).

Mary's response (v. 38) in her precarious situation is a model of faithfulness.[10]

Mary travels to visit Elizabeth—whom she now knows to be pregnant (Luke 1:36)—and immediately Elizabeth recognizes not only that Mary is herself pregnant but also the exalted status of the fruit of her womb.

> Why has this happened to me, that the mother
> of my Lord comes to me? (Luke 1:43)[11]

The Magnificat and the Benedictus

These are the titles traditionally associated with Mary's song (Luke 1:46–55) and Zechariah's prophecy (1:67–79), taken from the first Latin word of each poem: magnificat ("magnifies") and benedictus ("blessed").

The themes of the poems are, perhaps, unexpected. They seemingly have very little to do with Christmas. There's nothing about peace on earth and goodwill to men (that comes later; 2:14)—almost the opposite. Mary sings:

> He has shown strength with his arm;
> he has scattered the proud in the thoughts of
> their hearts.

---

[10] Jennifer Powell McNutt and Amy Beverage Peeler, "The First Christian," *Christianity Today* (Nov 22, 2019).

[11] On the significance of Elizabeth's acclamation of Mary's child as her "Lord," see Rowe, *Early Narrative Christology*, 34–49.

He has brought down the powerful from their
thrones. (Luke 1:51–52)

These words are much more ... what? militaristic? polemical?
aggressive? ... than the customary songs we sing in December,
whether "Winter Wonderland" or "Deck the Halls" or "Silent
Night." Mary interprets her situation as an action by which God
is bringing justice to the world, setting at naught the usual
markers of power. In that way, Mary's song is very much like
Hannah's prayer of thanksgiving upon the birth of her son
Samuel, a prayer that also omits any mention of the child and
instead dwells on God's character and power.

> The bows of the mighty are broken,
>> but the feeble gird on strength.
> Those who were full have hired themselves out
>> for bread,
>> but those who were hungry are fat with
>> spoil.
> The barren has borne seven,
>> but she who has many children is
>> forlorn.
> YHWH kills and brings to life;
>> he brings down to Sheol and raises up.
> YHWH makes poor and makes rich;
>> he brings low, he also exalts.
> (1 Sam 2:4–7)

Hannah sees that ultimately God calls the shots in this world, and
he is concerned for justice. While it often seems that the wicked

prosper while the righteous suffer, God's act of mercy toward Hannah—the birth of her son—demonstrates yet again that appearances are deceiving, and that God is interested in setting things right, reversing the injustice so prevalent in the world. God's choice of Mary as the mother of Jesus (or, can we even say the mother of God?)[12] is the supreme act in the great reversal brought about by the gospel. The very next lines in Mary's song continue the theme:

> ...and lifted up the lowly;
> he has filled the hungry with good things,
> and sent the rich away empty. (Luke 1:52–53)

The birth of Jesus to such a mother in the little town of Bethlehem, with no crib for a bed,[13] acclaimed by Shepherds and not kings, shows God as one who lifts up the lowly and nullifies the power of the wicked.

And, of course, all of this is in fulfillment of the ancient promises God has made to his people. Mary concludes:

> He has helped his servant Israel,

---

[12] Wikipedia: "Theotokos."

[13] But Luke probably does not locate the birth in a stable. Listen to Mark Goodacre's NTPod (https://podacre.blogspot.com/), episode 46, "Was Jesus Born in a Stable?" (Dec 15, 2010), or see the academic article by Stephen Carlson (to which Goodacre refers): Stephen C. Carlson, "The Accommodations of Joseph and Mary in Bethlehem: κατάλυμα in Luke 2.7," *New Testament Studies* 56 (2010): 326–42, available online: http://www.hypotyposeis.org/papers/Carlson%202010%20NTS.pdf.

in remembrance of his mercy,
according to the promise he made to our
ancestors,
to Abraham and to his descendants forever.
(Luke 1:54–55)

God promised long ago to Abraham that his descendants would bring blessing to the world (Gen 12:3; 22:18). Mary knows that her child ultimately fulfills these ancient promises.

Zechariah also mentions "the oath that [God] swore to our ancestor Abraham" (Luke 1:73), but he takes it in a different direction than what we might expect.

Thus he has shown the mercy promised to our
ancestors,
and has remembered his holy covenant,
the oath that he swore to our ancestor Abraham,
to grant us that we, being rescued from the hands
of our enemies,
might serve him without fear, in holiness and
righteousness
before him all our days. (Luke 1:72–75)

Here again we have a somewhat militaristic or aggressive interpretation of the birth of a child. Zechariah—when he is finally able to speak—sees his son's birth in terms of God's redemption of Israel (1:68). It should cause us no surprise that Zechariah connects this redemption to the long-promised Davidic king (1:69), but it might surprise us that Zechariah thinks this king is going to save Israel "from our enemies and from the hand of all who hate us" (1:71). What exactly does he think this king is going to do? He apparently thinks the king will establish Israel in safety, defeating her enemies, so that Israel can serve God without fear (1:74–75).

What do you imagine someone listening to Zechariah would have thought about these words? Whatever they thought about the accuracy of Zechariah's prophecy—is God really going to do these things now and through these children?—they would have understood the hopes that he was communicating. But they wouldn't have wanted to communicate those hopes too loudly for fear that the Romans might hear. It was those same hopes that eventually led to Jesus's death, with the charge against him being that he was "The King of the Jews" (Luke 23:38).[14] The kingship of Jesus was interpreted as a threat to Rome. And many Jews longed for this exact thing: for the long-promised Davidic Messiah to defeat the Roman enemy and establish Israel as a strong and secure empire.

Maybe Zechariah held this view, as well, but clearly Luke did not. Luke was writing several decades after these events, and he knew very well that the kingship of Jesus was not a direct threat to Roman rule in the way imagined by both Jews and Romans at the time. But Luke included this prophecy within his Gospel because he considered it an accurate account of the significance of these births—whether or not Zechariah himself understood the full import of his own words. God had, in fact, finally sent his king to defeat the enemies of Israel and establish God's people in security to worship him without fear (cf. Luke

---

[14] Mark 15:26 makes it clear that this is the "charge" (αἰτία) against Jesus.

12:4–5). And Luke shows throughout his Gospel Jesus fighting and defeating Israel's enemies (cf. 13:10–17, esp. v. 18).

Zechariah touches on more themes in the conclusion to his prophecy, and we will briefly touch on them here. His son John will be "prophet of the Most High" who will "go before the Lord to prepare his ways" (1:76). This description connects John's role as Elijah (cf. Mal 4:5) with Isaiah's prophecy in Isaiah 40:3. John will prepare a people for the Lord by teaching about salvation and the forgiveness of sins (1:77). And this will all result in light breaking out for those in darkness (1:78–79; cf. Isa 9:2; 42:6; 49:6). As should be obvious, Zechariah is very familiar with the ancient prophecies and believes that he is a witness to their fulfillment.

AT THE TEMPLE

There is so much in the first two chapters of Luke—such theological richness packed into a tight space—that we need to skip over something. (Actually, we've already skipped over quite a bit!) It might seem heretical to skip over the actual birth of Jesus in Luke 2:1–7, but we're going to. My excuse is that we need to pay more attention to the interpretations of the birth in these chapters. What does this birth represent? What does it mean? Mary tells us, and Zechariah, and Simeon, and Anna. It's to Simeon and Anna that we now turn. (That also means that we're skipping over the announcement to the Shepherds, which—as Linus tells us, quoting Luke 2:8–14—reveals the true meaning of Christmas.)[15]

In accordance with the Torah—Luke (2:23–24) quotes Exodus 13:2 and Leviticus 12:8—Mary and Joseph take their newborn to the temple in Jerusalem, where they meet a man and a woman, who tell them more about the significance of their child.

Simeon comes first. He is introduced as "righteous and devout" and anticipating the consolation of Israel. What does this mean? First of all, notice how this idea of anticipating stands at the beginning and end of this narrative about the temple.

[Simeon was] anticipating the consolation of Israel. (2:25)

[Anna told] about the child to all who were anticipating the redemption of Jerusalem. (2:38)

There were ancient Jews who were longing for (anticipating) God's action, and they might express that hope in terms of the consolation of Israel, or the redemption of Jerusalem. Remember that Zechariah also was hoping for the redemption (1:68) that would come by way of the Messiah (1:69), who would deliver Israel from their enemies (1:71). In the case of Simeon and the people to whom Anna spoke, we can't know exactly what they were hoping for, how they

---

[15] If you want to see what I'm talking about, go to YouTube and search "Linus Christmas Speech."

imagined the consolation of Israel or the redemption of Jerusalem, but I would not be shocked to learn that they thought it would entail the overthrow of the Romans. After all, Simeon already knows that he will live to see the Messiah (2:26), which most people (everybody?) interpreted in militaristic ways. The son of David would be just like his father David in killing the enemies of God (cf. 1 Sam 18:7). Or so they hoped.

Perhaps like Zechariah, Simeon's words may have meant more than he knew. Taking up the infant Jesus, the (elderly?)[16] man proclaimed:

> Master, now you are dismissing your servant in
> > peace,
> > according to your word;
> for my eyes have seen your salvation,
> > which you have prepared in the presence
> > of all peoples,
> light for revelation to the Gentiles
> > and for glory to your people Israel.
> (Luke 2:29–32)

Whatever Simeon may have been thinking, those who heard him might well have thought about salvation in physical terms, as in Israel being saved from the foreign oppressor, just as, long beforehand, God had saved his people from Egypt. Whereas such a salvation might well enlighten the nations about the nature of Israel's God (after all, that was part of the point of the

---

[16] Luke doesn't actually tell us that Simeon is old, but he does think he's going to die soon, it seems (2:26, 29).

exodus; cf. Exod 7:5; 9:16), the child in Simeon's arms would serve as a "light for revelation to the Gentiles" in a different way—or, at least, Jesus would reveal to the nations things about God that mere rescue from the Romans would not have done.

So far so good. But what Simeon says next entails the first hints that this whole story might contain some darker elements.

> This child is destined for the falling and the rising of many in Israel, and to be a sign that will be opposed so that the inner thoughts of many will be revealed—and a sword will pierce your own soul too. (Luke 2:34–35)

It is not clear at this point in the story what this prophecy might mean, but it is ominous. This little baby is "destined … to be a sign that will be opposed." Perhaps someone at the time would have said that the Messiah would be opposed by the enemies of God, and that the Messiah would bring about "the falling and rising of many in Israel" in the sense that those Jews who have been complicit with Roman rule (such as the Herods) would come on hard times. Greg Carey points out that several of the parables that Jesus later tells (especially the ones unique to Luke's Gospel) "depict sudden turns of fortune and the dramatic consequences of human decisions."[17] We can think of the Prodigal Son (Luke 15) or the Rich Man and Lazarus (Luke 16)

---

[17] Carey, *Luke*, 29.

or the Pharisee and Publican (Luke 18). So, interpreted narrowly, maybe Simeon just means that the wicked in Israel would receive their just desserts. But that last line is hard to interpret so positively: "a sword will pierce your own soul too." Things are going to get worse than this young mother hitherto imagines. This somber declaration only hints at the coming tragedy.

That's all in the future. For now, as with the birth of any baby, there is only rejoicing. And so we end with Anna, the elderly prophetess who worshiped in the temple "with fasting and prayer night and day" (Luke 2:37). Anna traced her ancestry to the tribe of Asher, one of the northern tribes, and so she here represents in incipient form the "all Israel" that God had promised to gather together under his king David (see, e.g., Ezek 37:21–25).[18] As we mentioned earlier, Anna becomes an evangelist, speaking about Jesus to those she meets who were "looking for the redemption of Jerusalem" (2:38).

Redemption is coming.

---

[18] For more on Anna and the significance of her tribe, see Richard Bauckham, *Gospel Women: Studies of the Named Women in the Gospels* (Grand Rapids: Eerdmans, 2002), 77–107.

2
JOHN THE BAPTIST
LUKE 3:1-20

> I myself did not know him; but I came baptizing
> with water for this reason, that he might be
> revealed to Israel. (John 1:31; cf. v. 26–27).

Israel's problem was its sin, and the people knew it. This had all been recorded in their Scriptures centuries earlier. Before the entrance into the Promised Land, Moses had warned the Israelites that failure to keep God's Torah would result in devastating consequences (Deut 28:15–68), including loss of that Promised Land (vv. 64–68). He had told them that if they acted like the previous inhabitants of the land, then the land itself would vomit them out (Lev 18:24–30; 20:22–24). As it turned out, the people did not keep the Torah, they did act like the Canaanites, and the land did vomit them out, into Babylonian exile (2 Kings 25). But God had also promised that even exile would not be the end of his people.

When all these things have happened to you, the blessings and the curses that I have set before you, if you call them to mind among all the nations where YHWH your God has driven you, and return to YHWH your God, and you and your children obey him with all your heart and with all your soul, just as I am commanding you today, then YHWH your God will restore your fortunes and have compassion on you, gathering you again from all the peoples among whom YHWH your God has scattered you. Even if you are exiled to the ends of the world, from there YHWH your God will gather you, and from there he will bring you back. YHWH your God will bring you into the land that your ancestors possessed, and you will possess it; he will make you more prosperous and numerous than your ancestors. (Deut 30:1–5)

This promise, too, God had kept, sort of. They had indeed returned from exile, when God used the Persian king, Cyrus the Great, to release them from their Babylonian captivity (Ezra 1:1–4) and allow them to return under Zerubbabel (Ezra 1–6) and later Ezra (Ezra 7) and Nehemiah. They were back in the land, to be sure, but it wasn't exactly like the old days. They were not anywhere close to being "more prosperous and numerous than your ancestors" (Deut 30:5), as God had promised. They were, in fact, still subject to a foreign overlord. There was no descendant of David on the throne, no divinely appointed king. In some ways they were still slaves even in their own land, as Nehemiah recognized: "Here we are, slaves to this day—slaves in the land that you gave to our ancestors to enjoy its fruit and its good gifts" (Neh 9:36; cf. Ezra 9:9). The exile was over, but it wasn't really over. Israel was still enduring the consequences of its sin.

But now there is a prophet in the desert, proclaiming a baptism of repentance for the remission of sins. This prophet is calling on people to repent and announcing the imminent arrival of Another One, who will execute God's wrath against the wicked and bring deliverance for God's people. The suffering of God's people will soon end. This prophet is preparing the way of the Lord.

THE EXPECTATION OF ELIJAH

The apocryphal book of Ben Sira, written in the early second century BC (about 200 years before John appeared in the desert), recalled the prophetic career of Elijah in these terms.

> [1]Then Elijah arose, a prophet like fire,
>   and his word burned like a torch.
> [2]He brought a famine upon them,
>   and by his zeal he made them few in
>   number.
> [3]By the word of the Lord he shut up the heavens,
>   and also three times brought down fire.
> [4]How glorious you were, Elijah, in your
>   wondrous deeds!
>   Whose glory is equal to yours?
> [5]You raised a corpse from death

and from Hades, by the word of the Most
High.
⁶You sent kings down to destruction,
and famous men, from their sickbeds.
⁷You heard rebuke at Sinai
and judgments of vengeance at Horeb.
⁸You anointed kings to inflict retribution,
and prophets to succeed you.
⁹You were taken up by a whirlwind of fire,
in a chariot with horses of fire.
**¹⁰At the appointed time, it is written, you are
destined
to calm the wrath of God before it breaks
out in fury,
to turn the hearts of parents to their
children,
and to restore the tribes of Jacob.**
¹¹Happy are those who saw you
and were adorned with your love!
For we also shall surely live.
(Sirach 48:1–11)

This passage shows that at least some Jews were
anticipating the return of Elijah, who would usher in some sort
of religious reform in Israel.[1] The disciples of Jesus were also

---

[1] Verse 10 is a little different in Greek. The *New English Translation of the
Septuagint* translates the first half of verse 10: "He who was recorded ready
for the times, to calm anger before wrath." The Hebrew text is preserved
in manuscript B from the Cairo Genizah, folio XVII verso, line 14,

anticipating the arrival of Elijah (Mark 9:11; Matt 17:10). The crowds thought Jesus might be Elijah (Matt 16:14; Mark 6:15; 8:28; Luke 9:8, 19). That expectation is based on Malachi, which ends with these words.

> Lo, I will send you the prophet Elijah before the great and terrible day of YHWH comes. He will turn the hearts of parents to their children and the hearts of children to their parents, so that I will not come and strike the land with a curse. (Mal 4:5–6)

Each of the Gospels mentions this expectation of Elijah and connects it in some way with John the Baptist. The most explicit are Matthew (11:4; 17:10–12) and Mark (9:11–13), while Luke is much more subtle. John's connection to Elijah is mentioned only in the angelic birth announcement: "With the spirit and power of Elijah he will go before him, to turn the hearts of parents to their children, and the disobedient to the wisdom of the righteous, to make ready a people prepared for the Lord" (Luke 1:17).

The point of the prophecy is not that Elijah would literally show up—though, in a way, he did at the Transfiguration (Luke 9:30)—but that a later prophet would embody "the spirit and power of Elijah," as Gabriel puts it. The people in the first century seem to have understood this significance since they

---

available online at bensira.org, where it is translated, "Who were appointed for the chosen time [[ ]] to cause wrath to cease befo[re]."

were wondering whether Jesus was Elijah or whether John might be (cf. John 1:21). John, like Elijah, was a rough looking man (though Luke does not describe his appearance as Matthew 3:4 and Mark 1:6 do) who lived in the desert and called the people to repentance. Elijah's appearance in the form of John the Baptist meant that "the great and terrible day of YHWH" was nigh.

Preparing a People

Aside from the Elijah prophecy, two other Old Testament prophecies are connected with John in Luke's Gospel (and the other Synoptic Gospels).

> See, I am sending my messenger to prepare the way before me, and the Lord whom you seek will suddenly come to his temple. The messenger of the covenant in whom you delight—indeed, he is coming, says YHWH of hosts. (Mal 3:1; cf. Luke 7:27)

A voice cries out:

> "In the wilderness prepare the way of YHWH,
>> make straight in the desert a highway for
>> our God.
> Every valley shall be lifted up,
>> and every mountain and hill be made low;
> the uneven ground shall become level,
>> and the rough places a plain.
> Then the glory of YHWH shall be revealed,

and all people shall see it together,
for the mouth of YHWH has spoken." (Isa
40:3–5; cf. Luke 3:4–6)

Israel anticipated the coming of the Lord to set things right. He would establish his kingdom and bring prosperity to his people, but before this could happen, as we've seen, the people's sin needed to be removed. There needed to be preparation for the coming of the Lord. And that meant repentance.

John's message was urgent because he was the forerunner for the Lord. He came announcing the imminent appearance of One much greater than himself. Whereas John used water for baptism, this Coming One would baptize with the Holy Spirit and fire (3:16). The cleansing symbolized by water baptism would be perfected (fulfilled) by the baptism of the Coming One. The next verse indicates that the Coming One would bring punishment for the wicked and blessing for the righteous, and that (I think) is also what the baptism with Holy Spirit and fire indicates. It would work like a refiner's fire, purifying the righteous and destroying the wicked. John's preaching is basically hellfire and damnation: "Even now the ax is lying at the root of the trees; every tree therefore that does not bear good fruit is cut down and thrown into the fire" (3:9).

This Coming One would, of course, not be fooled by any false claims of righteousness, whether those false claims were based on ancestry (3:8) or pretended repentance. The idea that descent from Abraham was irrelevant was shocking, but not completely unanticipated in the Old Testament. After all, the Old Testament contains those stories of non-Israelites joining with

Israel and being considered a part of God's people, whether we're talking about Rahab (Josh 2; 6:22–25) or Ruth or, to a lesser extent, Naaman (2 Kgs 5). Moreover, there were plenty of Israelites who were punished for their sin despite their descent from Abraham: Achan is a good example (Josh 7), but so is the entire nation, since they all suffered exile. Descent from righteous Abraham is no guarantee of God's favor.

What was needed was action. Repentance is not just about being sorry about how you've been living, it's about action—doing something different. This theme is highlighted in the material shared by Matthew and Luke (not in Mark), but Luke emphasizes it even more than Matthew, because he includes a passage with specific examples.

> And the crowds asked him, "What then should we do?" In reply he said to them, "Whoever has two coats must share with anyone who has none; and whoever has food must do likewise." Even tax collectors came to be baptized, and they asked him, "Teacher, what should we do?" He said to them, "Collect no more than the amount prescribed for you." Soldiers also asked him, "And we, what should we do?" He said to them, "Do not extort money from anyone by threats or false accusation, and be satisfied with your wages." (Luke 3:10–14)

This is (I guess) the first example of a prominent theme in Luke's Gospel—repentance. Think about the Prodigal Son (Luke 15) or Zacchaeus (Luke 19) or the dire warning, stated twice, "unless you repent, you will all perish" (13:3, 5). Luke's is the Gospel that specifies that it was "to repentance" that Jesus came to call sinners and not the righteous (Luke 5:32; cf. Mark 2:17; Matt 9:13).

But it's not like the call to repentance was anything new. The prophets had always called on God's people to repent.

> Seek YHWH while he may be found, call upon him while he is near; let the wicked forsake their way, and the unrighteous their thoughts; let them return to YHWH, that he may have mercy on them, and to our God, for he will abundantly pardon. (Isa 55:6–7)

> Repent and turn from all your transgressions; otherwise iniquity will be your ruin. (Ezek 18:30)

And often the people did not listen to the call for repentance.

> And though YHWH persistently sent you all his servants the prophets, you have neither listened nor inclined your ears to hear when they said, "Turn now, everyone of you, from your evil way and wicked doings, and you will remain upon the land that YHWH has given to you and your ancestors from of old and forever; do not go after other gods to serve and worship them, and do not provoke me to anger with the work of your hands. Then I will do you no harm." Yet

you did not listen to me, says YHWH, and so
you have provoked me to anger with the work of
your hands to your own harm. (Jer 25:4–7)

So John stands in a tradition as another prophet calling
the people to repent. If there is anything that sets John apart, it is
the urgency with which he issues his call to repentance. Things
are about to change. God is about to keep his promises, which
will spell doom for some people and blessing for others.

The fruit of repentance that John advises his audience to
produce all have to do with treatment of other people. Those who
have some worldly goods should share with those who lack. Tax
collectors, who might easily abuse their status as Rome's
appointee, should refrain from lining their own pockets by
mistreating others. Soldiers, who might easily abuse their power,
should take care to treat others with respect.

Incidentally, what message is communicated by the fact
that tax collectors and soldiers were submitting to John's
baptism? I think it means at least two things. (1) They recognized
their own sin. Even though the types of things they did were
completely normal, they realized that it was wrong. (2) They
were scared. John preached hellfire and damnation, and they
believed him. Tax collectors and soldiers were not the most
obvious candidates for religion, but they knew their need for
repentance and were willing to take the hard steps toward
changing their lives. While the religious leaders were promoting
the status quo, the tax collectors were acknowledging the justice
God (7:29–30).

Forgiveness of Sins

At John's birth, his father spoke this prophecy.

> And you, child, will be called the prophet of the
> Most High; for you will go before the Lord to
> prepare his ways, to give knowledge of salvation
> to his people by the forgiveness of their sins. By
> the tender mercy of our God, the dawn from on
> high will break upon us, to give light to those
> who sit in darkness and in the shadow of death,
> to guide our feet into the way of peace. (Luke
> 1:76–79)

The people were sinful, and the Lord was coming. The people
needed to be prepared for the coming of the Lord, and that meant
repentance, and repentance resulted in the forgiveness of sins.
That was John's mission, "to give knowledge of salvation to his
people, by the forgiveness of their sins."

John preached a "baptism of repentance for the
forgiveness of sins" (Luke 3:3), a phrase used only of John's
baptism. The baptism was a definite action symbolizing the
changed life (repentance) and resulting in forgiveness of sins. It
was similar to Christian baptism in that the main point is the
"pledge of a good conscience toward God," as Peter puts it (1 Pet
3:21).

God had promised to establish a new covenant with his people
(Jer 31:31–34), as a part of which God would forgive his people's
iniquity and remember their sin no more (v. 34). John's ministry

was the sign that all this was about to take place. The wait was over. The Lord was coming.

Dateline: Palestine

Before Luke tells us about John's ministry, he situates his narrative in a historical context.

> In the fifteenth year of the reign of Emperor Tiberius, when Pontius Pilate was governor of Judea, and Herod was ruler of Galilee, and his brother Philip ruler of the region of Ituraea and Trachonitis, and Lysanias ruler of Abilene, during the high priesthood of Annas and Caiaphas, the word of God came to John son of Zechariah in the wilderness. (Luke 3:1–2)

Tiberius was the second Roman Emperor, after Augustus, who had died on August 19 in the year AD 14. So the fifteenth year of Tiberius would be about AD 29. Pontius Pilate was the governor or prefect of Judea during the years 26–36. The Herod that is mentioned here would be Herod Antipas, the son of Herod the Great. It was Herod the Great who had been king when Jesus was born, when the Magi came to visit, and who had slaughtered the children of Bethlehem (not narrated in Luke; see Matt 2). After Herod the Great died in 4 BC, his kingdom was divided among his sons, as explained below. Two of the sons are mentioned here by Luke: Herod (Antipas) and Philip. Lysanias was a relatively unimportant ruler of a relatively unimportant location, Abilene. And the priests mentioned here, Annas and

Caiaphas, were related: Annas was the father-in-law of Caiaphas (cf. John 18:13). There would have been only one high priest at a time, which at this time was Caiaphas (serving as high priest during the years AD 18–36), but Annas, who had earlier been high priest (during the years AD 6–15), retained considerable power.[2]

Now let's take a closer look at the Herods. Herod the Great had ten wives and fifteen children, but he killed several of his sons due to his (perhaps justified) fear that they were plotting against him. After his death (4 BC), the Roman emperor Augustus divided Herod's territory among three of his sons.[3] Josephus describes the situation this way.

> [Caesar Augustus] gave half the kingdom to Archelaus, with the title of ethnarch, promising, moreover, to make him king, should he prove his deserts; the other half he divided into two tetrarchies, which he presented to two other sons of Herod, one to Philip, the other to Antipas, who had disputed the throne with Archelaus. Antipas had for his province Peraea and Galilee, with a revenue of two hundred talents. Batanaea, Trachonitis, Auranitis and certain portions of the domain of Zeno in the neighbourhood of Panias, producing a revenue

---

[2] On these priests, see James C. VanderKam, *From Joshua to Caiaphas: High Priests after the Exile* (Minneapolis: Fortress, 2004), 420–24 (Annas), 426–36 (Caiaphas). Annas is called Ananus by Josephus (*Ant.* 18.26).

[3] Wikipedia: "Herodian Tetrarchy."

of a hundred talents, were allotted to Philip. The ethnarchy of Archelaus comprised the whole of Idumaea and Judaea, besides the district of Samaria. (Josephus, *Jewish War* 2.93–96)[4]

These rulers, sons of Herod the Great, include the following:

- Archelaus, born 27 BC, oldest son of Herod's wife Malthace. He was made ruler of half of his father's kingdom and received the title Ethnarch ("ruler of the nation"). His territory included Judea, Idumea and Samaria. He was deposed in AD 6, after only a decade in power, and banished to Vienne in Gaul (according to the first century Roman writer Strabo, *Geography* 16.765).[5] Archelaus was replaced by direct Roman rule (i.e., a Roman prefect—eventually Pontius Pilate).

- Philip, born 26 BC, son of Herod's wife Cleopatra of Jerusalem. He was appointed by Augustus "Tetrarch" ("ruler of a fourth [of the nation]"). His territory included Iturea, Panias, Gaulanitis, Batanea, Trachonitis, and northern Auranitis. Reigned for 37 years. Died in 33 or 34 without an heir.

- Antipas, born 25 BC, a son of Malthace, thus a full brother to Archelaus. He was appointed Tetrarch over the territories of Galilee and Parea (which do not touch

---

[4] Translation by H. St. J. Thackeray in Josephus, *The Jewish War, Books I–II*, Loeb Classical Library (Cambridge, MA: Harvard University Press, 1927), 357–59.

[5] Wikipedia: "Vienne, Isère."

each other). He adopted the title "Herod" as a dynastic title (similar to the way "Caesar" became a title; cf. Josephus, *Jewish War* 2.167). He reigned for 43 years. His marriage to Herodias, his own half-niece and the former wife of his half-brother Herod II (called Philip at Mark 6:17 // Matt 14:3, but not the same person as Philip the tetrarch) is described by Josephus (*Antiquities* 18.110, 136). The marriage between Herod and Herodias produced a daughter (named Salome, according to Josephus, *Antiquities* 18.136), who danced for Antipas at his birthday party (Mark 6:21). In AD 39, Antipas was deposed by the emperor Caligula and exiled to Spain, while his territory was added to that of his nephew, King Agrippa I (the "King Herod" of Acts 12).

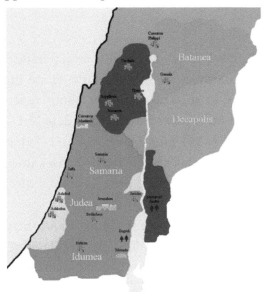

Map 1. Map of the Herodian Tetrarchy as established by Augustus in 4 BCE until 6 CE. Rh0809, CC BY-SA 4.0 <https://creativecommons.org/licenses/by-sa/4.0>, via Wikimedia Commons.

The blue area is the territory of Archelaus that became a prefecture in AD 6. The brown at the top right is the territory of Philip. The two purple spots are the territories of Antipas.

JOHN THE BAPTIST IN LUKE AND JOSEPHUS

Each of the Gospels includes John the Baptist. The story of Jesus cannot be told without mentioning the forerunner of the Lord, who prepared his way. But Luke has more material about John than any other Gospel, not only narrating his ministry in extended detail (3:1–20), but also his birth (ch. 1). The birth narrative is unique to Luke, but most of the other material on John does have parallels in the other Gospels. This other material includes:

- John's ministry (Luke 3:1–20), with parallels at Mark 1:1–8 and Matthew 3:1–12, but Luke alone includes John's response to specific questions about repentance (3:10–14), and Luke provides a specific date (3:1–2).
- Luke (7:18–35) and Matthew (11:2–19) record John's question to Jesus as to whether he was the Coming One, along with Jesus's response to John's disciples and his speech to the crowd in praise of John.
- Luke does not include the story about the death of John as instigated by Herodias and her daughter's dance for Herod Antipas, which is instead recorded in Mark 6:14–29 and Matthew 14:1–12. But Luke does include the material at the beginning of these accounts of John's

death, when Herod Antipas wondered whether Jesus might be John raised from the dead (9:7–9).

Outside the New Testament, Josephus (the late-first-century Jewish historian) also provides an account of John the Baptist. This is in the context of Josephus' description of a battle between Herod Antipas and Aretas IV, the king of Nabataea. Antipas suffered a devastating defeat, and Josephus explains one theory why:

> But to some of the Jews the destruction of Herod's army seemed to be divine vengeance, and certainly a just vengeance, for his treatment of John, surnamed the Baptist (Ἰωάννου τοῦ ἐπικαλουμένου βαπτιστοῦ). (§117) For Herod had put him to death, though he was a good man (ἀγαθὸν ἄνδρα) and had exhorted the Jews to lead righteous lives, to practise justice towards their fellows and piety towards God, and so doing to join in baptism (καὶ τοῖς Ἰουδαίοις κελεύοντα ἀρετὴν ἐπασκοῦσιν καὶ τὰ πρὸς ἀλλήλους δικαιοσύνῃ καὶ πρὸς τὸν θεὸν εὐσεβείᾳ χρωμένοις βαπτισμῷ συνιέναι). In his view this was a necessary preliminary if baptism was to be acceptable to God (οὕτω γὰρ δὴ καὶ τὴν βάπτισιν ἀποδεκτὴν αὐτῷ φανεῖσθαι). They must not employ it to gain pardon for whatever sins they committed (μὴ ἐπί τινων ἁμαρτάδων παραιτήσει χρωμένων), but as a consecration of the body (ἀλλ’ ἐφ’ ἁγνείᾳ τοῦ σώματος)

implying that the soul was already thoroughly cleansed by right behaviour (ἄτε δὴ καὶ τῆς ψυχῆς δικαιοσύνῃ προεκκεκαθαρμένης). (§118) When others too joined the crowds about him, because they were aroused to the highest degree by his sermons, Herod became alarmed. Eloquence that had so great an effect on mankind might lead to some form of sedition, for it looked as if they would be guided by John in everything that they did. Herod decided therefore that it would be much better to strike first and be rid of him before his work led to an uprising, than to wait for an upheaval, get involved in a difficult situation and see his mistake. (§119) Though John, because of Herod's suspicions, was brought in chains to Machaerus, the stronghold that we have previously mentioned, and there put to death, yet the verdict of the Jews was that the destruction visited upon Herod's army was a vindication of John, since God saw fit to inflict such a blow on Herod. (Josephus, *Antiquities* 18.116–119)[6]

There are two main differences between what Josephus says about John and what the New Testament says about him: (1)

---

[6] Translation by Louis H. Feldman in Josephus, *Jewish Antiquities, Books XVIII–XIX*, Loeb Classical Library (Cambridge, MA: Harvard University Press, 1965), 81–85.

the reason for his death, and (2) the purpose of his baptism. As to the first, the reason for his death, Josephus can be harmonized with the New Testament, assuming that the New Testament reported one side of Herod's fear of John (the moral side) and Josephus emphasized the other (the political side).[7] As for the purpose of John's baptism, Josephus says it was not for forgiveness of sins (§117), and the New Testament says it was. Probably Josephus, who was not a contemporary of John—he was probably born about the time John died—was simply not properly informed about John's preaching.

THE VOICE IN THE DESERT

Isaiah 40 begins a series of prophecies about the return of the Judeans from Babylonian exile. The first words of Isaiah 40 are "Comfort, O Comfort, my people," and the reason God's people need comfort is because they have suffered the punishment of captivity. The words of Isaiah 40 announce the end of that punishment, the return from exile. Israel has paid for her sins. But we've already noticed that in some ways the return to the Promised Land did not actually mark the end of the exile. The people were still slaves in their own land. And so while the words of Isaiah 40 had been fulfilled to some extent, at least some Jews in the first century thought that these words looked forward to a future time when God would act, when he would forgive his people of their sin and establish his kingdom.

---

[7] This is the explanation offered by Feldman in the LCL edition (previous note), p. 83, note e.

The community of the Dead Sea Scrolls were out at Qumran in the Judean desert in an attempt to prepare the way of the Lord. One of their important documents applies the words of Isaiah 40 to the community: they were "preparing the way in the desert."[8]

The New Testament links this prophecy with John the Baptist (Luke 3:4–6; cf. Isa 40:3–5). He was the voice in the desert, preparing the way of the Lord. His ministry signaled the salvation of God.

By the way, there was probably some sort of connection between John and the people out at Qumran. Some people have thought that John may at one time have been a part of that desert community, but that is only speculation.[9] Regardless, as Beasley-Murray has said, "it is nevertheless impossible that he [John] could have been ignorant of their existence."[10] That is because of their similar location out in the desert at the same time, their similar emphasis on baptism, and their similar relation to the prophecy of Isaiah 40:3 as preparers of the way of the Lord. But John's baptism was unlike that at Qumran in the sense that it was

---

[8] See *The Community Rule*, column 9, lines 19–20, in Michael Wise, Martin Abegg, Jr., and Edward Cook, *The Dead Sea Scrolls: A New Translation* (San Francisco: HarperSanFrancisco, 2005), 131.

[9] Everett Ferguson, *Baptism in the Early Church: History, Theology, and Liturgy in the First Five Centuries* (Grand Rapids: Eerdmans, 2009), 87.

[10] G. R. Beasley-Murray, *Baptism in the New Testament* (Paternoster, 1972; repr. Eugene, Or.: Wipf and Stock, 2006), 39.

a once-for-all baptism, whereas at Qumran they immersed themselves frequently for ritual cleansing.[11]

Baptism

We've just seen that not only John but also the Qumran community practiced a type of baptism. This is a practice that developed in the centuries before Jesus. We read nothing of baptism as such in the Old Testament, but there is plenty about ritual cleansing through water in the Old Testament. For instance, water is used in the priestly ordination ritual in Leviticus 8:6, and on the Day of Atonement (Lev 16: 4, 24, 26, 28), and frequently for cleansing in Leviticus 15, and for cleansing after sickness (14:8).

There are also prophecies that God would one day cleanse his people by means of water.

> On that day a fountain shall be opened for the house of David and the inhabitants of Jerusalem, to cleanse them from sin and impurity. (Zech 13:1)

> I will sprinkle clean water upon you, and you shall be clean from all your uncleannesses, and from all your idols I will cleanse you. (Ezek 36:25)

---

[11] For ritual cleansing at Qumran, see Jodi Magness, *The Archaeology of Qumran and the Dead Sea Scrolls*, 2d ed. (Grand Rapids: Eerdmans, 2021), ch. 7.

Such Old Testament passages probably motivated people to seek cleansing through ritual immersion (called in Greek "baptism"). In fact, if you want to convert to Judaism today, you will have to get baptized. This "proselyte baptism" goes back a long way, but probably not quite to the first century. The earliest evidence for it is second- or third-century.[12] At any rate, ritual immersion was commonly practiced in the first century, and archaeologists have dug up all kinds of mikva'oth, what Christians would call "baptistries." According to Everett Ferguson, "Excavations have revealed hundreds of mikvaoth in Israel, over 150 from the first century in Jerusalem alone (including those adjoining the temple mount) as well as many at Jericho, Gamla, Masada, and Herodium from the period before the destruction of the temple."[13]

---

[12] There is no mention of proselyte baptism in Philo or Josephus, or in the pseudepigraphon *Joseph and Aseneth*. In the apocryphal book of Judith, Achior received circumcision (14:10) but there is no mention of baptism. Some see proselyte baptism at *m. Eduyyoth* 5.2 (trans. Herbert Danby, *The Mishnah* [Oxford: Oxford University Press, 1933], 431), but see Shaye J. D. Cohen, "Is 'Proselyte Baptism' Mentioned in the Mishnah? The Interpretation of *M. Pesahim* 8.8 (= *M. Eduyot* 5.2)" in *Pursuing the Text: Studies in Honor of Ben Zion Wacholder on the Occasion of His Seventieth Birthday*, ed. John C. Reeves and John Kampen (Sheffield: Sheffield Academic, 1994), 278–92. On what is probably the earliest reference to the rabbinic conversion ceremony (*b. Yebamoth* 47a–b), see Shaye J. D. Cohen, *The Beginnings of Jewishness: Boundaries, Varieties, Uncertainties* (Berkeley: University of California Press, 1999), 209–11.

[13] Ferguson, *Baptism*, 64.

John the Baptist didn't use a mikveh; instead, he used the Jordan River. This use of the Jordan was probably symbolic.[14] The Jordan River was the barrier between the Promised Land and the territory outside Israel. When Joshua led the Israelites into the Promised Land, they had to cross the Jordan. In a re-enactment of the Red Sea crossing, God stopped the flow of the Jordan so that the people could cross on dry ground (Josh 3:14–17). Now John is at the Jordan, baptizing people in its waters, offering forgiveness of sins, announcing that One is coming who will be God's representative, who will execute God's judgment.

There were a few differences between other Jewish forms of baptism and what John was doing. Jews do not "get baptized"; they immerse themselves. They walk down into the water and cover their head rather than having someone else dunk them. John the Baptist is the first person we know about who had a practice of dunking other people under the water. That's probably why he became known as "the baptist" or "the baptizer": he wasn't the only person practicing baptism, but he was the only one baptizing other people. Ferguson suggests that perhaps John administered the baptism in order to communicate a particular symbolism, perhaps: "one cannot effect one's own cleansing."[15]

Another difference between John's baptism and other Jewish baptism is that it was a one-time act, not something that a person would do for routine ritual cleansing. That point is

---

[14] See Colin Brown, "What Was John the Baptist Doing?" *Bulletin for Biblical Research* 7 (1997): 37–50.

[15] Ferguson, *Baptism*, 95–96.

linked to the purpose of John's baptism; he proclaimed "a baptism of repentance for the forgiveness of sins" (Luke 3:3). This purpose connects John's baptism to Christian baptism, but there are differences here as well, in that John's baptism required a confession of sins (Mark 1:5) rather than a confession of faith, and John's baptism does not impart the Holy Spirit.[16]

---

[16] Ferguson, *Baptism*, 89. On the similarities between John's baptism and Christian baptism, see also Andrew B. McGowan, *Ancient Christian Worship: Early Church Practices in Social, Historical, and Theological Perspective* (Grand Rapids: Baker, 2013), 139.

3
The Genealogy of Jesus

Luke 3:21-38

> Jesus was about thirty years old when he began
> his work. He was the son (as was thought) of
> Joseph son of Heli. (Luke 3:23)

I have no interest in getting my DNA tested to find out where my ancestors came from.[1] It is not an issue that intrigues me at all. I have always thought of my ancestry as Irish, but I don't really care if that is fiction and I've actually inherited more DNA from the Germans or the Native Americans or Asians or Africans or whatever. Nor do I watch the television shows featuring celebrities who get their DNA tested to discover such revelations. But I guess my lack of interest is not universal because, well …

---

[1] Beyond my lack of interest, there is also apparently a negative side to the whole genealogy industry; see the *Washington Post* column by Honor Sachs, "The Dark Side of Our Genealogy Craze" (Dec 13, 2019).

those television programs are still on the air, and I continue to see advertisements for websites that are supposed to help you find out about your ancestors. And I've got a family member, my Aunt Jo, who has done a lot of genealogical research on our family and traced our ancestors back, I don't know, a few centuries, I guess. Some people are interested in that sort of thing.

Ancient Jews were interested in that sort of thing. The Bible likes genealogies. It has a bunch of them. There's one book of the Bible, Chronicles, that starts with nine chapters of genealogies. Some people think Leviticus is the toughest book of the Bible to make it through when you're trying to read through the Bible in a year, but to me that award goes to Chronicles simply because of all those names.

What's the problem with all those names? Well, it's sort of like when a missionary comes to church to give a report on what he's been doing in darkest Peru or wherever, and he runs through 75 pictures of people we've never heard of and will never see again. Such a brief encounter with a person without really knowing anything about them makes little impact on us. But— to go a different direction—each year my family gets out the Christmas decorations, which include photos of our past visits to the mall's Santa Claus. We love looking at these pictures because they call to mind what our kids looked like back then, and the kind of people they were and have become. We like looking at pictures of our kids because we know them. We don't know these people in the missionary's presentation.

So also a list of names: each one represents a person, a story, a life, but that doesn't mean much to you if you don't know anything about that person's life. If you know the person, or the story, the name itself holds immense interest for you and evokes all kinds of images of that person's story. Back in my college days I had to learn the names of the Roman emperors during the first and second centuries. When I first did that exercise, it was just a list of names, but the more I've learned about the first and second centuries, the more I have fleshed out that list of names in my own mind with other information about those emperors, so that Tiberius or Caligula or Hadrian is not just a name to me now but evokes stories and data about that person. I've been to Washington, D.C., to the Vietnam Wall with my grandma, years ago, when I was young, and I remember the columns and columns of names, and my grandma going up to the wall to find particular names—which were, to her, not just names.

I suspect that ancient Jews (at least, some of the time) thought that way about their genealogies. They had studied their history; they had heard stories about these ancestors; the names were more than just names.[2]

Another way of looking at the significance of genealogies—probably even more important (at least, for ancient Jews) than knowing stories associated with the names—is locating yourself within the history of a people, as part of a community. The Old Testament highlights the tribal structure of ancient Israel, so that identity within a tribe, or even within a clan within a tribe, was an important element of society. So, you sort of have to know your ancestry to know which tribe you belong to. Josephus attests that in the first century, this kind of thing was

---

[2] This is the point that Fred Craddock makes on Romans 16 in a wonderful sermon titled "When the Roll Is Called Down Here." You can find it at YouTube.

still important, at least as it pertained to Jewish priests, who kept records of their genealogies in the temple.[3] This sort of thing is much less prominent in twenty-first-century American society, but we still have analogies. Pretty much the entire plot of the first few seasons of the show Downton Abbey was based on genealogy, as the estate of the Earl of Grantham was entailed to the unknown relative Matthew Crawley just because he had the right ancestry. And, closer to home, there are groups like Daughters of the American Revolution ("a lineage-based membership service organization for women," as their Wikipedia page says) and Sons of Confederate Veterans (look at their Wikipedia page under eligibility) that you can't get into unless you have the right ancestry.

For many people, genealogy is important. For Jesus, genealogy is important.

The Two Genealogies

Probably the first thing that will occur to you as you look at the genealogy of Jesus in Luke (3:23–38) is that this is not the only genealogy of Jesus we have in Scripture. Matthew begins his Gospel with a genealogy, which is probably much more familiar to Christians since it begins the New Testament. And the other thing that will occur to you is that there are a bunch of differences between the two genealogies. These differences have been talked about for a long time, and there are various solutions proposed

---

[3] Josephus talks about this, for instance, in his work called *Against Apion* 1.29–36.

to explain the differences, but all the solutions are really only guesses.

Let's notice some of the obvious differences, and let's use a chart.

Matthew 1:1–17	Luke 3:23–38
moves forward historically (with Jesus at the end)	moves backward historically (with Jesus at the beginning)
earliest name is Abraham	earliest name is Adam (or even God)
Joseph's father: Jacob (v. 16)	Joseph's father: Heli (v. 23)
David's son: Solomon (v. 6)	David's son: Nathan (v. 31)
mentions a few women (vv. 3, 5, 6)	only men
explicitly organized into three sections of 14 generations (v. 17)	no explicit organization

The structural differences between the two genealogies are not that big of a deal, but the different names that appear in the list do cause some problems. (For a full comparison, see Exploration 3.1.) It's not just that Jesus's earthly father Joseph has a father called Heli in Luke and a father called Jacob in Matthew. If that were the only difference, maybe we could offer some sort of explanation, like the one I've often heard, that Luke gives us the genealogy of Mary and Matthew gives us the genealogy of Joseph. If we assumed that solution, then Heli would actually be Mary's father, and Jacob would be Joseph's father. But that explanation doesn't solve all the difficulties.

Notice that both genealogies more-or-less agree from Abraham to David (Matt 1:2–6; Luke 3:31–34), and the genealogies diverge with the son of David: Matthew traces the genealogy through Solomon, but Luke traces it through a different son of David named Nathan (not the prophet; cf. 2 Sam 5:14; 1 Chron 3:5; 14:4). But then the genealogies come back together with the two names Shealtiel and Zerubbabel (Matt 1:12; Luke 3:27),[4] only to diverge again. That's what can't really be explained by the idea that one genealogy presents Mary's ancestors and the other presents Joseph's ancestors; if that were the case, why would they come together and diverge, come together and diverge? Even if we could explain how Joseph has two fathers (Jacob and Heli), how can we explain that Shealtiel has two fathers (Jeconiah, Matt 1:12; Neri, Luke 3:27)?

EXPLORATION 3.1.

THE GENEALOGIES COMPARED. SHARED NAMES IN RED.

Matthew 1:2–16	Luke 3:23–38
	God
	1. Adam
	2. Seth
	3. Enosh

---

[4] It is also hard to reconcile these genealogies with 1 Chronicles 3:16–19, where Zerubbabel is the nephew of Shealtiel. For Zerubbabel as the son of Shealtiel, see Ezra 3:2, 8; 5:2; Nehemiah 12:1; Haggai 1:1, 12, 14; 2:2, 23.

	4. Cainan
	5. Mahalaleel
	6. Jared
	7. Enoch
	8. Methuselah
	9. Lamech
	10. Noah
	11. Shem
	12. Arphaxad
	13. Cainan
	14. Shelah
	15. Heber
	16. Peleg
	17. Reu
	18. Serug
	19. Nahor
	20. Terah

Abraham	21. Abraham
Isaac	22. Isaac
Jacob	23. Jacob
Judah **m. Tamar**	24. Judah
Perez	25. Perez
Hezron	26. Hezron
Ram	**27. Arni (= Ram?)**
	28. Admin
Amminadab	29. Amminadab
Nahshon	30. Nahson
Salmon **m. Rahab**	31. Salmon
Boaz **m. Ruth**	32. Boaz
Obed	33. Obed
Jesse	34. Jesse
David **m. Bathsheba**	35. David
Solomon	**36. Nathan**
Rehoboam	**37. Mattatha**

Abijah	38. Menna
Asa	39. Melea
Jehoshaphat	40. Eliakim
Joram	41. Jonam
Uzziah	42. Joseph
Jotham	43. Judah
Ahaz	44. Simeon
Hezekiah	45. Levi
Manasseh	46. Matthat
Amon	47. Jorim
Josiah	48. Eliezer
Jeconiah	49. Joshua
	50. Er
	51. Elmadam
	52. Cosam
	53. Addi
	54. Melchi

	55. Neri
Shealtiel	56. Shealtiel
Zerubbabel	57. Zerubbabel
Abihud	58. Rhesa
Eliakim	59. Joanan
Azor	60. Joda
Zadok	61. Josech
Achim	62. Semein
Eliud	63. Mattathias
Eleazar	64. Maath
Matthan	65. Naggai
Jacob	66. Hesli
	67. Nahum
	68. Amos
	69. Mattathias
	70. Joseph
	71. Jannai

	72. Melchi
	73. Levi
	74. Matthat
	75. Eli
Joseph **m. Mary**	76. Joseph
Jesus	77. Jesus

These are the sorts of issues that have exercised Christian scholars throughout the past couple millennia. We are certainly not the first generation to have noticed these differences. Already in the third century AD, Julius Africanus wrote a letter to a certain Aristides in which he attempted to harmonize the two genealogies by hypothesizing levirate marriage (Deut 25:5–10) at work a few times in Jesus's ancestry. Africanus even attributes his information to the descendants of Jesus's own family.[5] In his commentary on Luke, Howard Marshall discusses three basic methods for harmonizing the two lists.[6]

---

[5] This letter was quoted by the fourth-century Christian author Eusebius in his *Ecclesiastical History* (book 1, chapter 7), which can easily be found online. Africanus mentions the family of Jesus as the source of his information at *Ecclesiastical History* 1.7.11.

[6] I. Howard Marshall, *The Gospel of Luke: A Commentary on the Greek Text*, NIGTC (Grand Rapids: Eerdmans, 1978), 158–59.

- First is the idea that I've heard most often in churches, that Matthew gives Joseph's ancestors and Luke gives Mary's. Apparently the first person to propose this interpretation was Annius of Viterbo in the fifteenth century.[7] Marshall considers this idea "not at all plausible, and the theory does not fit in with 1:27 where the Davidic descent of *Joseph* is stressed." By the way, one time I encountered in church the reverse view, that Matthew gives the ancestry of Mary and Luke gives the ancestry of Joseph, but I have never run across that view in a publication.

- The view of Julius Africanus mentioned above goes like this, in the summary given by Marshall: "Matthan (Matt 1:15) married a certain Estha, by whom he had a son, Jacob; when Matthan died, his widow married Malchi (Luke 3:24) and had a son Eli (Luke 3:23; note that Africanus did not apparently know of Levi and Matthat who come between Malchi and Eli in Luke's list). The second of these two half-brothers, Eli, married but died without issue; his half-brother Jacob took his wife in levirate marriage, so that his physical son, Joseph, was regarded as the legal son of Eli. Africanus admits that this theory is uncorroborated, but worthy of belief." Marshall concludes that this idea is pretty improbable, and I must say I agree with that assessment.

---

[7] Wikipedia: "Annio da Viterbo." The Wikipedia article briefly mentions (under "works") that Annio developed this idea.

- I am most partial to the third idea listed by Marshall, and it seems that Marshall is, too. I think I came upon this idea independently, without reading about it in any other source—which I say not to toot my own horn but in order to suggest that it has a certain plausibility to it. The idea is that Luke presents the actual biological ancestry of Jesus, and Matthew does not, nor does he even try to do so. Matthew instead presents the "royal line," and that's why he traces the genealogy through Solomon and all those kings. Matthew's point is that Jesus stands in the line of the rulers of Israel. Luke's point is different, that Joseph, the ostensible father of Jesus, is biologically descended from David. For this idea to work, you'd have to assume that Shealtiel and Zerubbabel were actually in the biological line leading to Jesus from David's son Nathan, but that they were also rulers (not kings) in post-exilic Judah, which they were, as the first few chapters of Ezra attest. That would mean that when Matthew says that Jeconiah was the father of Shealtiel, he was the "father" only in a manner of speaking, because they were both rulers over God's people, though Shealtiel was not actually physically descended from Jeconiah.[8] That

---

[8] There may be a similar thing going on in the book of Daniel, where Belshazzar, king of Babylon, is presented as the son of Nebuchadnezzar (cf. Dan 5:2, 11, etc.), even though we know through other sources that Belshazzar's actual father was Nabonidus, and Nabonidus was not physically descended from Nebuchadnezzar at all. Perhaps Belshazzar was the "son" of Nebuchadnezzar in the sense that they were both kings of Babylon?

doesn't solve all the problems, like: who are all these supposed rulers (on the theory) mentioned by Matthew between Zerubbabel and Joseph? As Marshall says, "There are undoubted difficulties with this theory, but they may not be altogether incapable of solution. But the solution depends upon conjecture, and there is no way of knowing whether the conjectures correspond to reality." In other words, we really don't know what the solution is, but this one may be it.

The Genealogy in Luke

It had never occurred to me to count the names. I feel foolish saying that, because we only have two genealogies for Jesus, and one of them makes it explicit that you're supposed to count the names. So why in the case of the other one had it never occurred to me that the number of names in the list might be significant? If I had counted, I would have seen that Jesus is number 77 in the genealogy presented by Luke. Given the importance of the number seven in the Bible, this simple interpretive procedure of counting the names yields surprising and significant results.

Matthew's presentation of the genealogy of Jesus is the one that makes it clear that the number of names is important. He tells his readers that there are three sections of fourteen generations (Matt 1:17). He doesn't tell us why that's important, but it clearly is; otherwise he wouldn't have pointed it out. My guess is that the number fourteen is important because it is symbolically associated (by means of gematria; see Wikipedia) with the name "David." Davies and Allison, in their commentary on Matthew, discuss this interpretation and conclude in its favor.

We suspect gematria because David's name has the value fourteen and because in Mt 1.2–16 there are 3 x 14 generations. But there is an additional observation to be made. David's name is fourteenth on the list. This is telling. In a genealogy of 3 x 14 generations, the one name with three consonants [remember: in Hebrew writing there are only consonants] and a value of fourteen is also placed in the fourteenth spot. When one adds that this name is mentioned immediately before the genealogy (1.1) and twice at its conclusion (1.17), and that it is honoured by the title, king, coincidence becomes effectively ruled out. The name, David, is the key to the pattern of Matthew's genealogy.[9]

Luke's genealogy is obviously structured much differently, but the comparison with Matthew's genealogy should lead us to consider whether we should count the names in Luke as well. Yes, we should.

Jesus is the 77th name in Luke's genealogy. As Richard Bauckham notes, "If seven indicates fullness, seventy-seven implies ultimacy, a fullness beyond measure."[10] As a point of

---

[9] W. D. Davies and Dale C. Allison, *The Gospel according to Saint Matthew*, vol. 1, ICC (Edinburgh: T&T Clark, 1988), 165.

[10] Richard Bauckham, "The Lukan Genealogy of Jesus," in *Jude and the Relatives of Jesus in the Early Church* (London: T&T Clark, 1990), 315–73, at 318.

comparison, note the words of Lamech: "If Cain is avenged sevenfold, truly Lamech seventy-sevenfold" (Gen 4:24). And note the words of Jesus, in response to Peter's question about whether he should forgive someone seven times: "Jesus said to him, "Not seven times, but, I tell you, seventy-seven times" (Matt 18:22). I know that Matthew 18:22 has traditionally been translated "seventy times seven," but take a look at some modern translations (NIV, ESV, NRSV, CEB) and you'll see that scholars these days are agreed that the best translation is "seventy-seven times." Those are just some examples to show that 77 is viewed in the Bible as something like "completeness squared." Since Jesus is name number 77, he is "completeness squared."

But there may be even more going on with these names. Remember that Matthew divided his genealogy into 3 x 14. Well, in this list of 77 names in Luke, we might divide it into 7 x 11, sort of like eleven weeks of generations.[11]

The idea that you might count time in terms of "weeks of generations" is unusual but not unheard of in ancient Jewish literature. For one thing, the patriarch Enoch had a high status not only because "he walked with God, and he was not, for God took him" (Gen 5:24), but also because it was well-known that he was the "seventh from Adam," i.e., he was at the end of the first week of generations in world history, a fact mentioned by Jude in his epistle (Jude 14).[12] The ancient Jewish work known as 1

---

[11] For a similar idea, where weeks = weeks of years, see Daniel 9:24–27.

[12] For other references to Enoch as the "seventh from Adam" in ancient Jewish literature, see the book known as *1 Enoch* (easily found online) at 60:8; 93:3; or also the book known as *Jubilees* 7:39; and the rabbinic work known as *Leviticus Rabbah* 29.11.

Enoch actually represents the patriarch Enoch saying this: "I was born the seventh in the first week" (93:3).[13]

So if we count these names in Luke's genealogy as a collection of "weeks of generations," the first and last name in each week are as follows.

1. Adam to Enoch
2. Methuselah to Shelah
3. Eber to Abraham
4. Isaac to Admin
5. Amminadab to David
6. Nathan to Joseph
7. Judah to Joshua
8. Er to Shealtiel
9. Zerubbabel to Mattathias
10. Maath to Joseph
11. Jannai to Jesus

It seems hardly accidental that the first and last names of each "week of generations" are such significant names. Note, for instance, that besides Jesus's supposed father, the name "Joseph" appears twice in this genealogy, both times at the end of a "week of generations," the sixth week (i.e., name #42, v. 30) and the tenth week (i.e., name #70, v. 24). The name Joshua appears once in this genealogy, at the end of the seventh week of generations (i.e., name #49, v. 29). You probably know that the name

---

[13] This is from the part of *1 Enoch* called "The Apocalypse of Weeks" and dating to the early second century BC.

"Joshua" is the same as the name "Jesus" in Greek and Hebrew (the Greek words are the exact same in our manuscripts of Luke). It seems significant, then, that "Jesus" is both the 77th name on this list and the 49th name (= 7 x 7).

What is the meaning of all this? Well, on one level I think it's just cool to see all these connections. But there might also be a deeper message, and that message might be that Jesus is the turning point in history. Here's how that would work.

There was an idea in ancient Judaism that at one point in the distant past angels had cohabited with human women, a sin for which they suffered the punishment of being chained in darkness. (Some Jews interpreted Genesis 6:1–4 in light of this idea.) In the book of *1 Enoch* again, the text represents God as commanding the angels to be bound for seventy generations until they are judged on the Day of Judgment (*1 Enoch* 10:12–14).[14] Assuming that the angels were bound in the generation after Enoch (i.e., the seventh generation of world history),[15] that would mean that the Day of Judgment would happen at the seventy-seventh generation. In the passage, quoted below, Michael is the archangel commissioned by God to bind the rebel angels, and Semyaza is one of the leaders of the rebel angels.

> And the Lord said to Michael, Go, inform Semyaza and the others with him who have associated with the women to corrupt

---

[14] This passage is in the part of *1 Enoch* called "The Book of Watchers" and dating to the third century BC.

[15] For an argument to this effect, see Bauckham, "Lukan Genealogy," 320. Bauckham's analysis of Luke's genealogy has been very influential in my presentation.

themselves with them in all their uncleanness. [12]When all their sons kill each other, and when they see the destruction of their beloved ones, bind them for seventy generations under the hills of the earth until the day of judgment and of their consummation, until the judgment which is for all eternity is accomplished. [13]And in those days they will lead them to the abyss of fire; in torment and in prison they will be shut up for all eternity. [14]And then he [Semyaza] will be burnt and from then on destroyed with them; together they will be bound until the end of all generations. (*1 Enoch* 10:11–14)[16]

So the idea here in *1 Enoch* is basically that world history will last 77 generations. Well, that's pretty interesting, since in Luke's genealogy Jesus is the 77th generation. Now I am not saying that Luke buys into the idea that the generation of Jesus represents the end of the world. How could he think that, since he's probably writing a generation or more after the time of Jesus? But what I do think is plausible is that this genealogy has exactly 77 names because it is playing with this ancient Jewish idea that we see in *1 Enoch*, and what the Lukan genealogy means is that Jesus is (not the end but) the culmination of world history, the turning point of world history, and in a sense the incarnation of Jesus represents the "Day of the Lord" or even a form of the

---

[16] Trans. Michael Knibb in Miryam T. Brand, "1 Enoch," in *Outside the Bible: Ancient Jewish Writings Related to Scripture*, 3 vols., ed. L.H. Feldman et al. (Philadelphia: JPS, 2013), 2.1359–1452, at 1373.

"Day of Judgment." Jesus is the pivot of history, and his is the decisive generation.

Beyond that, it is also significant that Luke traces the genealogy of Jesus through David's son Nathan rather than through Solomon. Solomon's progeny, of course, were the kings of Judah, who ended with Jeconiah (= Jehoiachin or sometimes Coniah), who was taken into exile by Nebuchadnezzar (2 Kgs 24:8–17). Jeremiah did not have nice things to say about Jeconiah.

> As I live, says YHWH, even if King Coniah son of Jehoiakim of Judah were the signet ring on my right hand, even from there I would tear you off and give you into the hands of those who seek your life, into the hands of those of whom you are afraid, even into the hands of King Nebuchadrezzar of Babylon and into the hands of the Chaldeans. I will hurl you and the mother who bore you into another country, where you were not born, and there you shall die. But they shall not return to the land to which they long to return. Is this man Coniah a despised broken pot, a vessel no one wants? Why are he and his offspring hurled out and cast away in a land that they do not know? O land, land, land, hear the word of YHWH! Thus says YHWH: Record this man as childless, a man who shall not succeed in his days; for none of his offspring shall succeed in sitting on the throne of David, and ruling again in Judah. (Jer 22:24–30)

There it is. According to Jeremiah, no descendant of Jeconiah will ever reign as king (Jer 22:30). About Jeconiah's father Jehoiakim, Jeremiah says the same thing (Jer 36:30). The line of kings descended from David had come to a dead-end, and we need to start over. That's probably part of the point of Isaiah's prophecy: "A shoot shall come out from the stump of Jesse, and a branch shall grow out of his roots" (Isa 11:1). Isaiah prophesies a king who will represent a new shoot from the stump of Jesse, meaning apparently not descended from the current line of kings, but rather representing new growth—not just a son of David, but a new David.

And so Luke presents Jesus as a descendant of David not through the line of wicked kings, but precisely in conformity with Isaiah's prophecy as descended through a new line, the line of Nathan.[17] While Nathan was a very obscure son of David in the Bible, he is mentioned in one later prophecy (Zech 12:12), and his very obscurity seems to be part of his appeal; he could not be associated with the line of failed kings.

Conclusion

Christians often think about the genealogy of Jesus in Luke only in terms of its problems, its differences from the genealogy as presented in Matthew. Those problems are real and the solutions to them are not obvious. But Luke does not offer us a genealogy

---

[17] Nevertheless, there does not seem to be much of a pre-Christian Jewish tradition tracing the Messiah's descent from David's son Nathan; see Bauckham, "Lukan Genealogy," 347–54, for some suggestions.

of Jesus in order to cause his readers problems but in order to explain some things about Jesus. Most basically, he uses the genealogy to connect Jesus to David through a non-kingly son (Nathan). Additionally, simply counting the names in the genealogy seems to be the key to its deeper mysteries pointing toward the culmination of world history in Jesus.

4
Launching a Ministry

Luke 4

The Spirit of the Lord is upon me, because he has anointed me to bring good news to the poor. He has sent me to proclaim release to the captives and recovery of sight to the blind, to let the oppressed go free, to proclaim the year of the Lord's favor. (Luke 4:18–19)

Every once in a while I go back to my hometown, Madisonville, Kentucky. I last lived there about twenty years ago, but before that I had spent all my life there up until I went to college. My parents still live there, so I take my family up to Kentucky a couple times a year to stay for a few days. Now, I am exceedingly bad at keeping up with people from high school, so I never schedule any sort of get-togethers. When I go back home, usually the only time I see people from my childhood besides my parents is when we go to church. I don't think the people at my parents' church, my childhood congregation, are resentful of me.

They know I got a PhD in biblical studies; they know I teach Scripture for a living. They generally seem to respect my understanding of the Bible, appreciate what I have to say. They've even invited me to preach for them on occasion, and never have they come close to running me out of town, or—worse—throwing me off a cliff. Some of them do remind me that they taught me when I was in kindergarten or first grade or high school, but—far from implying that they could not possibly learn anything from me—they seem to be relatively proud of what I've been able to do. I have never had occasion to cite the proverb about myself, "A prophet is not without honor except in his hometown."

Then again, I'm not a prophet. A prophet's job is to hold up society to the light of God's standards, and almost always that means being critical of one's society. As we think back to the prophets in the Old Testament, we remember plenty of them that suffered for their ministry. Elijah fled from Jezebel (1 Kgs 19). Jeremiah was beaten, imprisoned (Jer 37:15), and thrown down a pit (38:6). Amos was from the south, and he went up north to prophesy against Israel at Bethel; the priest of Bethel, a man named Amaziah, told him to go back home (Amos 7:10–13). Even today, if you're critical of your society, you might be told to go home.

Jesus was critical of his society. Yes, he was all about love and acceptance. But he was also all about change. He told people to repent. The Son of Man did not come to affirm people in their lifestyles, but to "seek and to save that which was lost" (Luke 19:10). Jesus's contemporaries were lost, and they needed saving. That's good news only if you're willing to accept the premise—that you're lost. If you think everything is just fine, you probably bristle at somebody coming to tell you that you need saving, especially if you've seen that particular somebody in diapers and you know he's no better than you are. Rather than putting on airs and acting holier than thou, he should learn respect and be thankful for where he came from! I imagine things would turn sour pretty quickly if I went back to my childhood congregation and started calling out people's sins.

BACK IN NAZARETH

Every so often a new church launches in our town. Sometimes it's an exceedingly quiet affair, and sometimes it's not. I remember a few years ago a church launched around here with a big advertising push. They were funded by a group outside the area who invested human and financial capital in starting the new church plant with a bang. And it worked, at least in terms of attracting attention and a crowd.

In the Gospel of Luke, Jesus goes to his hometown of Nazareth to launch his ministry. Well, sort of. As soon as he gets baptized (3:21–22) and overcomes the temptations in the wilderness (4:1–13), Luke reports that he "returned to Galilee .... He began to teach in their synagogues and was praised by everyone" (4:14–15). It's at that point that he goes to Nazareth (4:16). So going to Nazareth wasn't the very first thing he did in his ministry; he had already been teaching in synagogues in Galilee. In fact, while he's at Nazareth, Jesus refers to his previous ministry in Capernaum (4:23), so we do get a sense that Jesus has already been doing some amazing things that for some reason Luke omits. The way Luke tells the story, the return of the 30-year-old Jesus to Nazareth is the first major thing he does in his ministry. In other words, Luke doesn't tell his readers anything at all about the kinds of things Jesus had been teaching in those other synagogues; he flies by those details so that he can spend some time telling us what happened in Nazareth.

We should notice that this whole account comes across much differently in Luke than in the other Synoptic Gospels. Matthew and Mark both explain that Jesus's first steps in ministry (after the wilderness temptations) were preaching the kingdom of God in Galilee (Matt 4:12–17; Mark 1:14–15), calling his first disciples, the fishermen (Matt 4:18–22; Mark 1:16–20), and then going to Capernaum, where he healed people (Matt 4:13, 23–25; Mark 1:21–28), including Peter's mother-in-law (Matt 8:14–15; Mark 1:29–31).[1] In Matthew and Mark, these episodes are what make Jesus's reputation. Only later does he visit Nazareth (Matt 13:54–58; Mark 6:1–6).

Luke wants to highlight the episode at Nazareth. He presents it as the launching point of Jesus's ministry. And if we're comparing it to a modern church launch, it'd be more like those churches with the big advertising campaigns than the ones that begin without notice. If there's one thing you can say about Jesus's ministry, it's that people took notice.

Jesus goes to the synagogue on the Sabbath, reads Isaiah 61:1–2, and declares that this ancient prophecy is being fulfilled today.

---

[1] Matthew has some other material here as well, including the Sermon on the Mount.

The Scroll of Isaiah

We don't know exactly how a synagogue service was conducted in the days of Jesus, but in later times (and still today) there is an assigned portion of the Torah (Pentateuch) to read on each Sabbath, and an assigned portion of another book from the Hebrew Bible (the Haftarah).[2] If the Nazareth synagogue in the first century followed this custom, then Jesus read the Haftarah, and Luke doesn't tell us about the Torah portion for that synagogue service.[3]

Another thing we don't know is the language in which worship was conducted in that Nazareth synagogue.[4] You would expect that the normal Jewish language in Galilee in the first century would be Aramaic, and most people think that's the language Jesus grew up speaking. But it seems likely that at least some Aramaic-speaking Jews attended synagogues in which the Bible was read in Hebrew. And then again, we have evidence that many synagogues (as many as fifty percent) in Palestine in the first century conducted their services in Greek (based on the

---

[2] Wikipedia: "Weekly Torah Portion" and "Haftarah."

[3] Note that Luke mentions the reading of the Torah and the Haftarah during Paul's visit to the synagogue at Pisidian Antioch (Acts 13:15). On the history of Torah reading and the Haftarah in synagogues of the Second Temple Period, see Lee I. Levine, *The Ancient Synagogue: The First Thousand Years* (New Haven, CT: Yale University Press, 2000), 135–43.

[4] See Michael Graves, "Languages of Palestine," in *Dictionary of Jesus and the Gospels*, 2d ed., ed. Joel B. Green (Downers Grove, IL: IVP, 2013), 484–92.

Greek inscriptions on their walls). The story that we have in Luke is written in Greek, including the quotation of Isaiah at Luke 4:18–19. Most scholars would say that the scroll of Isaiah would have actually been read in Hebrew (or Aramaic?) and Luke presents to us a translation, but possibly Jesus could speak Greek (but would he have been able to read Greek?).

Jesus read Isaiah 61:1–2 in some language, and he declared that it had been fulfilled. What is it that Jesus was claiming? Let's look at the text as it was quoted by Luke.

> The Spirit of the Lord is upon me, because he has anointed me to bring good news to the poor. He has sent me to proclaim release to the captives and recovery of sight to the blind, to let the oppressed go free, to proclaim the year of the Lord's favor. (Luke 4:18–19)

The quotation corresponds more-or-less to the text of Isaiah 61:1–2, though including only about the first half of the second verse. There are a few differences. First of all, whatever language Jesus used in that synagogue, the quotation as Luke presents it in his Gospel corresponds to the Greek version of Isaiah (the Septuagint).[5] This becomes clear because of the phrase "recovery of sight to the blind" (Luke 4:18; Isa 61:1), which does not precisely correspond to the Hebrew text, which

---

[5] On the Septuagint, see Edmon L. Gallagher, *The Translation of the Seventy: History, Reception, and Contemporary Use of the Septuagint* (Abilene, TX: ACU Press, 2021), which discusses the New Testament's use of the Septuagint in chapter 6.

has instead "release to the prisoners." But the underlying Hebrew is difficult, and "recovery of sight to the blind" might be the Greek translator's best guess at what it meant (and he might have been right).[6] In any case, Luke no doubt considered the line in the Greek translation to be perfectly suited to Jesus's ministry (Luke 7:21; 18:35–43). A second difference between the quotation in Luke and the text of Isaiah 61 is that Luke for some reason omits the phrase "bind up or heal the brokenhearted" (which is present in the Hebrew and the Greek version of Isaiah). And third, Luke inserts a phrase, "let the oppressed go free," which is not in Isaiah 61:1–2. Luke seems to have gotten the phrase Isaiah 58:6.[7]

In Isaiah, the full passage goes like this (according to the NRSV, translating the Hebrew text).

> The spirit of the Lord YHWH is upon me,
>> because YHWH has anointed me;
> he has sent me to bring good news to the oppressed,
>> to bind up the brokenhearted,
> to proclaim liberty to the captives,
>> and release to the prisoners;
> to proclaim the year of YHWH's favor,

---

[6] See Mark S. Gignilliat, "God Speaks Hebrew: The Hebrew Text and Septuagint in the Search for the Christian Bible," *Pro Ecclesia* 25 (2016): 154–72, esp. 160–61.

[7] I keep saying that Luke is doing these things, making these changes, because he's the one who gives us the quotation in Greek. But I realize that he might be just giving us exactly what Jesus said (in Greek? in Hebrew? in Aramaic?), and so maybe it was Jesus who made these changes.

and the day of vengeance of our God;
to comfort all who mourn;
to provide for those who mourn in Zion—
to give them a garland instead of ashes,
the oil of gladness instead of mourning,
the mantle of praise instead of a faint spirit.
They will be called oaks of righteousness,
the planting of YHWH, to display his glory.
They shall build up the ancient ruins,
they shall raise up the former devastations;
they shall repair the ruined cities,
the devastations of many generations.
Strangers shall stand and feed your flocks,
foreigners shall till your land and dress your vines;
but you shall be called priests of YHWH,
you shall be named ministers of our God;
you shall enjoy the wealth of the nations,
and in their riches you shall glory.
Because their shame was double,
and dishonor was proclaimed as their lot,
therefore they shall possess a double portion;
everlasting joy shall be theirs. (Isa 61:1–7)

Why does Jesus choose this passage to read in that synagogue?[8] He obviously thought it was peculiarly appropriate

---

[8] Or was it chosen for him? If the synagogue had an appointed Haftarah reading for the day, maybe it happened to be Isaiah 61. I agree with Levine,

for his own ministry. In fact, later when the imprisoned John the Baptist sends delegates to ask Jesus whether he was "the one to come," Jesus responds with allusions to this passage of Isaiah.

> And he answered them, "Go and tell John what you have seen and heard: the blind receive their sight, the lame walk, the lepers are cleansed, the deaf hear, the dead are raised, the poor have good news brought to them." (Luke 7:22)

Jesus doesn't say he's citing Isaiah at all here, but his words are reminiscent of Isaiah 35:5–6 and Isaiah 61:1–2. Particularly the last phrase of Luke 7:22 about the poor having good news brought to them sounds like Isaiah 61:1.

So Jesus thinks this passage from Isaiah 61 provides a good summary, or maybe introduction, to his own ministry. He identifies himself with this character from Isaiah. As we read the passage in Isaiah, we can imagine several features of the description that Jesus likely thought appropriate to himself. In the Greek Septuagint, the word for "anointing" at Isaiah 61:1 is a verbal form of the word Christos. This prophet in Isaiah is anointed with the Spirit of the Lord, an image reminiscent of Jesus's baptism (Luke 3:21–22). Isaiah's prophet was "sent" by God—note that Jesus uses this same word (ἀποστέλλω, *apostellō*) for himself (Luke 4:43; 9:48; 10:16)[9]—to preach "good news" to poor people. The word for "good news" here is, in

---

Ancient Synagogue, 47, that "Luke's account seems to allude to the fact that Jesus himself chose the passage."

[9] He uses a different word for "send" (πέμπω, *pempō*) at Luke 20:13.

Greek, a verbal form of *euangelion* (εὐαγγέλιον), the Greek term that gives us English words like "evangelism."[10] This same word is used earlier in Isaiah, at 52:7, in a passage quoted by Paul at Romans 10:15: "How beautiful are the feet of those who bring good news!" Of course, this same word for "good news" (*euangelion*) is the very word often translated "gospel." So here is an Old Testament passage talking about the announcement of the gospel. Little wonder Jesus found this passage to be appropriate to the inauguration of his own ministry.

Moreover, this good news is supposed to be announced specifically to the poor or oppressed.[11] Whether we interpret "poor" here in a literal, economic sense or in a spiritual sense, the ministry of Jesus was especially directed at the poor. Or, let's say, his announcement of good news was especially directed at the poor; his ministry also dealt a lot with the rich and powerful, but it was not good news that he was announcing to those people, but rather the judgment of God. Examples in Luke are too numerous to list, but see especially the beatitudes (Luke 6:20–26), the story of the rich man and Lazarus (Luke 16:19–31), and the Parable of the Pharisee and the Publican (Luke 18:9–14).

---

[10] The Hebrew word in Isaiah 61:1 is *bisser*, which doesn't appear a whole lot (only twenty-four times in the Hebrew Bible and six times in the Dead Sea Scrolls).

[11] The Hebrew word at Isaiah 61:1 (עֲנָוִים, *anavim*), which is not a common word (only six times in the Bible, though twenty-one times in the Dead Sea Scrolls), is probably better rendered "oppressed" or "humble." The Greek word used in the Septuagint and in Luke 4:18 (πτωχός, *ptōchos*) means "poor." Obviously, these concepts (humble/oppressed and poor) are closely related.

The other elements in this Isaiah passage that Jesus reads to the Nazareth audience include release for captives, healing for blind people, and the proclamation of the year of the Lord's favor. We've already talked about the healing for blind people, so let's talk about these other elements. Actually, the way Luke presents this quotation from Isaiah, the matter of "release" comes up twice. Here's a translation of Luke 4:18–19 that displays this feature.

> ... to proclaim release to the captives
> and recovery of sight to the blind,
> to send away the oppressed in a release
> to proclaim a favorable year of the Lord.

As I mentioned earlier, that third line ("to send away the oppressed in a release") is not in Isaiah 61, but seems to have come from Isaiah 58:6 (where the Greek for "let the oppressed go free" is basically identical with what we have in Luke 4:18).[12] This is such an important passage from Isaiah that it bears quoting.

> Is not this the fast that I choose:
>> to loose the bonds of injustice,
>> to undo the thongs of the yoke,
> to let the oppressed go free,
>> and to break every yoke?
> Is it not to share your bread with the hungry,

---

[12] On what follows, see Richard B. Hays, *Echoes of Scripture in the Gospels* (Waco, TX: Baylor University Press, 2016), 225–30.

and bring the homeless poor into your house;
when you see the naked, to cover them,
and not to hide yourself from your own kin?
Then your light shall break forth like the dawn,
and your healing shall spring up quickly;
your vindicator shall go before you,
the glory of YHWH shall be your rear guard.
Then you shall call, and YHWH will answer;
you shall cry for help, and he will say, Here I am.
(Isa 58:6–9)

God is calling upon Israel here to behave like his children, to obey the Torah, to live lives worthy of the calling they have received, and he is promising that if they will do that, God will bless them exceedingly (see the rest of the passage, vv. 10–14). Part of this great blessing God wants to accomplish for his people is something like a "new exodus." Notice that God says "your vindicator shall go before you, the glory of YHWH shall be your rear guard" (v. 8). This description is reminiscent of the pillar of cloud that led Israel in the wilderness following their escape from Egypt (e.g., Exod 13:21–22; 14:19–20). A new exodus would mean that the oppressed would go free, just like they did in the first exodus. Isaiah was originally referring to the end of the Babylonian exile, when God would lead the captives back to their homeland. But the same message continued to resonate with many first-century Jews, who were also longing for a new exodus: freedom from the oppressor.

The promise of "release" that Jesus twice mentions in his reading from Isaiah is tied to another biblical theme, which Jesus also mentions: the favorable year of the Lord. This is a reference to the Jubilee Year.

> And you shall hallow the fiftieth year and you shall proclaim liberty throughout the land to all its inhabitants. It shall be a jubilee for you: you shall return, every one of you, to your property and every one of you to your family. (Lev 25:10)

This is a translation of the Hebrew text of Leviticus. The Greek Septuagint does not have the term Jubilee (which is a Hebrew word) but instead has the phrase "year of release" (ἐνιαυτὸς ἀφέσεως), using the same word for "release" that Jesus twice uses in his reading of Isaiah 61. Actually, Isaiah was himself alluding to the Jubilee Year by proclaiming a release from captivity, since that was the main feature of the Jubilee: no more debt, no more slavery.

At least some first-century Jews were anticipating the fulfillment of Isaiah 61. There are a couple of scrolls from the Dead Sea Scrolls that explicitly quote Isaiah 61:1–2 as a prophecy relating to messianic times. One of them (called 11Q13) features a figure named Melchizedek who will usher in the Jubilee Year and do the things mentioned in Isaiah 61.[13] The other text (4Q521) talks about the Messiah and (at the very end of the preserved fragment) says that he will "bring good news to the poor," exactly as in Isaiah 61:1.[14] What these Dead Sea Scrolls

---

[13] You can read the whole, brief text in English at Wikipedia, "11Q13."

[14] Again, read the whole thing in English at Wikipedia, "4Q521." You can also see the actual scroll online; here is the address for an infrared image:

show us is that some ancient Jews, more-or-less contemporary with Jesus, were looking forward to the messianic fulfillment of Isaiah 61 at the end times.

This passage from Isaiah that Jesus reads goes in multiple directions. This section of Isaiah is about the end of the Babylonian exile, and it (especially Isa 58) speaks about that period of captivity in terms of a new exodus. And Isaiah 61 is about the year of Jubilee. All of that is already at work in the passage that Jesus chooses to read. And his simple and brief sermon explodes with significance: "Today this scripture has been fulfilled in your hearing" (Luke 4:21).

The Reaction to Jesus

If the long-anticipated hopes of Israel were about to be fulfilled, you would think that maybe people would be happy. But claiming to embody the promises of God also sounds incredibly presumptuous, especially when you're around people who know better because they've seen you grow up. The reaction in that Nazareth synagogue to the words of Jesus is somewhat mixed, and then Jesus seems intentionally to push them over the edge. At first "all spoke well of him and were amazed at the gracious words that came from his mouth, and they were saying, 'Is not this Joseph's son?'" (4:22). It is not clear to me what we are

---

https://www.deadseascrolls.org.il/explore-the-archive/image/B-513138. The unmarked quotation from Isaiah 61:1, amounting to only two Hebrew words (ענוים יבשר), is in the middle column, third line from the bottom (line 12), at the end of the line. The official publication is in volume 25 of Discoveries in the Judean Desert.

supposed to make of this reaction. Is the crowd excited about the prospect of Israel's hopes finally coming to fruition, or are they just proud of the local boy who has started to make his mark on the world? And the question they ask— "Is not this Joseph's son?"—are we supposed to read it as a sign of local pride (as in, "wow, Joseph's boy has really done well!") or as an accusation ("why should we listen to you? aren't you just that local carpenter's boy?").[15]

Whatever verse 22 means, it seems that Jesus is then intentionally provocative in what he says next. I think we can say that Jesus senses some hesitation on the part of the hometown crowd, or some downright hardness of heart. That's certainly the way the story goes in Mark and Matthew, where the people of Nazareth take offense at Jesus and demonstrate such lack of faith that Jesus performed no sign for them (Mark 6:1–6; Matt 13:54–58). Here in Luke, it's almost like Jesus is goading the people into displaying their obstinance.

To accomplish this, Jesus cites two episodes from the Old Testament. The first concerns Elijah, who went to Zarephath during a famine in Israel (1 Kgs 17:8), more than 100 miles north of Samaria (Israel's capital).[16] While there, Elijah saved a widow and her son from starving to death in the famine (1 Kgs 17:8–16), and he raised the widow's son from death (17:17–24). The second story Jesus mentions is the story of Naaman (2 Kgs 5), whose leprosy brought him down to Israel from his own country of Aram so that he could consult with the prophet Elisha.

---

[15] C. F. Evans, *Saint Luke* (Philadelphia: Trinity Press International, 1990), 273, thinks the question does signal the crowd's "incredulity and hostility."

[16] On Zarephath, see https://www.bibleplaces.com/zarephath/.

Naaman was healed of his leprosy after dipping seven times in the Jordan River, according to the instructions from Elisha. The point that Jesus makes from these two stories is that in both cases God's grace was transmitted to people outside Israel because the Israelites themselves had rejected God. On the one hand, Jesus here anticipates themes that will find their fulfillment only in Luke's second volume, when the gospel spreads among gentiles. On the other hand, Jesus is implying here that Israel's own scriptures attest God's favor toward all who have faith rather than those with the right bloodline.

The implication is enough. The synagogue-attendees that day so despised the implication, especially coming from the lips of this carpenter's boy, that they tried to kill Jesus. Of course, they did not accomplish their task (v. 30) because, as Evans says, "Jesus possesses a mysterious invulnerability" (cf. John 8:59; 10:39).[17] But this rejection by Jesus's hometown is, in some ways, a foregone conclusion, because Jesus is here announcing his prophetic ministry and is thus standing in a long line of prophets who were rejected by God's people. That's the point, for instance, of the Parable of the Tenants (Luke 20:9–19): what the Jewish leadership is doing to Jesus by rejecting him is nothing new but is rather what they have always done with God's prophets. But just as Jesus is the fulfillment of the ancient words of Isaiah 61, so also he is the fulfillment of God's prophets, and his ultimate rejection by his own people through the cross would embody and fulfill all the prior rejections of God's servants.

---

[17] Evans, *Saint Luke*, 275.

He came to his own, and his own did not receive
him. (John 1:11)

That is the story of Jesus's ministry, resulting in his death
on a cross. And since that is the pattern of his life (and again, the
pattern of life for all God's prophets), this rejection at his
hometown of Nazareth is a fitting beginning to a prophetic
career that Jesus knows will end in his own death. And it is his
very death that ushers in the favorable year of the Lord, the
proclamation of good news, liberty to those in bondage.

5

In the Home of a Pharisee

Luke 7:36-50

Wherefore I say unto thee, Her sins, which are many, are forgiven; for she loved much: but to whom little is forgiven, the same loveth little. (Luke 7:47)

I never wear cologne and rarely lotion. I do use deodorant. In the winter, my hands get all dry, and sometimes I remember to rub some lotion into them, so they don't crack so much. That's about it for me. But my wife uses lotion a lot more than I do, every day, I think. And then one of my sons will get really dry skin if I don't lotion him up really well all over his body after every bath. So even though I personally don't use lotion much, we always have a supply at the house and our family uses it constantly. None of us care too much about making ourselves smell a certain way with cologne or perfume, but we all would like to avoid stinking. If I were in a situation in which I couldn't take a shower every day, I would probably use cologne, to try to counteract the stench.

In the first century, I would have used cologne, or whatever oil was the equivalent. This practice is sometimes mentioned in the Bible.

> Go, eat your bread with enjoyment, and drink your wine with a merry heart; for God has long ago approved what you do. Let your garments always be white; do not let oil be lacking on your head. Enjoy life with the wife whom you love, all the days of your vain life that are given you under the sun, because that is your portion in life and in your toil at which you toil under the sun. (Eccl 9:7–9)

Jesus tells people to conceal the fact that they are fasting by washing their face and anointing their head (Matt 6:17). Some ancient Jewish literature, like the apocryphal stories of Susannah (v. 17) and Judith (10:3), mentions the use of oils and ointments after baths. If you were in a state of mourning, you would avoid using oils (2 Sam 14:2; Dan 10:3).

The Bible uses several different words for the oil used on such occasions. The story of the woman who anoints Jesus for burial in Mark (14:3) and John (12:3) uses the term nard (from the Greek νάρδος, *nardos*, which itself comes from the Hebrew word nard [נֵרְדְּ]), which also appears in the Old Testament a few times, all in the Song of Solomon (1:12; 4:13, 14).[1] In Luke's

---

[1] Wikipedia: "Spikenard."

telling of the woman anointing the feet of Jesus (7:36–50, the focus of this chapter), a couple other words are used. There is olive oil (Greek ἔλαιον, *elaion*)—still one of the best oils for healthy skin (as the internet tells me)—which Jesus notes was not supplied to him by his host (Luke 7:46), and there is the oil that the woman uses on Jesus's feet, called "ointment" or "perfume" in most translations, from the Greek word *muron* (μύρον, vv. 37, 38, 46).[2]

Of course, Luke doesn't tell us this story because he's interested in the ointment—he doesn't even tell us whether it was especially high quality ointment, or expensive—or because he wants us to know that Jesus had the very human needs of keeping his skin moist and fragrant, but because of the way Jesus interacts with the woman and with the Pharisee who had invited him to the meal.

Comparison with the Other Gospels

Before examining the story in Luke, let's notice how it is similar in some ways to stories told in Matthew, Mark, and John, while there are also many differences. Matthew and Mark tell the same story, about Jesus going to the home of Simon the leper in Bethany during the week before his crucifixion, and at this home, a woman (not labeled a "sinful" woman) pours expensive perfume on his head. Despite criticism from his disciples against

---

[2] This same word also appears in each of the other Gospels in reference to their stories of a woman anointing Jesus (Matt 26:7, 12; Mark 14:3, 4, 5; John 11:2; 12:3, 5). The only other appearances in the New Testament are at Luke 23:56 and Revelation 18:13.

wasting money, Jesus interprets this action as an anointing for his burial.

Matthew 26:6–13	Mark 14:3–9
[6]Now while Jesus was at Bethany in the house of Simon the leper,	[3]While he was at Bethany in the house of Simon the leper, as he sat at the table,
[7]a woman came to him with an alabaster jar of very costly ointment, and she poured it on his head as he sat at the table.	a woman came with an alabaster jar of very costly ointment of nard, and she broke open the jar and poured the ointment on his head.
[8]But when the disciples saw it, they were angry and said, "Why this waste? [9]For this ointment could have been sold for a large sum, and the money given to the poor."	[4]But some were there who said to one another in anger, "Why was the ointment wasted in this way? [5]For this ointment could have been sold for more than three hundred denarii, and the money given to the poor." And they scolded her.
[10]But Jesus, aware of this, said to them, "Why do you trouble the woman? She has performed a good service for me.	[6]But Jesus said, "Let her alone; why do you trouble her? She has performed a good service for me.

¹¹For you always have the poor with you, but you will not always have me.	⁷For you always have the poor with you, and you can show kindness to them whenever you wish; but you will not always have me.
¹²By pouring this ointment on my body she has prepared me for burial.	⁸She has done what she could; she has anointed my body beforehand for its burial.
¹³Truly I tell you, wherever this good news is proclaimed in the whole world, what she has done will be told in remembrance of her."	⁹Truly I tell you, wherever the good news is proclaimed in the whole world, what she has done will be told in remembrance of her."

Immediately after narrating this incident, both Matthew (26:14) and Mark (14:10) report that Judas Iscariot went to the chief priests to cut a deal to betray Jesus in exchange for thirty pieces of silver.

John tells maybe the same story, but the details are different.

> Six days before the Passover Jesus came to Bethany, the home of Lazarus, whom he had raised from the dead. There they gave a dinner for him. Martha served, and Lazarus was one of those at the table with him. Mary took a pound

of costly perfume made of pure nard, anointed Jesus's feet, and wiped them with her hair. The house was filled with the fragrance of the perfume. But Judas Iscariot, one of his disciples (the one who was about to betray him), said, "Why was this perfume not sold for three hundred denarii and the money given to the poor?" (He said this not because he cared about the poor, but because he was a thief; he kept the common purse and used to steal what was put into it.) Jesus said, "Leave her alone. She bought it so that she might keep it for the day of my burial. You always have the poor with you, but you do not always have me." (John 12:1–8)

Here, though the story takes place in Bethany (as in the story reported by Matthew and Mark), the home belongs to Lazarus and not Simon the leper. Like the story in Matthew and Mark, John's story involves a woman anointing Jesus with expensive perfume (and the perfume is "nard," as at Mark 14:3), but instead of pouring the perfume on the head of Jesus (as in Matthew and Mark), the woman pours it on his feet. And the woman is named Mary, whom we've already met in John 11. The question of reprimand is largely the same (John 12:5; cf. Matt 26:8–9 // Mark 14:4–5), but in John's story the question comes from Judas Iscariot rather than from "some" who were there (Mark) or from "the disciples" in general (Matthew). The response of Jesus to this question is also largely the same across both stories, connecting the woman's actions to Jesus's burial (John 12:7; cf. Matt 26:12 // Mark 14:8) and reminding his listeners that the poor are always with them (John 12:8; cf. Matt 26:11 // Mark 14:7).

Luke's story of a woman anointing Jesus (Luke 7:36–50) is similar to both of these stories in a lot of ways, and yet further from these other stories than John's story is from the one in Matthew and Mark. For one thing, the story in Luke does not take place in Bethany but in Galilee, and it's at the home of a Simon (as in Matthew and Mark) but this Simon is not "the leper" but "the Pharisee." There is nothing to suggest that the woman in Matthew/Mark is an outcast or immoral; indeed, quite the opposite—the fact that she has an expensive bottle of perfume suggests that she is not without significant resources. The woman in John's story is Mary of Bethany, obviously not an outcast but a member of a respected family. But the woman in Luke's story is labeled several times "a sinner." This sinful woman brings "an alabaster jar of ointment" (Luke 7:37), which is reminiscent of the alabaster jar owned by the woman in the story in Matthew/Mark. (No jar is mentioned in John's story.) The sinful woman seems to engage in a series of actions: first she cleans Jesus's feet with her tears, dries them with her hair, and finally anoints them with the perfume while also kissing his feet (v. 38). These actions have very little resemblance to the actions of the woman in Matthew/Mark, though in John's story Mary of Bethany also anointed Jesus's feet with the perfume and used her hair to dry them (not of her tears but of the perfume, apparently). In Luke, as in the other stories, the response to the woman's actions is indignation on the part of the bystanders, but the actual words used in Luke do not correspond to the wording in the other stories. The continuation of the story in Luke is nothing like the stories in John or Matthew/Mark.

Odd Features of Luke's Story

Luke's story of Jesus's encounter with the sinful woman at the home of a Pharisee is wonderful and inspiring in several ways, which we will mention in a moment, but it also presents, perhaps, a few odd features that are worth thinking about.

First of all, Jesus was eating with a Pharisee. This never happens in the other Gospels, but in Luke it happens twice more after this time in Luke 7 (cf. 11:37; 14:1). Jesus's eating with Pharisees seems odd because usually we think of Jesus as at odds with the Pharisees; it seems like neither Jesus nor any Pharisee would want to sit down and share a meal together. The appearance of the Pharisees so far in Luke's Gospel probably confirms us in our view of the Pharisees as typically opponents of Jesus. They make their first appearance at 5:17, where they are present to hear Jesus teach, but they soon complain about Jesus when he pronounces forgiveness of sins on the paralytic carried by his four friends. That's the first in a series of confrontations with the Pharisees. The Pharisees complain at Jesus's eating with Levi and his sinful friends (5:30), and they twice complain at him for healing on the Sabbath (6:2, 6). This last event made the Pharisees so mad they "discussed with one another what they might do to Jesus" (6:11). There has not been a positive encounter between Jesus and Pharisees up to this point in the narrative.

So what do we make of this dinner at the home of Simon the Pharisee? The text says that the Pharisee invited Jesus for dinner (7:36), but it doesn't say why. I guess we could imagine all kinds of reasons. Sometimes a Gospel story specifically says that a person approaches Jesus with the intention of trapping him (Matt 22:15, 35). Could Simon be doing that? Well, sure, I guess we could read the story in that way. But let's also remember that Pharisees were not monolithic. We should resist the temptation—so common today, just like always—to give someone a label (Pharisee) and then interpret that person completely through our views on that label. In the Gospels, we usually get the stories about the conflict that Jesus had with Pharisees, because the Gospel writers need to explain why Jesus ended up dead (before he ended up alive), and stories of conflict tend toward that end better than stories of harmony. The Gospels also give us glimpses into these stories of harmony, like when Nicodemus came to visit Jesus, apparently with a genuine desire to understand him better (John 3). Joseph of Arimathea was not a Pharisee, as far as we know, but he was a member of the same Sanhedrin that condemned Jesus (Luke 22:66–71), and yet he took care of Jesus's corpse (Luke 23:50–53), because, as John says, he was a secret disciple of Jesus (John 19:38). And in Acts, Luke reports that some Pharisees became Christians (Acts 15:5).

I don't know why Simon invited Jesus home, but I lean toward thinking that he wanted to learn more about him. Simon had heard a lot of grand things about this itinerant prophet and healer, and he had heard some negative things about him, and Simon just wanted to see for himself. I interpret this invitation positively.

We shouldn't miss the fact that Jesus accepted the invitation. Simon and Jesus present a good model for engagement with people with whom we will likely have disagreements. Simon extended an invitation; Jesus accepted. Those excellent first steps toward understanding are too often neglected, even intentionally shunned. This point deserves much thought and emphasis (and enacting), but we will move on.

A second odd thing about the story: this lady is there. Who is this lady? Why is she in this Pharisee's house? Simon seems surprised to see her, or repulsed by her, so it seems like she hasn't been invited. I don't know why she's there. Maybe this Pharisee's house was a little more open than we usually consider our houses. Like, maybe, it wasn't a complete breach of social etiquette to walk into someone's house. (I'm just spit balling here.) Or maybe this little dinner party was on a patio or something such that this lady didn't have to actually walk into the house to get at Jesus.

Third odd thing: what's the deal with the lady being behind Jesus and getting at his feet (7:38)? Can you picture that? I do have an answer to this one, and it has something to do with the way ancient people sat at a meal. Luke says explicitly that Jesus "reclined" to eat (7:36), though translations often obscure this word, using instead "sat down" or some such (the ESV is a good exception). For the lady to be behind Jesus and touching his feet, you've got to imagine Jesus either lying on his belly or on his side. Strange to say, that's the way people liked to eat in antiquity. I wouldn't want to eat like that, but they did.[3]

---

[3] You can find some drawings of what that would look like by going to Google Images and searching "reclining at table."

A Woman Who Is a Sinner

Luke's story identifies the woman as a sinner. It's not just that Simon the Pharisee thinks she's a sinner–which he does (7:39)—but the narrator of the story says the woman is a sinner (7:37), and Jesus says that she has many sins (7:47).

What kind of sins? The story does not say.

People often think she's a prostitute. I suppose what gives that impression is that any woman who is a known sinner—well, we figure we know what she's been up to. If she's not actually a prostitute, then she's been passed around like that Samaritan Woman in John 4 (see v. 18). And also Jesus has that saying about prostitutes preceding religious leaders into God's kingdom (Matt 21:31).

Maybe. Biblical scholar Michael Bird, for instance, thinks she's a prostitute because of "her access to expensive perfume."[4] Sometimes people cite her hair—the fact that it's unbound, hanging free—as an indication that she might be a prostitute: loose hair, loose woman.

I myself am not convinced, and I think it would be better to leave the matter open. First of all, Luke does not actually say that this perfume is expensive, but even if it were, access to expensive perfume is not a very good clue that this woman is a prostitute. I guess we also imagine that she is poor, but that might not be the case. Certainly, we should not interpret the story in the other Gospels, where the perfume is explicitly identified as

---

[4] Michael F. Bird, "Sin, Sinner," in *Dictionary of Jesus and the Gospels*, 2nd ed., ed. Joel B. Green (Downers Grove, IL: IVP, 2013), 863–69, at 866.

"expensive," as if the woman anointing Jesus is a prostitute. Mary of Bethany (in John) is not a prostitute.

Second, the hair thing is not in any way definitive. Loose hair sometimes did indicate a sexually provocative woman, but that was just one possible meaning among many.

> When a woman wears her hair unbound/unbinds her hair, this can be a sexually suggestive act, an expression of religious devotion, a hairstyle for unmarried girls, a sign of mourning, a symbolic expression of distress or proleptic grief in the face of impending danger (and a way of pleading with or currying the favor of those in power, whether gods or men), a hairstyle associated with conjury, a means of presenting oneself in a natural state in religious initiations, and a precaution against carrying demons or foreign objects into the waters of baptism.[5]

Cosgrove points out that the woman apparently does not look like a "sinner" since Simon thinks that Jesus should have known her character because he was a prophet (7:39)—not that

---

[5] Charles H. Cosgrove, "A Woman's Unbound Hair in the Greco-Roman World, with Special Reference to the Story of the 'Sinful Woman' in Luke 7:36–50," *Journal of Biblical Literature* 124 (2005): 675–92, at 691. Cosgrove surveys ancient accounts of women with loose hair (pp. 678–86) and finds that their unbound hair has widely varying significations.

just anyone would have known.[6] Cosgrove suggests that a first century audience hearing Luke's Gospel would most likely interpret the woman's unbound hair "as a gesture expressing grief, gratefulness, or solicitation."[7]

Third, the word "sinner" itself does not really narrow things down very much. This is one of the distinctive things about Luke: he talks about "sinners" a lot more (eighteen times)[8] than the other Gospels (fifteen times combined). Think about these verses and what kind of "sinners" we're talking about.

> The Pharisees and their scribes were complaining to his disciples, saying, "Why do you eat and drink with tax collectors and sinners?" (Luke 5:30)

> If you love those who love you, what credit is that to you? For even sinners love those who love them. (6:32)

> The Son of Man has come eating and drinking, and you say, "Look, a glutton and a drunkard, a friend of tax collectors and sinners." (7:34)

> All who saw it began to grumble and said, "He has gone to be the guest of one who is a sinner" (= Zacchaeus). (19:7)

---

[6] Cosgrove, "A Woman's Unbound Hair," 689.

[7] Cosgrove, "A Woman's Unbound Hair," 692.

[8] Luke 5:8, 30, 32; 6:32–34; 7:34, 37, 39; 13:2; 15:1–2, 7, 10; 18:13; 19:7; 24:7.

> The Son of Man must be handed over to sinners,
> and be crucified, and on the third day rise again.
> (24:7)

Sometimes Luke associates sinners with Gentiles (24:7; note 6:32; cf. Matt 5:47). Often he associates sinners with tax collectors (see also Luke 15:1–2). In ancient Jewish literature, a "sinner" was one who had abandoned the Law of Moses, especially in two ways: by adapting to the wider Gentile society, or by oppressing the poor.[9] The rich man in Luke 16:19–31 is not identified as a "sinner," but he clearly is one (notice where he ends up).

It's at least possible that this lady who comes to Jesus in the Pharisee's house is a well-to-do woman, who has, let us say, oppressed her workers, or profaned the Sabbath to advance her business interests, or eaten unclean foods with Gentiles, or in some other way not maintained her distinctive Jewish identity.

We like to think of sinners as the oppressed, the downcast or the outcast—partly, maybe, because we feel like we have something to offer them: a word, a gesture of love, a gift of grace. I'm not sure that the sinners in the Gospels are the outcast. Certainly the sinners in Luke 24:7 are not outcasts. Zacchaeus was not an outcast. The problem with the sinners in Luke 7:34 was not that they were lonely, but almost the opposite: they fit into society too well. Tax collectors had plenty of money, and

---

[9] For the range of meanings for "sinners" in the Gospel, see Bird, "Sin, Sinner."

therefore plenty of friends. (I know I'm generalizing.) These were successful people, who might look down their noses on "the God-fearing" as poor schlubs who haven't learned how to make it in the world. But they themselves were sinners, and they needed to repent. That's what Jesus told them (Luke 5:32), just as John the Baptist had (Luke 3:10–14).

And sinners came to Jesus, just as they had come to John. They recognized their sin, and they sought redemption. That's what Jesus offered them. He had earned a reputation as a friend of sinners (Luke 7:34). Other Jews looked at tax collectors the way we might look at loan sharks, or a small-time mafioso. Everybody saw them as sinners; Jesus became their friend and called them to repent. And they did.

I don't know what this woman had done, how she had earned a reputation as a sinner, and Luke doesn't help us narrow it down. But like other sinners who encountered Jesus, she recognized a friend, someone who was calling her out of her sin, someone calling her to God.

As for her precise motivation for coming to Jesus at this time (in Simon's home), the story can be read in a couple different ways: either she is looking for forgiveness right now, or she is expressing gratitude for forgiveness previously granted. If the latter, then we'd have to imagine that Luke omits a story in which this woman has already met Jesus, and Jesus has already offered her forgiveness. That's the way I take it, because it makes better sense of the parable Jesus tells. Taking it in this way would mean that this act of anointing the feet of Jesus is this woman's expression of gratitude, of love, because she has been forgiven much. Whereas we might imagine that Jesus pronounces her sins forgiven at vv. 48 and 50, we could also interpret those statements as reassurances that she really has been forgiven (as Jesus had, hypothetically, already told her in their hypothetical initial encounter).

THE POINT OF THE STORY

> Then turning toward the woman, he said to Simon, "Do you see this woman? I entered your house; you gave me no water for my feet, but she has bathed my feet with her tears and dried them with her hair. You gave me no kiss, but from the time I came in she has not stopped kissing my feet. You did not anoint my head with oil, but she has anointed my feet with ointment. Therefore, I tell you, her sins, which were many, have been forgiven; hence she has shown great love. But the one to whom little is forgiven, loves little." (Luke 7:44–47)

Jesus interprets the woman's actions as if she has played the host better than Simon. And Jesus related it all to the woman's, and Simon's, perception of their own sinfulness.

The point seems to be twofold: Jesus welcomes sinners (who repent); and—this one is more subtle—Simon ought to recognize his own sinfulness. After all, the greatest commandment in the Torah (recognized by everyone; cf. Luke 10:25–28) is to love God. Simon the Pharisee knows full well that this commandment is the *sine qua non* of Judaism; he recites that commandment to himself twice daily.[10] Jesus says that you can accomplish this commandment really only if you recognize how much God has forgiven you. The woman does a better job than Simon of obeying the greatest command because she recognizes that "her sins, which were many, are forgiven" (7:47).

In other stories, Jesus condemns the Pharisees, pronounces woes upon them, warns against them. Not in this story. Yes, Jesus welcomes this sinful woman who has recognized her own sinfulness. But Jesus also welcomes the Pharisee and invites Simon also to recognize his own sinfulness.

And the story ends, like so much in the Gospel, without perfect resolution. What did Simon do? The others sitting around the table still display hard hearts (7:49, echoing 5:21), but Simon's response is not recorded. Luke leaves his readers to reflect on what Simon's response likely was, and on what it should have been. And in reflecting on Simon's response, we reflect on our own response, as well.

---

[10] Wikipedia: "Shema Yisrael." There is more on the *Shema* in the next chapter.

6

The Good Samaritan

Luke 10:25-37

But wanting to justify himself, he asked Jesus,
"And who is my neighbor?" (Luke 10:29)

We've heard stories about the search for eternal life. I seem
to remember learning during my school days that the
conquistador Ponce de León was searching for the fountain of
youth in Florida, but apparently that's just a legend.[1] King Arthur
and his knights were allegedly on the lookout for the Holy Grail,
which was also supposed to be a source of eternal life. Of course,
Indiana Jones found the Holy Grail, and it did give him eternal
life (on a limited basis). Early in the movie *Indiana Jones and the
Last Crusade* (1989), the antiquities collector (and villain) Walter
Donovan explains the significance of the lost cup of Christ:
"Eternal life, Dr. Jones. The gift of youth to whoever drinks from
the grail … every man's dream." A real example: the baseball

---

[1] Wikipedia: "Ponce de León," under the section "First Voyage to Florida:
Fountain of Youth."

player Ted Williams is frozen (in two pieces!) so that he can someday come back to life.[2]

Ancient Jews were also interested in eternal life, sort of. Their conception of what that entailed was quite a bit different from what Ponce de León might have been looking for, or what the Holy Grail reputedly offered. When ancient Jews thought about eternal life, it wasn't a continuation of the current life without any death; it was life in a new manner of existence, in the age of eternity.[3]

But how does one achieve this vision of eternal life? How does one qualify for life in the age to come?

That was a question upon which Jesus had something to say. Particularly in the Gospel of John, Jesus has quite a bit to say about eternal life. For instance: "those who drink of the water that I will give them will never be thirsty. The water that I will give will become in them a spring of water gushing up to eternal life" (John 4:14).[4] The way to attain eternal life is to believe in him, or to drink the water he provides, or to eat his flesh. The theme occasionally comes up in the other Gospels, such as when Jesus promises that the sheep on the right of the enthroned Son of Man will enter into eternal life (Matt 25:46). Here, the sheep that enter eternal life are those who feed Jesus, or give him drink,

---

[2] I bet you can find information on Ted Williams without my needing to cite anything for you.

[3] On the hopes of Jews contemporary with Jesus, see E. P. Sanders, *Judaism: Practice & Belief, 63 BCE–66 CE* (Philadelphia: TPI, 1992), 279–303.

[4] For the phrase "eternal life" in the Gospel of John, see also 3:15, 16, 36; 4:36; 5:24, 39; 6:27, 40, 47, 54, 68; 10:28; 12:25, 50; 17:2, 3.

or clothe him, etc., by means of performing these acts of service for "the least of these my brethren."[5]

Sometimes people flat-out asked Jesus how to attain life in the coming age, or how to inherit eternal life. Each of the Synoptic Gospels records this exact question from the Rich Young Ruler to Jesus (Matt 19:16; Mark 10:17; Luke 18:18). The gospel of Luke also records an incident in which a "lawyer" asked Jesus this question. The answer to this question led to the Parable of the Good Samaritan.

SITUATING THE ENCOUNTER

Luke does not tell us exactly where Jesus's encounter with the lawyer took place. By this point in Luke's Gospel, Jesus is already on his way to Jerusalem to accept crucifixion (cf. 9:51). He must be still somewhere in Galilee in Luke 10 because in Luke 17:51 he is still in the area between Samaria and Galilee. He won't arrive in the area around Jerusalem until 19:29.

---

[5] Similar in concept to eternal life, the kingdom of God was more frequently the object of Jesus's proclamation in the Synoptic Gospels (e.g., Luke 4:43; 8:1). The "kingdom of God" referred to the coming age, when God would reign through his Messiah and God's people would dwell securely. The way to get into the kingdom of God is to do the will of the Father (Matt 7:21). One must enter God's kingdom like a child (Mark 10:15). Rich people will only with difficulty enter God's kingdom (Mark 10:23–25). One should strive for (Luke 12:31) or seek God's kingdom (Matt 6:31). Sometimes people asked Jesus when God's kingdom would become manifest (Luke 17:20; 19:11). It would take nothing short of a birth from above to enter God's kingdom (John 3:3, 5).

The Greatest Commandment

Luke records no incident in which someone asks Jesus about the most important commandment in the Torah. Such an episode does appear in Matthew (22:34–40) and Mark (12:28–34). Apparently Luke did not feel it necessary to include that story since he includes this similar story. In Matthew, a Pharisee lawyer approached Jesus with the question about which commandment in the Torah was the most important. In Mark, the person who asks this question is a scribe (and Mark's story generally seems more positive toward this scribe). Jesus's answer according to both Matthew and Mark is to highlight a commandment in Deuteronomy and another in Leviticus. These same two commandments are also cited by the lawyer in Luke 10:27 as summarizing the means by which one may inherit eternal life, a summary with which Jesus heartily agrees: "You have given the right answer; do this, and you will live" (Luke 10:28).

The Shema

The most important commandment, according to Jesus and the lawyer of Luke 10:25, is taken from Deuteronomy 6:5, "You shall love the Lord your God with all your heart, and with all your soul, and with all your strength, and with all your mind." Actually, this is the way the lawyer says it in Luke 10:27, which doesn't precisely match what we find in Deuteronomy 6:5, where the "mind" is not mentioned. I have no good explanation for why the "mind" comes up in all three Synoptic presentations of this commandment (Matt 22:37; Mark 12:30), or why Matthew's version omits "strength."[6] At any rate, the original command in Deuteronomy—love God with all your heart, soul, and strength—surely intended to require complete devotion, and the New Testament quotations reflect this same requirement.[7] "[O]ne should love God with every globule of one's being."[8]

The passage from Deuteronomy is the first part of the Shema, a Jewish prayer traditionally recited twice each day, morning and evening, a practice perhaps going back to the time of Jesus.[9] The beginning of the Shema is Deuteronomy 6:4, "Hear, O Israel," words that give the prayer its name ("hear" in Hebrew is *shema*). The whole prayer, or confession of faith, includes Deuteronomy 6:4–9; 11:13–21; and Numbers 15:37–41. Detailed instructions about how to recite the Shema are given in the Mishnah,[10] the earliest rabbinic document, dating to around

---

[6] The scribe speaking to Jesus in Mark 12 repeats the commandment after Jesus and omits "soul" and substitutes "understanding" (σύνεσις) for "mind" (διάνοια).

[7] On the various forms of the Shema in the Bible, see the chart at W. D. Davies and D. C. Allison, *The Gospel according to Saint Matthew*, 3 vols., International Critical Commentary (London: T&T Clark, 1988–1997), 3.242.

[8] Davies and Allison, *Gospel according to Saint Matthew*, 3.241.

[9] Please, please watch the Bible Project's video on "Shema/Listen" (https://bibleproject.com/explore/video/shema-listen/), which is actually the first of a series on the Shema covering every major word in Deuteronomy 6:4. If then you get lost on the Bible Project's website (or their YouTube page) watching all their wonderful videos, good for you!

[10] This is the very first topic addressed in the Mishnah, in the opening tractate *Berakhot*. On the recitation of the Shema, see Emil Schürer, *The History of the Jewish People in the Age of Jesus Christ*, rev. ed., 3 vols. (Edinburgh: T&T Clark, 1973–87), 2.454–55.

AD 200 but often preserving earlier material. Josephus seems to assume that Moses himself instituted the practice of reciting the Shema twice each day.[11] Tiny scrolls called in Hebrew *tefillin* (or, in Greek, phylacteries) containing the Shema have been found among the Dead Sea Scrolls.[12]

So it is no surprise at all that Jesus would consider the command to love God to be the most important commandment in the Torah, nor that the lawyer in Luke 10 would suggest that it is the primary avenue to eternal life.

The Neighbor Command

The lawyer in Luke 10 tacks on to the end of his answer, "and your neighbor as yourself," as if this phrase was part of the same law. In fact, the command to "love your neighbor as yourself" comes from a different book of the Torah, Leviticus (19:18). In

---

[11] See Josephus, *Antiquities of the Jews*, 4.212, with the commentary of Louis H. Feldman, *Flavius Josephus: Judean Antiquities 1–4* (Leiden: Brill, 2000), 406–7.

[12] In general, see Wikipedia: "Tefillin." For the Dead Sea Scrolls, see the phylacteries called Mur4 edited by J. T. Milik and published in *Les Grottes de Murabba'ât*, Discoveries in the Judean Desert 2 (Oxford: Oxford University Press, 1961), 85, with digital images at the Leon Levy Dead Sea Scrolls Digital Library (https://www.deadseascrolls.org.il/home). Go to "Explore the Archive" and search "Mur4." In this picture (https://www.deadseascrolls.org.il/explore-the-archive/image/B-278148), at the very top, you can see the Hebrew word *shema* (שמע). See also Phylactère C (4Q130), ed. J. T. Milik, in *Qumran Grotte 4, II*, Discoveries in the Judean Desert 6 (Oxford: Oxford University Press, 1977), 55, starting at line 15.

his response to the question about the greatest command, Jesus (in both Matthew and Luke) adds this quotation from Leviticus 19:18 as the second most important commandment. According to Jesus, no commandment is greater than these (Mark 12:31), and all the Law and the Prophets depend on these two commandments (Matt 22:40). What Jesus seems to be saying here is that these two commandments, Deuteronomy 6:5 and Leviticus 19:18, encapsulate all of the laws in the Torah.

In the New Testament, it is the second greatest commandment that actually appears more often than the Shema.

> Owe no one anything, except to love one another; for the one who loves another has fulfilled the law. The commandments, "You shall not commit adultery; You shall not murder; You shall not steal; You shall not covet"; and any other commandment, are summed up in this word, "Love your neighbor as yourself." Love does no wrong to a neighbor; therefore, love is the fulfilling of the law. (Rom 13:8–10).

> For the whole law is summed up in a single commandment, "You shall love your neighbor as yourself." (Gal 5:14)

> You do well if you really fulfill the royal law according to the scripture, "You shall love your neighbor as yourself." (Jas 2:8)

All these passages indicate that you can summarize the entire Torah, all 613 commandments (according to the traditional Jewish reckoning),[13] in the one commandment, "Love your neighbor."

This way of summarizing the Torah would have seemed very normal within first-century Judaism. The two same commandments, Deuteronomy 6:5 and Leviticus 19:18, were also brought together in a work known as *The Testament of the Twelve Patriarchs*,[14] though this work may be not a Jewish composition but a Christian one.[15] But Philo provides a Jewish source contemporary with Jesus who summarized the Torah essentially just as Jesus did, without citing the specific commandments of Deuteronomy 6:5 and Leviticus 19:18.

---

[13] The number 613 is found in the Babylonian Talmud, tractate *Makkot*, 23b–24a.

[14] You can find the text in English online; go to the Issachar section and look at ch. 5. The Greek is ἀλλ᾽ ἀγαπᾶτε κύριον καὶ τὸν πλησίον; see M. de Jonge, ed., *The Testaments of the Twelve Patriarchs: A Critical Edition of the Greek Text* (Leiden: Brill, 1978), 85. On love of neighbor in the *Testaments*, see H. W. Hollander and M. de Jonge, *The Testaments of the Twelve Patriarchs: A Commentary* (Leiden: Brill, 1985), 418, commenting on *Testament of Benjamin* 3.3. See also M. de Jonge, "The Two Great Commandments in the Testaments of the Twelve Patriarchs," in *Pseudepigrapha of the Old Testament as Part of Christian Literature: The case of The* Testaments of the Twelve Patriarchs *and the Greek* Life of Adam and Eve (Leiden: Brill, 2003), 141–59.

[15] See Hollander and De Jonge, *Testaments*, 82–85; and M. de Jonge, "*The Testaments of the Twelve Patriarchs* as a Document Transmitted by Christians," in *Pseudepigrapha of the Old Testament*, 84–106.

But among the vast number of particular truths and principles there studied [i.e., in the Torah], there stand out practically high above the others two main heads: one of duty to God as shown by piety and holiness, one of duty to people as shown by humanity (*philanthrōpia*) and justice.[16]

In fact, Philo indicates that the Ten Commandments are already a summary of the entire Torah, and the Ten Commandments can themselves be summarized as two: the first five commandments (he says) correspond to love of God, and the second set of five commandments correspond to love of people.[17] Moreover, there were summaries of the Torah along the lines of something like the Golden Rule,[18] showing that Jews in the first century understood that the Law was essentially calling on them to treat others well. This is illustrated by the famous story in the

---

[16] See Philo's work called *On the Special Laws* 2.63. I have used the translation (slightly adapted) by F. H. Colson in *Philo*, vol. 7, Loeb Classical Library (Cambridge, MA: Harvard University Press, 1937), 347. For other Jewish parallels to the Torah summary offered by Jesus, see Dale C. Allison, Jr., "Mark 12.28–31 and the Decalogue," in *The Gospels and the Scriptures of Israel*, ed. Craig A. Evans and W. Richard Stegner (Sheffield: Sheffield Academic, 1994), 270–78.

[17] Philo sets out this understanding of the Ten Commandments in his work called *On the Decalogue* §§106–10, but for the interpretation see Allison (previous note).

[18] Wikipedia: "Golden Rule." For other reflections on such summaries, see Jeffrey Peterson, "The First and Second Tables of the Law in the New Testament," *Christian Studies* 23 (2009): 47–58.

Talmud about the Gentile asking Rabbi Hillel to recite the Torah while standing on one foot; Hillel responds, "What is hateful to you, do not do to your neighbor; that is the whole Torah, the rest is commentary; go and learn it."[19] There's a statement attributed to the important second-century AD Rabbi Akiva labeling Leviticus 19:18 "an all-embracing principle לכל דגוף] in the Torah."[20]

Luke presents these two commandments as the lawyer's understanding of how to inherit eternal life. There is nothing at all unusual about this way of thinking for a first-century Jew. The rub, as always, is, "Who is my neighbor?"

IDENTIFYING NEIGHBORS

If we need to love neighbors like ourselves, then it's perfectly reasonable to ask who this includes. I don't mean that the lawyer was perfectly reasonable; Luke says he was trying to justify himself (Luke 10:29), which I think means that he was pretty sure Jesus was going to tell him what he already believed to be true: that the law of Leviticus 19:18 is limited to people who think and act like you do.

Is it really necessary to point out that people today are just like this lawyer, looking to confirm our own biases? People watch the news channel that tells them the kinds of things they want to hear: that their lifestyle is right and everyone else is wrong. We like to justify ourselves in this way. The books we read

---

[19] This story is found in the Babylonian Talmud, tractate *Shabbat* 31a.

[20] This is in the rabbinic document called *Sifra*, a type of legal-based commentary on Leviticus, in the section *Kedoshim* 4.12.

or the people we're willing to listen to are determined, often, by whether or not we are likely to agree with the argument. We want to justify ourselves.

Yes, Jesus does justify people (Rom 5:9!), but not without calling for repentance. He's certainly not into confirming our own biases. What he offers this lawyer is a story so clear that the lawyer is forced to admit the very point that he had wanted to avoid.

First of all, in the context of Leviticus 19, two things are clear: (1) love is not so much an emotion as an action; and (2) the idea of "neighbor" excludes no one. As for the idea that "love" entails action, look at the commandments in Leviticus 19:9–18. That's not to say no emotion is involved (Lev 19:17), but there must be a practical outcome of love (cf. 1 John 3:16–18). And as for the identity of the neighbor,[21] note that sometimes the Torah refers to Canaanites as neighbors of God's people (Gen 38:12, 20), and to Egyptians as neighbors (Exod 11:2). Moreover, the Torah commands Israel repeatedly to love the "alien" (52x). For instance, later in the same chapter of Leviticus:

> When an alien resides with you in your land, you shall not oppress the alien. The alien who resides with you shall be to you as the citizen among you; you shall love the alien as yourself, for you were aliens in the land of Egypt: I am YHWH your God. (Lev 19:33–34)

---

[21] On this topic, see Richard Elliott Friedman, "Love Your Neighbor: Only Israelites or Everyone?" *Biblical Archaeology Review* 40.5 (September/October 2014), 48–52.

Both the command about loving neighbors (Lev 19:18) and the command about loving aliens (Lev 19:34) concludes with the affirmation, "I am YHWH," as if the identity and character of God is bound up with the principle of treating others fairly.

Samaritans

The parable that Jesus tells in response to the lawyer's question, "Who is my neighbor?" features a Samaritan as the hero. So before we get to the parable itself, let's review a little bit about Samaritans.

The Samaritans are a religious group that still exists today, numbering 820 people (in 2021),[22] centered around Mt. Gerizim in Israel (cf. John 4:20), about forty miles north of Jerusalem. They are not a sect of Judaism, they are a different religion. Samaritans do accept the Torah as God's law, revealed to Moses on Mt. Sinai, but they have their own version of the Torah, somewhat different from the Jewish version.[23] The main difference in terms of doctrine is that the Samaritan Torah has

---

[22] For the latest news about the Samaritan community, go to the Samaritan Update online: http://www.thesamaritanupdate.com/.

[23] The Samaritan Pentateuch is available in an English translation: Benyamin Tsedaka, *The Israelite Samaritan Version of the Torah: First English Translation Compared with the Masoretic Version* (Grand Rapids: Eerdmans, 2013). For an overview of the Samaritans, see Reinhard Pummer, *The Samaritans: A Profile* (Grand Rapids: Eerdmans, 2016).

an extra paragraph within the Ten Commandments that explicitly commands worship on Mt. Gerizim.[24]

The Samaritans do not call themselves Samaritans. They refer to themselves as Israelites, or as "Keepers" (of the commandments).

It's not clear when the Samaritan religion began as a distinct form of Torah-observance separate from Jews. The story told in 2 Kings 17 about a group of people mixed between pagans and Israelites does not seem to describe the group later known as Samaritans. Archaeologists have uncovered a temple on Mt. Gerizim dated to the fifth century BC. This temple was destroyed by the Jewish high priest John Hyrcanus in about 111 BC, in an effort to forcibly convert the Samaritans to Judaism. It didn't work; it just made them mad. In the first century, there was much animosity between Samaritans and Jews.

Luke's Gospel represents a Samaritan as the hero of two stories: the Parable of the Good Samaritan, and the story in Luke 17:11–19 about the grateful Samaritan. But there's another story in Luke about Samaritans that illustrates the animosity that Jews harbored against them (and vice versa). As soon as the Travel Narrative in Luke begins, this happens:

> And he sent messengers ahead of him. On their
> way they entered a village of the Samaritans to
> make ready for him; but they did not receive
> him, because his face was set toward Jerusalem.

---

[24] You can read the Samaritan tenth commandment at Wikipedia: "Ten Commandments," under the section on the Samaritan version.

When his disciples James and John saw it, they said, "Lord, do you want us to command fire to come down from heaven and consume them?" But he turned and rebuked them. (Luke 9:52–55)

It's hard to imagine that James and John would have been so ready to obliterate a Jewish village that didn't receive Jesus, such as Nazareth, or even Capernaum (cf. Luke 10:13–16). But they seem pretty eager to wipe out this Samaritan village.

Jesus did not approve of the Samaritan religion. When he was speaking to the Samaritan Woman in John 4 about the appropriate place of worship, he basically told her that Jews are right (Jerusalem) and Samaritans are wrong (Mt. Gerizim), though pretty soon it wouldn't matter. He told her that "salvation is from the Jews," i.e., not from the Samaritans (John 4:22). Just because Jesus thought we ought to show love to the Samaritan does not mean that he approved of the doctrines of the Samaritan.

To whom should we compare a "Samaritan" in our own context? Of course, there are still Samaritans today, but most American Christians I know do not hold much animosity toward Samaritans. It might be useful to think about the Parable of the Good Samaritan in terms of someone conservative American Christians typically do not like. I think we could nominate several candidates: Muslims, illegal immigrants, abortion providers, homosexuals, Democrats.

We might also think about these verses, a few chapters earlier in Luke.

> But I say to you that listen, Love your enemies,
> do good to those who hate you. (Luke 6:27)

> But love your enemies, do good, and lend,
> expecting nothing in return. Your reward will be
> great, and you will be children of the Most High;
> for he is kind to the ungrateful and the wicked.
> (Luke 6:35)

The Parable

A man was going down from Jerusalem (2,500 feet above sea level) to Jericho (800 feet below sea level), and he fell among robbers. A priest and a Levite ignored him, but a Samaritan took care of all his needs, thus proving to be a neighbor.

Why did the priest and Levite pass the man by? Notice that Jesus says in regard to both of them that they "saw" the wounded man. One would think that if anyone was religious, if anyone kept the Law of God, it would be a priest or a Levite, and yet Jesus has these two people breaking the second most important commandment.

I like the way the VeggieTales—yes, that's right, I said the VeggieTales—interpret the actions of these two characters.[25]

> We're busy, busy, dreadfully busy.
> You've no idea what we have to do.
> Busy, busy, shockingly busy.

---

[25] YouTube: "VeggieTales: Busy, Busy."

Much, much too busy for you.

I like that interpretation for two reasons. One, I identify with it. I'm busy, much too busy to be spending my time helping people I don't know. I mean, just look at the amount of time the Samaritan spent with this wounded man. I don't have time for that! Two, it nicely leads into the very next story in Luke, the one about Mary and Martha. Jesus was talking to Mary, and Martha didn't have time to join her. She was busy, busy, dreadfully busy. But Jesus said Mary had chosen better than Martha how to spend her time.

So I don't really think about the priest and the Levite as unusually bad people, just completely normal people. It's the Samaritan here who is unusual. Look again at what he does for this wounded man—bandaged his wounds, put him on his donkey and walked beside it, paid for a room in the inn and spent more time there taking care of the man, actually spending the night with him. Then he made arrangements to return to the inn at some later date to check on the wounded man.

Good grief! That is not a normal display of concern. That is extravagant generosity. That is an imitation of God.

When Jesus got to the question at the end of the parable, the lawyer could not deny that the Samaritan had proven to be more of a neighbor to the wounded man than had the priest or Levite. But Jesus does not then tell the lawyer to go and love Samaritans because Samaritans, too, are our neighbors. Rather, Jesus tells him to go act like the Samaritan. Prove yourself to be a neighbor and thus worthy of love.

Conclusion

Martha was too busy to be with Jesus (Luke 10:38–42). Jesus tells us that he is with the poor and oppressed (Matt 25:31–46), so if we are too busy for the poor and oppressed, we're too busy for Jesus. We fill our lives with so many things, it may be that we need to let something go. It may be that we need to sacrifice something that we really want to do in order to leave us time to love our neighbor. Would I rather my sons learn baseball or learn to serve the homeless? Would I rather my girls take piano or take care of widows? I'm not saying that you have to choose, but if you find that your life is too full to love your neighbor, you might have a tough decision to make. You might have to let something go, or run the risk of being too busy for Jesus.

7

The Prodigal Son

Luke 15:11-32

Then the father said to him, "Son, you are always with me, and all that is mine is yours." (Luke 15:31)

I've been lost before—literally, a few times, and then many, many times metaphorically. First, literally. I was 10 or 11 years old, at church camp, Western Kentucky Youth Camp, outside Marion, Kentucky (population in 2010: 3,039). On Thursday evenings every year at WKYC we would go on the hike to Mad Myrtle's house, back in the woods, where this old shack was. The counselors would tell us scary stories, especially about Mad Myrtle, the legendary former occupant of said shack. We'd spend 30-45 minutes there around the campfire, then head back through the woods to the main part of the camp. One year when we had started the hike back to camp, my friend and I decided to take one of the side trails, just to be rebellious, or adventurous, or whatever. It was pitch black, and even though we had flashlights, we had no idea where we were going, and after losing sight of the big caravan of campers on the main trail, we were utterly lost. Apparently once everybody else got back to camp, the counselors took roll call and discovered that we were missing, so they organized a search party. We ended up lost in the woods—and it was raining!—for probably 30 minutes. I was scared. Finally, we saw the lights of a pickup truck coming at us, and some men jumped out of the truck, including my cabin counselor. The first thing he did when he saw me was yell, "What were you thinking?!," and then without waiting for an answer, he just hugged me, relieved. He had left the ninety-nine campers (or thereabouts) to look for the one (or two) who were lost.

We may have eventually found our way back to camp, I don't know—maybe only when the night was over. Really, I had no idea where to go. It was like a maze in those woods, in the dark. I needed someone to look for me.

Now, metaphorically. Much more recently, I was in Oxford, England, at an academic conference. Just a refresher: whenever we Americans meet someone from another country, we expect them to speak English to us. And more often than not that is what happens. Well, I met this lady, a professor originally from Italy now teaching in Switzerland, delivering her lectures in French. She spoke to me in English, but she was not very confident in her English. The session began, and she read her paper in English, and I read a paper (in English, of course), and after our papers, there was time for question and answer. The audience asked a few questions. But then, it happened. This Italian Professor who regularly lectures in French started talking in French, and looking at me ... and I was thinking, "I hope she's not asking me a question." She was—she was asking me a question, in front of everybody, in French. Of course, most of the people there could understand French, but I'm the fool who only speaks one language. Why do they let such ignorant people attend international conferences? That's how I felt. So she speaks for about a minute in French and then stops, and looks at me, waiting for me to respond. And my necessary response was, "I don't know what you just said." I was lost. Then she started speaking Italian to this Italian guy right next to her, and they were both trying to figure out how to ask her question in English. And I just hung my head in shame.

That's just a recent example of how I have been lost. I'm sure you have your stories as well. In those situations, it is such a relief—so joyful—to find your way, or to get found.

Luke 15

Jesus tells three consecutive parables about something that is lost in Luke 15: first, a sheep (vv. 3–7); second, a coin (vv. 8–10); third, a son (vv. 11–32).[1] The first two parables, helpfully, come with their own interpretation.

> Just so, I tell you, there will be more joy in heaven over one sinner who repents than over ninety-nine righteous persons who need no repentance. (v. 7)

---

[1] The only one of these parables that finds a near parallel in the other Gospels is the Lost Sheep (cf. Matt 18:10–14). There is also a version of this parable in the *Gospel of Thomas* (saying 107).

Just so, I tell you, there is joy in the presence of
the angels of God over one sinner who repents.
(v. 10)

The point of the parables is about how much God loves
it when sinners repent. Now, the third parable, the one about the
lost son, does not have an explicit interpretation attached to the
parable like the first two do, but it does show the father in the
parable throwing a party once the lost son has been found (vv.
22–24). "And they began to celebrate" (v. 24). The point of this
third parable is the same as in the first two, though there is also
a complication at the end of the parable that we will have to
address in a little bit.

There is joy in heaven when a sinner repents. That gives
the lie to the old idea that we are "sinners in the hands of an angry
God." Okay, yes, there is some truth even in that characterization
of God, but not as much truth as there is in this:

As I live, says the Lord YHWH, I have no
pleasure in the death of the wicked, but that the
wicked turn from their ways and live. (Ezek
33:11; cf. 18:23, 32)

What gives God joy is not punishing sinners but repentant
sinners.

Why is Jesus telling parables about how much God loves
it when sinners repent? Because Jesus has been hanging out with
some sinners, and some people who are supposed to represent
the interests of God—the Pharisees and the scribes—are
grumbling, "This fellow welcomes sinners and eats with them"

(vv. 1–2). So Jesus tells these parables to justify his decision to hang out with sinners. Why is Jesus hanging out with sinners? Because he's trying to get them to repent! And there's nothing God loves more than when a sinner repents.

Notice, again, that the reason Jesus is hanging out with sinners is not because sinners are the cool crowd. It's not that sinners know how to have a good time better than those stuffy ole Pharisees. No, Jesus is hanging with sinners because those are the people that need to repent. He wants the sinners to stop being sinners.

"Between two evils I pick the one I haven't tried before." That's Mae West, and when she said it, it was funny. But that is not Jesus's motto. He has no interest in trying a new evil. He wants to be with sinners because he wants them to change their lives. I'm sure he was relatively nice to them, gentle, patient—but he wasn't affirming them in their lifestyle. He was telling them to abandon their lifestyle and to adopt a more godly lifestyle. Remember his response on a prior occasion when the Pharisees were grumbling about his decision to "eat and drink with tax collectors and sinners" (5:30).

> I have come to call not the righteous but sinners
> to repentance. (5:32)

He was after repentance. That was the goal.

But he told these parables not so much for the sake of the sinners as for the sake of the Pharisees who didn't understand the goal. If the Pharisees were grumbling about Jesus because of the company he kept, I suppose that means they had completely written off these people to whom Jesus was reaching out. These particular Pharisees doing the grumbling presumably didn't want to be associated with sinners, wanted to maintain their own purity which would be compromised by association with sinners, and didn't want to give the impression that they approved of sin. I guess these particular Pharisees assumed that what made God happy was when his people maintained purity. And—let's be honest—there are good reasons to think such a thing, because the Bible is filled with passages where God pleads with his people to maintain their purity, and not just in the Old Testament (2 Cor 6:14–7:1)! But what Jesus wanted to show was that the most joyful thing of all is when something lost has been found. After all, "the Son of Man came to seek and save the lost" (19:10).

Stories of Desperation

These are stories of desperation.

First, we have a shepherd who is desperate to find his sheep. Then we have a woman who is desperate to find her coin. I understand completely their desperation.

I've never lost a sheep or helped someone look for a sheep, but I have helped someone look for a lost dog. In our neighborhood, a few times a year we'll run into someone looking for their dog. They're usually in a hurry; they quickly ask if we've seen a dog wandering around, and when we say no, they quickly move on. I myself wouldn't be too upset if our dog ran away, but my oldest daughter would be frantic, and that means I'd be out looking, driving around, frantic, too.

What would I do if I lost a silver coin? The lady in Jesus's parable had ten silver coins, so she lost a tenth of her holdings. What would you do in that situation? The scene that pops into my head is Uncle Billy losing the $8,000 when he accidentally folded it up in Potter's newspaper. (Of course, I'm talking about *It's a Wonderful Life*.) You remember how frantic they were, how desperate? George Bailey yells at his uncle:

> Where's that money you silly, stupid old fool?! Where's that money?! You realize what this means? It means bankruptcy and scandal and prison. That's what it means. One of us is going to jail! Well, it's not gonna be me!

Desperation.

In these stories told by Jesus, it is the character representing God that is desperate. God is like a shepherd hunting for his sheep. God is like a woman turning her house upside down in search of her coin. And in both situations, when what was lost has been found, God is like someone calling up his friends, saying, "Rejoice with me, for I have found what I had lost!"

And God is like a father missing his son, hoping—desperately—for his son to come back.

THE PRODIGAL SON

Dividing the Estate

My sister has already called dibs on some of our parents' possessions. Really, I think she's called dibs on everything; I'm definitely getting the leftovers. But what my sister hasn't done is asked for my parents—who are in fine health close to ending their seventh decade—to go ahead and give her the inheritance. She has declared some of the things she wants when it's time to settle their estate, but she hasn't demanded to settle their estate now, while they're still alive. She knows—everyone knows—that to do so would be incredibly disrespectful, heartless, callous.

That's what the younger son does. "Father, give me the share of the property that will belong to me" (v. 12). Yeah, it's not really a surprise that if one of the two sons was going to do such a thing, it would be the younger son. The first child tends to be more obedient, more responsible; the second child tends to be more rebellious. That's not always the case, but it fits a lot of the families I know. It certainly fits the family that Jesus describes in Luke 15:11–32.

We might wonder what kind of parent would raise a child who would end up saying something like this to his father. How does the opening of this parable cohere with Proverbs 22:6?

> Train up a child in the way he should go:
> and when he is old, he will not depart from it.

Does the opening of Jesus's parable show that parenting is really just a crap shoot; if even God can't parent very well (since the father of the prodigal son represents God), what hope is there for us? There are a few responses to this line of thinking. First, we shouldn't press the details of these opening verses too far. This is all part of the set-up, not the main point. Jesus wants to tell a story about a rebellious son who repented, and a heart-broken father rejoicing over the repentance of this son. To tell such a story, the son has to rebel. Second, one could argue very easily that Proverbs 22:6 turns out to be exactly on point in the life of this prodigal son: he was trained up in the way he should go, and when he was old, he did not depart from it. The proverb does not mean that there will be no bumps along the road. The prodigal son, in the pig pen, remembers his training, and directs his life accordingly. This story might be interesting to think about in terms of parenting, but Jesus did not design it to go in that direction. (Except for the joy that a parent feels when reuniting with a child—that is the main point of the parable.)

We could say the same thing about the father's response to the son's demand. The father acquiesces and gives the younger son what he requested. One might look at that action and say, since the father represents God, then it provides an example to human fathers. I don't think so.

Again, verse 12 is all set-up, not main point, so we shouldn't press these details. I, for one, think it would be unwise (to say the least) to give in to such a request from such a son. What the son ended up doing with the money demonstrates how unwise it would be.

Tangent

Let's imagine for a moment that the father here is not a picture of our God, that the only correspondence between our God and this father is at the end, when he welcomes his son back joyfully, and not at the beginning, when the father acts sort of foolishly. That is, for a moment, those details I said we should not press— let's press them.

I'll say it again: it's foolish for this father to divide his estate and give so much to his son. Such an action suggests a father who spoils his child. Here we might think of Jacob's favoritism of Joseph, and how Joseph was a bit of a brat early on (Gen 39). When you've got a father who so readily gives a son anything he asks for, you'll get a son who nearly ruins his life.

ROCK BOTTOM

What the son ended up doing with the money was taking it to a far country and burning through it with riotous living (v. 13). That's what "prodigal" means—"wasteful," "reckless." Later, the elder brother accuses his sibling of wasting the money on prostitutes (v. 30), and he might be right. Rembrandt thought so, anyway. Here's his 1637 painting called *The Prodigal Son in the Brothel*.

Figure 3. Rembrandt's *The Prodigal Son in the Brothel*
c. 1635. Public domain, via Wikimedia Commons.

We've seen this story many times, the fool who comes in to some money and pretty soon has no money and nothing to show for it. Back to Proverbs:

Precious treasure remains in the house of the wise,
but the fool devours it. (Prov 21:20)

> Anyone who tills the land will have plenty of bread,
> but one who follows worthless pursuits will have
> plenty of poverty. (Prov 28:19)

When we hear that a lottery-winner later declared bankruptcy, we are not surprised. We might wonder what they spent it all on, but, really, we already know: some combination of cars and houses and clothes and vacations and exotic pets and whatever else popped into their heads. Apparently, sixty percent of NBA players go broke within five years of exiting the league, and seventy-eight percent of former NFL players experience financial hardship within a couple years of leaving the league.[2] We know what the riotous living is. We see it on TV all the time.

Of course the prodigal went to the Far Country to engage in his riotous living. That's where the riotous living happens, far away from everyone that knows you, around whom you'd be ashamed to live riotously. That's why Paul calls that lifestyle "the unfruitful deeds of darkness" (Eph 5:11), because they're the types of things you do in the dark where no one can see ("secretly"; Eph 5:12). "Those who are drunk get drunk at night" (1 Thess 5:7). They want the cover of darkness to hide their sin. But the nighttime isn't good enough for the prodigal, so he goes to the Far Country, where he can do anything he wants without any prying eyes.

The problem with the Far Country, though, is that it's real far away. When something bad happens, who's there to offer

---

[2] Chris Dudley, "Money Lessons Learned from Pro Atheletes' Financial Fouls," *CNBC.com* (May 14, 2018).

a helping hand? You've cut yourself off from your network, from the people that care about you, so you're going to end up in the pig pen. Things go south for the prodigal pretty quickly. He blows through his inheritance, and then there's a famine, and he ends up feeding pigs—not owning pigs, but just feeding them. Of course, for a Jew, that would be pretty low, but, really, there's no society on earth that would consider pig farming a particularly glamorous profession. But it gets worse: the prodigal—who just moments before had been living high on the hog (sorry for that)—now wants to eat the pig food. Have you ever wanted to eat dog food? Me neither.

I guess we could call that rock bottom.

Repentance

That's when the prodigal gets an idea. He decides to go back home and ask his father for a job (vv. 17–19). There are different ways of interpreting this plan from the prodigal. If you're the skeptical type, you might see in here a wonderful-awful idea, a scheme by which to get his father to give him even more money, knowing that his father will do anything he asks. David Buttrick summarizes the prodigal's idea this way: "I'll go to Daddy and sound religious."[3] And I must say, that way of reading the prodigal is attractive, not least because we see that exact scenario play out so frequently, if not in our own communities, at least in the movies.

---

[3] David Buttrick, *Speaking Parables: A Homiletic Guide* (Louisville: WJK, 2000), 43.

But that is not how I interpret the prodigal's intentions. If you just took this parable by itself—if you just read Luke 15:11–32—I guess you could get that meaning out of it, since we don't ever really hear whether the prodigal ended up being a good and faithful son, or whether he once again took advantage of his old man's soft heart. But this parable does not come to us as a stand-alone but as part of a Gospel that emphasizes repentance (as we saw earlier in this chapter). Luke presents these three parables as illustrations of God's joy at seeing sinners repent. So I think we have to understand, in the context of Luke's Gospel, that the prodigal son genuinely, sincerely repented.

And taking it in that way, as a sincere act of remorse, means that the speech by the prodigal is an excellent example of what repentance should look like. We need such examples. That's why Luke offers so many to us, whether in the encounter of John the Baptist with the tax collectors and soldiers (3:10–14), or the sinful woman at the pharisee's house (7:36–50), or the tax collector who prays in the temple (18:9–14), or Zacchaeus (19:1–10). Whenever my kids do wrong, especially the younger ones, I have to feed them all the words they need to say in order to make it right, to reconcile with the person they've offended. They don't come by it naturally. It doesn't occur to them to say sorry. They have to be trained. The speech that the prodigal plans to say (vv. 18–19), if it is sincere, is what repentance ought to look like. It is training for us.

Amy Winehouse sang a song about how people were trying to get her to go to rehab. In the song, she resists, in part because she hates the idea that "everyone [will] think I'm on the mend." I think I know what she means. She hates the idea of people condescendingly telling her, "Oh, you're doing really well.

You look so good." She hates that going to rehab would represent a public admission that she had problems that she couldn't solve, that the life she had been living was out of control. It's an insightful lyric. Some people who are in a bad situation stay away from the people who could help them because they don't want to hear, "We're so proud of you!" I imagine the prodigal son had to get over that exact fear. He knew if he went home, he would have to deal with whatever his father would say. Maybe he could deal with that because he had treated his father carelessly. But then there are the servants. What would they think? What would they say? And, of course, there's brother. What comes with repentance is sucking it up and recognizing—and accepting— that people are going to say what they're going to say. And they might hold your past transgressions against you, or forever judge you by your worst faults, or constantly wonder when you're going to fall off the wagon again. If the prodigal had such fears, they do not stop him from returning home in repentance.

Joy

But even more than repentance, this parable is about the reaction of the father. Jesus says that "while [the prodigal] was still far off, his father saw him" (v. 20). I don't know what this could mean other than that the father was looking for him. The father didn't leave and search in the Far Country the way the shepherd left the ninety-nine to look for the lost sheep, or the way the woman scoured her house in search of her coin, but the father was on the lookout. The apocryphal book of Tobit tells a similar story, though it doesn't involve a rebellious son. Instead, an obedient son leaves home on a mission, but that boy's mama "would rush out every day and watch the road her son had taken" (Tobit 10:7); she "sat looking intently down the road" (11:5). I imagine this father doing something like that.

The father "ran and put his arms around him and kissed him" (Luke 15:20). The scene is reminiscent of Esau's reconciliation with his brother Jacob (Gen 33:4). The prodigal can't get his whole speech out before his father interrupts him. The father orders a robe and a ring and sandals and a feast (Luke 15:22–23), "for this son of mine was dead and is alive again; he was lost and is found" (v. 24).

Rembrandt again:

Figure 4. Rembrandt's *The Return of the Prodigal Son*
c. 1668. Public domain, via Wikimedia Commons.

Notice what is absent. All those years ago, the first thing out of my camp counselor's mouth were words of rebuke—followed quickly, to be sure, by the very gestures performed by the father toward the prodigal in verse 20. The father manages to suppress even the hint of rebuke. No doubt the father had thought about this scene over the past weeks or months or years, considering what he would do. No doubt the father had thoughts—perhaps fleeting, perhaps regular—that if he ever saw his son again, he would tell him what for, or tell him how thoughtlessly he had acted, or tell him about all the nights the father had stayed up worrying, or tell him how he had broken his father's heart. But in the moment of reconciliation, we see no anger or resentment or sadness or frustration. We see only joy.

And that's the point of the parable.

Except that Jesus keeps talking.

THE ELDER BROTHER

There's another brother, and he's not happy. Unlike with the younger brother, we never really question whether this elder brother is sincere in what he says to his father. He doesn't try to flatter his father like the younger brother does. It sounds like this stuff has been boiling inside him for a while and now it's time to let it out. But, man, what a warped view of his life this boy has! Unfortunately this view of life, too, is very common, very familiar to us. We know people like this.

In verse 7, Jesus mentions "righteous persons who need no repentance." Here we meet an example of someone who is righteous and needs no repentance—and it becomes clear that there is no one who is righteous and without need of repentance.

The main problem here is that the elder brother has misinterpreted his relationship to his father. Here's what he says: "For all these years I have been working like a slave for you, and I have never disobeyed your command; yet you have never given me even a young goat so that I might celebrate with my friends" (v. 29). He thinks he's a slave, receiving and executing commands, able to enjoy the bounty of the estate only when given explicit permission. But the father interprets their relationship completely differently. He addresses him as "son," not "slave." "Son, you are always with me, and all that is mine is yours" (v. 31).

The elder brother needn't have waited for a written invitation to throw a party for his friends. He was son of the owner. Everything belonged to him already. If he wanted a goat, he should have just taken a goat. That means also that the younger brother could equally have enjoyed the estate and stayed home; there was no need to ask for his share of the inheritance early (except, of course, that the younger son wanted to be prodigal with the money; he wanted to do things he didn't want his dad to know about).

Just like his younger brother, this elder brother needed to change. He needed to recognize his own role as son and heir rather than slave. Most of all, rather than harboring anger and hatred, he needed to share in the joy of the moment, because it was necessary to celebrate (v. 32).

Conclusion

It's a story about loss and redemption and more. Like a lot of Jesus's parables, it ends without a neat conclusion, leaving us wondering whether the elder brother recognized his own folly, whether he accepted the younger brother, whether the younger brother was genuine in his repentance, whether the father's joy lasted. The parable is open-ended, and life is open-ended. As we reflect on these characters, and what we wish each of them would do, we form our own character, preparing ourselves to offer a proper response to God and others. And the proper response is twofold: repentance and joy.

8

Two Parables on Money

Luke 16

You are those who justify yourselves in the sight
of others; but God knows your hearts; for what
is prized by human beings is an abomination in
the sight of God. (Luke 16:15)

On Saturday I went to the gym to get on the elliptical
machine. The place was packed. I spent thirty minutes
working out. A lot of the people who were there when I showed
up were still there when I left. It won't be the last time I go to the
gym; if you really want it to do any good, you've got to go back
pretty frequently. But isn't it all pretty ridiculous? We have a
culture in which we eat so much and move so little that we
regularly have to schedule time, significant amounts of time in
our week, to work off the calories we refuse to stop consuming.
The point that I'm driving at is not about gluttony, though I
definitely need to hear that lesson. But I'm talking about money.
We pay money to join a gym to counteract the fact that we eat so

much. That's just one example of the fact that a lot of us have money (and calories) to burn.

We tend to think of Jesus as talking to an audience without a whole lot of money. Sometimes he talked to the Jewish leadership, and they probably had a bit of money, but for the most part he directed his comments to the poor and outcast. Let me just say, if that's true, he sure did talk a lot about money to these people without any money—especially in Luke. "Luke's Gospel is renowned for having a large amount to say on the topic of riches and poverty."[1] Now, it may be that Jesus wanted to fire up his base by condemning other people; that is, maybe he talked about the evil One Percent to a bunch of poor people. That doesn't strike me as the kind of thing Jesus would do. And as we look at his audience of outcasts, we might notice that they are not necessarily outcasts (I've mentioned this before: see Chapter 5), and they weren't necessarily poor. Remember the folks that Jesus is talking with at the beginning of Luke 15? It's the tax collectors and sinners, along with the scribes and Pharisees. Everything we know about tax collectors suggests that these are people with money, who are friends with other wealthy people. So maybe Jesus's audience was more diverse than we usually imagine.[2]

At any rate, we also are a part of Jesus's audience—or, at any rate, the audience of the Gospel of Luke. Surely Luke chose the particular stories and episodes for his portrayal of Jesus

---

[1] Christopher M. Tuckett, *Luke*, New Testament Guides (Sheffield: JSOT Press, 1996), 94.

[2] See Greg Carey, *Luke: All Flesh Shall See God's Salvation*, An Introduction and Study Guide (London: Bloomsbury, 2017), 12–13.

because he intended, in part, for wealthy people to hear Jesus's teaching on wealth. So let's listen closely.

Money in Luke

Luke 16 is our focus here, and it is a chapter about money (and a little bit extra, vv. 16–18, which we won't discuss here).[3] The chapter is dominated by two parables, one at the beginning (vv. 1–9) and one at the end (vv. 19–31), that both start the same way: "There was a rich man." When Jesus talks about wealth, he usually has some pretty annoying things to say about it—annoying for someone who likes money.

For instance:

> Sell your possessions, and give alms. Make purses for yourselves that do not wear out, an unfailing treasure in heaven, where no thief comes near and no moth destroys. For where your treasure is, there your heart will be also. (Luke 12:33–34)

Or remember this one?

---

[3] These three verses are paralleled in the Sermon on the Mount (Matt 5–7). If you want my thoughts on the themes of Luke 16:16–18, find my treatment of the parallel verses in *The Sermon on the Mount: Explorations in Christian Practice*, Cypress Bible Study Series (Florence, AL: HCU Press, 2021).

> How hard it is for those who have wealth to
> enter the kingdom of God! Indeed, it is easier for
> a camel to go through the eye of a needle than
> for someone who is rich to enter the kingdom of
> God. (Luke 18:24–25)

And, no, sorry, the "eye of a needle" was not a reference to a short
or narrow gate in Jerusalem that a camel could go through only
with difficulty.[4] That interpretation is no earlier than Medieval,
and it was probably developed by someone with money, or
someone who wanted to win the favor of a patron.

And he even says the same thing another time.

> So therefore, none of you can become my
> disciple if you do not give up all your
> possessions. (Luke 14:33).

There are more annoying passages in the Sermon on the Plain
(Luke 6).

> Blessed are you who are poor, for yours is the
> kingdom of God.
> Blessed are you who are hungry now, for you
> will be filled.
> (6:20–21)

---

[4] On that interpretation, see Wikipedia: "Eye of a Needle," at the section,
"Gate."

Woe to you who are rich, for you have received
your consolation.
Woe to you who are full now, for you will be
hungry.
(6:24–25)

A little later Jesus repeatedly tells his followers to give their stuff
away without expecting anything in return (6:30, 34, 35).

There's also the rich fool, who builds storerooms for all
his stuff but is not rich toward God (12:13–21). Speaking of the
rich fool, some people today have so much stuff that they literally
rent out storage units in order to store their stuff. I'm glad I don't
do that. (I have a detached garage where I can put my junk.)

Even in contexts that shouldn't have anything to do with
money, somehow money comes up. Like when Mary is rejoicing
about God's mercy upon her in the form of her pregnancy—
which seems to have nothing to do with money—Mary talks
about how God "has filled the hungry with good things, and sent
the rich away empty" (1:53).

The Gospel of Luke, more than the other Gospels, seems
to be against rich people. One rich guy who comes off pretty good
is Zacchaeus, but that's only because he (more-or-less) does what
Jesus commands and gives away his money (19:8).

I've tried to paint the picture as starkly as possible so that
we will get as uncomfortable about our wealth as I think Jesus
wants us to be. But, actually, I have painted the picture more
starkly than even Luke painted it. Not everything in Luke's
Gospel that concerns money is wholly negative toward it. Some
wealthy women are credited with providing for Jesus and his
followers during the Galilean ministry (8:1–3). Joseph of

Arimathea, who seems to have money, is represented positively as giving Jesus an honorable burial (23:50–53). And, of course, the Good Samaritan (10:30–37) provides an example for our imitation because he used his money on behalf of others. And then if we look ahead to Acts, there's not really an emphasis on giving away all possessions but instead on using those possessions for others (and, of course, not lying about it; Acts 5:1–11).

What I think we can say, then, is that Luke's Gospel tends to present a very provocative and negative impression of the value of money, but when we try to reconcile everything in the Gospel, and especially when we add in Acts, it seems that Luke's view would not be very far from what we read in 1 Timothy.

> As for those who in the present age are rich, command them not to be haughty, or to set their hopes on the uncertainty of riches, but rather on God who richly provides us with everything for our enjoyment. They are to do good, to be rich in good works, generous, and ready to share, thus storing up for themselves the treasure of a good foundation for the future, so that they may take hold of the life that really is life. (1 Tim 6:17–19)

The Unrighteous Steward

This parable is one of the most difficult in the Gospels. Is the unrighteous steward an example for us to imitate or an example of what not to do? And what is going on with his telling the people to reduce their bills? How does that help him? And why is the master happy about it? These are hard questions that I don't have the answers to. But I'll offer a possible way of understanding what's going on.

The parable begins by noting that the unrighteous steward had been squandering his master's money (16:1), just as the prodigal son had squandered his inheritance (15:13). Just last night I saw a commercial on TV—one of those AT&T commercials about how it's not okay to be okay—and this commercial involved a financial advisor who had several pictures showing the nice vacations he enjoyed, with the implication that he was using other people's money for his own enjoyment. I imagine this unrighteous steward was doing something like that—putting personal expenses on the company credit card or something.

The manager gets fired (v. 2) and develops a plan "so that, when I am dismissed as manager"—which apparently hasn't quite happened yet—"people may welcome me into their homes" (v. 4). So it looks like to me his idea is to use his quickly expiring power to get some of his master's clients to owe him a favor (like a lame duck president pardoning his friends). The manager wants them to "welcome me into their homes"—maybe to offer him a job as their house's manager. So he calls them and reduces their bills (vv. 5–7). It seems a little sneaky, but the manager's desperate. The weird thing is that the master ends up praising the manager (v. 8), which seems odd since the manager has just apparently cheated the master out of some significant income. My guess at why the master views this as a good thing is that he will come off as generous and a benefactor, and these clients will view the master even more highly. They will be loyal to him. So even though the manager was working in his own best interests, he ended up serving his master's interests, as well. So is the manager still fired? Who knows.

I'm not sure I've interpreted the parable correctly. If you look in some Luke commentaries, you'll probably find a different interpretation in each commentary. But Jesus is explicit about the point he wants to derive from the parable.

> And I tell you, make friends for yourselves by means of the mammon of unrighteousness so that when it is gone, they may welcome you into the eternal homes. (Luke 16:9)[5]

In that way, the unrighteous steward is an example for us. Maybe we shouldn't imitate exactly his methods, but he did make friends with the unrighteous mammon. The point is: use your unrighteous mammon to "make friends"; use it on behalf of others.

Faithful with a Little

The parable of the unrighteous steward leads immediately to Jesus's more explicit teaching on money (vv. 10–13), culminating in the familiar statement, "You cannot serve God and Mammon" (v. 13; cf. Matt 6:24). Here the main thing I want to stress—and I think it's also what Jesus wanted to stress—is (1) that our

---

[5] The quotation is a mixture of the NRSV with the KJV. The latter uses the phrase "mammon of unrighteousness," a more literal translation of the Greek than the NRSV's "dishonest wealth."

unrighteous mammon is a "very little thing" in the grand scheme of things (v. 10) and (2) our unrighteous mammon doesn't belong to us (v. 12). We are in the same position as that unrighteous steward, taking care of what belongs to someone else.

Listen, the fact that we have a bunch of money has almost nothing to do with our own wonderful qualities as human beings. Well, yes, it has something to do with those things. If we were stupid and lazy, we probably wouldn't have money. The book of Proverbs talks about that. But there are a lot of relatively intelligent people who also work pretty hard who do not have anywhere near as much money as many people in America have. I know; I've met some of these people. They certainly work harder than I do. But the reason I have more money than them is because I happened to be born in America and they weren't. Or I happened to be born to the right set of parents, who trained me in how to navigate opportunities and made sure I got plenty of them. I can't really claim that I have money while people in Haiti and other places don't because I'm a better person than they are. No, it's just that somehow I got the job to manage some of God's money. I don't see how we can interpret Luke 16:10–13 in any way other than that the money we have is not our own. It belongs to another. So unless we use it the way our Master wants us to use it, we're going to get fired like that unrighteous steward—by which I do not mean that we won't have the money anymore (well, we won't), but rather that we'll be expelled from our Master's presence (cf. 13:27; cf. Matt 7:23).

THE RICH MAN AND LAZARUS

This parable is more familiar and more straightforward than the one at the start of the chapter. I'm just going to highlight a few aspects of the parable here. Earlier Jesus had pronounced a "woe" upon the rich (6:24) in these terms: "Woe to you who are rich, for you have received your consolation." Here we have a parable illustrating this woe. Abraham says to the rich man: "Child, remember that during your lifetime you received your good things, and Lazarus in like manner evil things; but now he is comforted here, and you are in agony" (v. 25). This is the great reversal that Mary had also mentioned (1:52–53).

What is quite disconcerting about the way Abraham words his rebuke to the rich man in verse 25 is that he does not say that the rich man is being punished for ignoring Lazarus or not using his wealth on behalf of others. He just says the rich man is being punished for being wealthy. The rich man had a comfortable life, so now it's his turn to suffer.

We've already seen, however, that Luke sometimes includes these sorts of black-and-white statements in his Gospel and he balances them out with more moderate statements about the proper use of wealth. I think we get a hint of that in this parable, as well. The rich man wants Lazarus to go and warn his brothers (v. 27). What does he want Lazarus to tell them? Surely it's that they need to use their money not on their own lavish lifestyles but rather on those poor people like Lazarus who are right outside their door.

Abraham tells him that the brothers need to listen to Moses and the prophets. The rich man actually says that his brothers are not going to listen to Moses and the prophets on this score. What passages of Moses and the Prophets do you think they have in mind? How about these?

> When you reap the harvest of your land, you shall not reap to the very edges of your field, or gather the gleanings of your harvest. You shall not strip your vineyard bare, or gather the fallen grapes of your vineyard; you shall leave them for the poor and the alien: I am YHWH your God. (Lev 19:9–10)

> Every third year you shall bring out the full tithe of your produce for that year, and store it within your towns; the Levites, because they have no allotment or inheritance with you, as well as the resident aliens, the orphans, and the widows in your towns, may come and eat their fill so that YHWH your God may bless you in all the work that you undertake. (Deut 14:28–29)

> If there is among you anyone in need, a member of your community in any of your towns within the land that YHWH your God is giving you, do not be hard-hearted or tight-fisted toward your needy neighbor. You should rather open your hand, willingly lending enough to meet the need, whatever it may be. (Deut 15:7–8)

> Hear this word, you cows of Bashan who are on Mount Samaria, who oppress the poor, who

crush the needy, who say to their husbands,
"Bring something to drink!" (Amos 4:1–2)

That's merely a sampling. Abraham knows what he's talking about: Moses and the prophets have a lot to say about how to use your money. And the way you're supposed to use it is for the benefit of the Lazaruses out there.

The rich man says his brothers are not going to listen to Moses and the prophets. Are we?

Conclusion

Ask yourself the question: "If I were going to glorify God with my money, what would I do? If I were going to be faithful with this unrighteous mammon, which my Lord calls a very little thing that doesn't even belong to me—if I were going to be faithful with what has been entrusted to me, what would I do?" Ask yourself that question, and then decide if you want to be faithful with your unrighteous mammon.

9

Two Tax Collectors

Luke 18:9-14; 19:1-10

> But the tax collector, standing far off, would not
> even look up to heaven, but was beating his
> breast and saying, "God, be merciful to me, a
> sinner!" (Luke 18:13)

The Bible is big on repentance. In the Gospel according to
Mark, the first words out of Jesus's mouth announced the
nearness of God's long-awaited kingdom and the concomitant
need for repentance (Mark 1:15). Fast forward a few years, and
the very first gospel sermon after the Ascension ends with a call
for repentance (and, of course, baptism; Acts 2:38). Paul told the
crowd on Mars Hill that God "now commands all people
everywhere to repent" (Acts 17:30), echoing the earlier statement
of Jesus that "except ye repent, ye shall all likewise perish" (Luke
13:3, 5).

The theme is found not just in the New Testament. The
Old Testament prophets were constantly calling on the people to
turn back to God, even if our English translations don't contain

the word "repent." To quote just one of the more famous examples:

> Wash you, make you clean; put away the evil of your doings from before mine eyes; cease to do evil; Learn to do well; seek judgment, relieve the oppressed, judge the fatherless, plead for the widow. Come now, and let us reason together, saith YHWH: though your sins be as scarlet, they shall be as white as snow; though they be red like crimson, they shall be as wool. (Isa 1:16–18)

One of those odd features of the Bible is that Paul doesn't use the word "repent" very often in his letters: the verb appears once (μετανοιέω, *metanoiéō*; 2 Cor 12:21) and the noun "repentance" a few times (μετανοία, *metanoia*; Rom 2:4; 2 Cor 7:9–10; 2 Tim 2:25). But like the Old Testament prophets, Paul talks about the concept a lot more than he uses the specific word. For instance, listen to what the Apostle says here:

> Now this I affirm and insist on in the Lord: you must no longer live as the Gentiles live, in the futility of their minds. They are darkened in their understanding, alienated from the life of God because of their ignorance and hardness of heart. They have lost all sensitivity and have abandoned themselves to licentiousness, greedy to practice every kind of impurity. That is not the way you learned Christ! For surely you have

heard about him and were taught in him, as truth is in Jesus. You were taught to put away your former way of life, your old self, corrupt and deluded by its lusts, and to be renewed in the spirit of your minds, and to clothe yourselves with the new self, created according to the likeness of God in true righteousness and holiness. (Eph 4:17–24)

You could hardly get a better description of repentance: no longer live that way, take off that old lifestyle, clothe yourself with a new lifestyle, and learn to think in a different way. Or consider this one:

Do you not know that wrongdoers will not inherit the kingdom of God? Do not be deceived! Fornicators, idolaters, adulterers, male prostitutes, sodomites, thieves, the greedy, drunkards, revilers, robbers—none of these will inherit the kingdom of God. And this is what some of you used to be. But you were washed, you were sanctified, you were justified in the name of the Lord Jesus Christ and in the Spirit of our God. (1 Cor 6:9–11)

In the KJV, verse 11 begins with the familiar "such were some of you"—you used to live in that sinful way, but no longer. And then there's Romans 8, which I will not quote, because I'd have to quote the whole chapter, but just take a look there at Paul's description of the new life characterized by the Spirit as opposed to the old life of the flesh. And while you're in Romans, take a look at chapter 6.

So, anyway, the Bible is big on repentance. And Luke is especially big on it. (And so this is not the first time we've talked about it in this series of studies.) Going back to counting words for just a moment, Luke uses the verb "repent" (*metanoiéō*) more than any other writer (nine times in the Gospel; five times in Acts),[1] and he is responsible for half of the appearances of the noun "repentance" (*metanoia*) in the New Testament (Gospel, five times; Acts, six times).[2] Jesus came to call sinners to repentance (Luke 5:32). He tells parables about how God loves repentance (15:7, 10). In Luke's Gospel, the resurrected Jesus sends the apostles out into the world to preach repentance (24:47). With all this emphasis on repentance, Luke makes sure to put plenty of examples of repentance in his Gospel. In this series of lessons, we've already looked at the sinful woman from Luke 7 and the parables from Luke 15. There's also the instruction by John the Baptist about what repentance should look like for people in general and specifically for tax collectors and soldiers (3:10–14). And then there are the stories we're considering in this chapter, also about tax collectors (18:9–14; 19:1–10).

---

[1] Luke 10:13; 11:32; 13:3, 5; 15:7, 10; 16:30; 17:3, 4; Acts 2:38; 3:19; 8:22; 17:30; 26:20.

[2] Luke 3:3, 8; 5:32; 15:7; 24:47; Acts 5:31; 11:18; 13:24; 19:4; 20:21; 26:20.

Tax Collectors

Tax collectors keep coming up in Luke's Gospel. The Greek term for tax collector (τελώνης, *telōnēs*) appears in the New Testament only in the Synoptic Gospels, and nearly half of the references are in Luke.[3] But, actually, "tax collector" is an inaccurate translation, as is "publican" (KJV). "Publican," from Latin *publicanus*, corresponds to the Greek term *dēmosiōnēs* (δημοσιώνης), a term that does not appear in the New Testament—and for good reason: "the classical publican system was abrogated in Palestine by the NT period."[4] Publicans were used by Rome to collect taxes in other parts of the empire, and in Palestine earlier than the time of Jesus. Publicans were a type of tax collector, but a different kind from the type that we read about in the Gospels. In the Gospels, we read about toll collectors, people who would work from a toll booth (*telōnion*)— like where Jesus met Levi (Luke 5:27)—and assess a tariff on transported goods. That's what the Greek word *telōnēs* indicates.[5] But, since we are used to thinking about these people

---

[3] Luke 3:12; 5:27, 29, 30; 7:29, 34; 15:1; 18:10, 11, 13.

[4] John R. Donahue, "Tax Collectors and Sinners: An Attempt at Identification," *Catholic Biblical Quarterly* 33 (1971): 39–61, at 54.

[5] Fabian E. Udoh, *To Caesar What Is Caesar's: Tribute, Taxes, and Imperial Administration in Early Roman Palestine (63 B.C.E.–70 C.E.)* (Providence, RI: Brown Judaic Studies, 2005), 239. Udoh discusses at length the system of direct taxation in Judea under the Roman governors of the first century (pp. 219–38). For a brief survey, see Emil Schürer, *The History of the Jewish People in the Age of Jesus Christ*, rev. ed., 3/4 vols. (Edinburgh: T&T Clark, 1973–1987), 1.401–4. The *telōnēs* was involved in the system of indirect taxation.

as tax collectors, and since our English Bibles routinely use this English term rather than toll collector, and since a toll is a type of (indirect) tax, I won't make a big deal out of the term. But before leaving this discussion of the term, let me reiterate that every time your English Bible mentions a tax collector, it's translating the same Greek term (*telōnēs*), and we should think of the tax collector as someone who collects tolls.

Tax collectors were well-known for their extortion. In a previous chapter (chapter 5), I suggested that we think of a tax collector like a small-time mafioso or perhaps a loan shark. I don't mean to say that they were violent, but they were crooked—or, at least, that was their reputation. Just look at what Jesus says about tax collectors in Matthew's Gospel.

> If [a straying brother] refuses to listen to them,
> tell it to the church, and if he refuses to listen
> even to the church, let him be to you as a Gentile
> and a tax collector. (Matt 18:17)

The implication is that you would normally have no association with a tax collector. What was wrong with a tax collector? In the Sermon on the Mount, Jesus could not imagine a bigger sinner than a tax collector (or, at least, he couldn't think of a better example of a sinner for his audience).

> For if you love those who love you, what reward
> do you have? Do not even the tax collectors do
> the same? (Matt 5:46)

We can get an idea of why tax collectors were considered so beyond the pale from Luke's Gospel. When the tax collectors asked John the Baptist what they should do in order to demonstrate their repentance, this is what he told them.

> Collect no more than the amount prescribed for you. (Luke 3:13).

And that's it; that's the sum total of John's advice. Apparently John thought it was a pretty big problem that tax collectors were taking in more money than their orders prescribed. Zacchaeus—a "chief" tax collector (*architelōnēs*; 19:2)—admits that it's possible (wink wink) that he may have defrauded some people (19:8).

How would this defrauding have worked? In the words of biblical scholar David J. Downs, "Rome exerted its power and raised funds to support its military activities through levies on conquered peoples."[6] Downs distinguishes tribute (paid to foreign rulers) from taxes (paid to local rulers), and he classifies tolls as a third type of tax. Tolls would usually support the local government but may also at times have contributed toward the tribute obligations of the local government to Rome. Downs describes the toll collectors in the Gospels as

> individuals contracted to extract tolls at transit and trade points. It is generally agreed

---

[6] David J. Downs, "Economics," in *Dictionary of Jesus and the Gospels*, 2d ed., ed. Joel B. Green (Downers Grove, IL: IVP, 2013), 219–26, at 223.

that these toll collectors were responsible for gathering local tolls (*telē*) levied by cities (*CIS* 3913), including duties on agricultural produce sold in Jerusalem (Josephus, *Ant.* 18.90), although they may also have played a part in the collection of tithes and the Roman tribute.[7]

Another biblical scholar has described the possibility for corruption among toll collectors in these terms:

> To stop people on the road and demand a portion of their goods certainly appeared to be institutionalized robbery, and the only apparent beneficiary was the tax farmer himself. Although the commission system was regulated, the power of the assessor to determine the value of some goods encouraged dishonesty.[8]

And the leading Greek-English dictionary for the New Testament describes the system of toll collecting as affording "a collector many opportunities to exercise greed and unfairness. Hence tax collectors were particularly hated and despised as a

---

[7] Downs, "Economics," 224.

[8] T. E. Schmidt, "Taxation: Jewish," in *Dictionary of New Testament Background*, ed. Craig A. Evans and Stanley E. Porter (Downers Grove, IL: IVP, 2000), 1163–66, at 1165. Donahue, "Tax Collectors and Sinners," surveys opinions on toll collectors in rabbinic literature.

class."[9] Of course, disdain for the taxman hasn't really changed in a couple thousand years. Just ask the Beatles.[10]

> Let me tell you how it will be
> There's one for you, nineteen for me
> 'Cause I'm the taxman
> Yeah, I'm the taxman
> Should five percent appear too small
> Be thankful I don't take it all
> 'Cause I'm the taxman
> Yeah, I'm the taxman

The IRS is hardly a popular institution in America. Still, taxmen and toll collectors in first century Jewish society had a reputation for being corrupt that the IRS does not exactly share. The system of toll collection in Roman Palestine was almost inherently dishonest. I have heard of the same sort of thing in some countries today, in which, for instance, church workers are pressed to provide a bribe to a government official to secure a permit or some such.

The system of taxes in Roman Palestine resulted in toll collectors being marginalized—but, of course, they would be marginalized only from a particular vantage point. They had their own circles, and as long as they stayed there, they probably felt very little marginalization. I want to avoid thinking in terms

---

[9] Frederick William Danker, ed., *A Greek-English Lexicon of the New Testament and Other Early Christian Literature*, 3d ed. (Chicago: University of Chicago Press, 2000), 999 s.v. τελώνης.

[10] From "Taxman" (1966), written by George Harrison.

of the poor, oppressed tax collector that is finally given value by Jesus. If I may attempt a modern analogy, we might think about the tax collectors as being "marginalized" or "outcasts" in the same way that the so-called "liberal elites" are marginalized. Or, to go back to my earlier suggestion, we might think about a loan shark, or a bookie. Are any of these groups marginalized or outcast today? They are, from the perspective of the circles to which they do not belong. (That makes the description "marginalized" almost a truism: they are marginalized among groups to which they don't belong.) I don't think we would say that the "liberal elites" live a marginalized or outcast life. But if they entered a conservative church, they would probably feel some marginalization. Loan sharks, I imagine, do not feel like outcasts because they quite reasonably avoid the kind of people who would give them such a feeling. So also do I avoid such situations. Again, the issue of marginalization really comes up only when someone tries to "cross over" into someone else's territory. I think we've all experienced that—we've all had the feeling, "I don't belong here." All of that to say, I bet toll collectors in the first century rarely felt marginalized; rather, they probably felt powerful, and they enjoyed the friendship of powerful people, and they could take care of their families, providing nice things for their wives and arranging for a good education for their children. But they knew they weren't welcome in conservative Jewish circles, for a variety of reasons: perhaps some Jews thought toll collectors were unclean because of their close association with Gentiles; probably most people suspected they were guilty of extortion; likely a lot of people were jealous of the comfortable lifestyle and protections enjoyed by toll collectors, especially in light of the way they came by this lifestyle and these protections; and such a lifestyle usually entailed a diminishing concern for the intricacies of God's law. Tax collectors were sinners, from the conservative Jewish perspective, and everybody knew it.

THE PHARISEE AND THE TAX COLLECTOR

If anyone needed to repent, the tax collector did. Certainly not the Pharisee. The Pharisee had a close relationship with God. He thought constantly about God, about how to please God, how to embody the Torah. That's why he became a Pharisee, because he wanted to live a life wholly devoted to God, with all his heart, all his soul, and all his strength. So, of course, a Pharisee—famous for piety—would be a perfect example of how anyone can become self-righteous.

Jesus uses a Pharisee in his parable at Luke 18:9–14 because everybody knew that Pharisees were the salt of the earth, calling Israel back to repentance, walking examples of how to please God and live according to the Torah in a modern, corrupt world. And Jesus used a tax collector in the parable because everybody knew tax collectors were the exact opposite of Pharisees: tax collectors didn't give a flip about God or his Torah, they cared only about themselves, certainly not about their nation. Whereas Moses "chose to share ill-treatment with the people of God rather than to enjoy the fleeting pleasures of sin" (Heb 11:25), the tax collectors made the opposite choice. They loved the fleeting pleasures of sin, and if enjoying those fleeting pleasures meant avoiding the ill-treatment of the people of God, all the better!

But Jesus came, in part, to inaugurate the great reversal (Luke 1:52–53). Remember the Beatitudes (Matt 5:3–12; cf. Luke 6:20–26)? The standards of this world are being flipped upside down. In the great reversal, you should invite people you don't know to your parties rather than your friends (Luke 14:12–24). You'll find your life by losing it, not by avoiding the cross (9:23–24). And even Pharisees may find themselves on the outside looking in—looking in at tax collectors enjoying fellowship with God.

That's the upshot of the last statement of this parable:

I tell you, this man [= the tax collector] went down to his home justified rather than the other [= the Pharisee]; for all who exalt themselves will be humbled, but all who humble themselves will be exalted. (Luke 18:14)

Jesus tells us what the problem is: the Pharisee exalted himself, and so in the great reversal he will be humbled. But the tax collector humbled himself, and so he will be exalted. This sounds similar to what Jesus had said earlier, about picking out the worst seat for yourself at dinner parties so that you can move to a better spot (14:7–11). In fact, that earlier teaching ends with the same punchline as our parable.

So, how did this Pharisee exalt himself? Here's his prayer:

God, I thank you that I am not like other people: thieves, rogues, adulterers, or even like this tax collector. I fast twice a week; I give a tenth of all my income. (Luke 18:11–12)

Wow, what a terrible prayer! So self-righteous, sanctimonious, proud! Let us pause to pray: "God, I thank thee that I am not like this Pharisee!"

Remember, this parable is told "to some who trusted in themselves that they were righteous and regarded others with contempt" (v. 9). Let's not fall into the trap of magnifying the folly of the Pharisee lest we suffer the same condemnation. The Pharisee was, by his own account (and it's believable), a very religious person, who constantly thought about how to live out his faith. The Pharisee's commitment to fasting and tithing is commendable, and an example to us. In fact, the things he mentions in verse 12 are not at all exaggerated; Jesus mentions how scrupulous the Pharisees were about tithing (11:42), and we've already heard of the "frequent" fasts of the Pharisees (5:33). But the prayer is a demonstration of someone "who trusted in himself that he was righteous," and that's what gets the Pharisee into trouble.

I don't think Jesus is here condemning all Pharisees, but he is presenting a believable portrait of someone who hasn't realized how far he is from God, how his very prayer condemns him, renders him unjustified (v. 14). Instead, his prayer should have been more like this:

God, be merciful to me, a sinner! (Luke 18:13)

But this is the prayer of the tax collector, who—Jesus tells us—"would not even look up to heaven, but was beating his breast." Yes, it would be shocking to a first-century Jewish audience that a tax collector would be justified before God rather than a

Pharisee, just as it is still shocking to religious people to think that prostitutes (along with some tax collectors!) "are going into the kingdom of God ahead of you" (Matt 21:31). But, of course, the reason is that the prostitutes repented of their sin (Matt 21:32), and our tax collector, beating his breast and crying out for God's mercy, is also an example of repentance.

If you want to learn how to repent, look at this tax collector.

Zacchaeus

Another example of repentance: Zacchaeus. The difference between Zacchaeus in Luke 19 and the tax collector from the previous chapter is that Zacchaeus is a "chief" tax collector (ἀρχιτελώνης, *architelōnēs*). Luke tells us that he was rich (19:2). If anything, a first-century audience probably would have said that Zacchaeus was more corrupt than the average tax collector.

But Zacchaeus has heard about Jesus, and he's curious. Maybe he's heard that one of Jesus's close companions is a former tax collector (Luke 5:27–32). Maybe he wants to see what could be so attractive about this wandering teacher that someone would leave a good paying job to become a vagabond. Maybe he feels like a sinner and he's wondering how to begin to change his life. Whatever the motivation, he wants to see Jesus, so he climbs that sycamore tree (v. 4).

Jesus initiates the encounter. He sees Zacchaeus up in the tree, calls him by name, and invites himself over to his house (v. 5). That did it: Zacchaeus "hurried down and was happy to welcome him" (v. 6). It's hard to quite know the motivation at this point, or what is going on in Zacchaeus' head, but it seems like he climbed the tree feeling pretty rotten about himself and looking for a way out. Like the woman who just wanted to touch the hem of Jesus's garment (8:43; cf. Mark 5:27–28), maybe Zacchaeus just wanted to get a glimpse and hear some words from this itinerant rabbi. Maybe he climbed the tree thinking that Jesus might say something that could offer Zacchaeus some direction in life. He probably didn't anticipate hosting Jesus in his own home; that result was better than what he could have hoped for. Jesus had come to call sinners to repentance (5:32), and he recognized a sinner ripe for repentance.

Of course, people grumbled (v. 7). But Zacchaeus wasn't just a sinner; he was a sinner ready to repent. And no doubt this is the part of story that suggested to Luke that it needed to be preserved, needed to become a part of his narrative of Jesus's life. Zacchaeus said:

> Look, half of my possessions, Lord, I will give to the poor; and if I have defrauded anyone of anything, I will pay back four times as much. (v. 8)

Zacchaeus knows how he has become rich, and he knows that it was by ignoring God's law, which calls for compassion on the poor and for "honest scales" (Lev 19:36). This is what repentance looks like: recompensing those to whom you've done wrong, and using your blessings on behalf of others.

It is interesting to compare this rich man's pledge to the response to Jesus from the other rich man, mentioned just a few verses earlier (18:18–23). Jesus had told that earlier rich man, "Sell all that you own and distribute the money to the poor, and you will have treasure in heaven" (18:22). Jesus made no similar demand on Zacchaeus, but Zacchaeus volunteers something close to it. Perhaps we can explain the difference in Jesus's demand this way: that earlier rich man was already a pious Jew (18:21), and Jesus challenged him to draw yet nearer to God. Zacchaeus had not been pious at all, and so these are his first steps in faith. Does this indicate that God meets us where we are? If so, where are we, and what would Jesus challenge us to do?

The story ends with the famous proclamation by Jesus, "The Son of Man has come to seek out and to save that which was lost" (19:10). Zacchaeus had been lost, but now he is found, he is saved, and salvation comes to his house (19:9). What did it require of him? Repentance, turning his life around. All it takes is giving up your life to God. Jesus demands nothing less (9:23).

The Future, According to Jesus

Luke 17:20-37; 21:5-36

> Once Jesus was asked by the Pharisees when the kingdom of God was coming, and he answered, "The kingdom of God is not coming with things that can be observed; nor will they say, 'Look, here it is!' or 'There it is!' For, in fact, the kingdom of God is among you." (Luke 17:20–21)

About a thousand years before Jesus was born, King Solomon built a grand temple in Jerusalem, on the very site where Abraham had once nearly sacrificed his own son (2 Chron 3:1; cf. Gen 22:2). But, of course, that temple was demolished just a few hundred years later, so thoroughly destroyed by the Babylonians that nothing of it remained for Jesus to admire. Why had God allowed his own house to be destroyed by these foreign enemies, Nebuchadnezzar's armies? According to the Israelite prophets, it was because of Israel's sin. Ezekiel the prophet was exiled to Babylon in 597 BC, with the temple still standing. He records his experience of being transported to Jerusalem— whether in the body or out of the body, I do not know; God knows—and seeing people in the temple worshiping foreign Gods (Ezek 8–11). This vision ends with God's abandonment of his temple, leaving it to its fate, while "the glory of the Lord ascended from the middle of the city and stopped on the mountain east of the city" (11:23). Instead of inhabiting the temple, God's glory would rest on a nearby mountain and watch the Babylonians destroy his house.

That was the first temple. There would be a second. When the Persians (led by Cyrus) defeated the Babylonians, they allowed the Jews to return to Jerusalem and rebuild the temple (Ezra 1:1–4). Zerubbabel and others did return to Jerusalem, and they did build a new temple, which was dedicated in 516 BC (Ezra 6:15). This second temple stood longer than the first one. Just before the birth of Jesus, Herod the Great directed a building project that expanded the Jerusalem Temple and rendered it much more glamorous. It was this temple that prompted the disciples of Jesus to exclaim during the last week of their Master's life, "Look, Teacher, what large stones and what large buildings!" (Mark 13:1).

If you go to Jerusalem today, you will probably want to visit the site of this temple, but you won't be able to visit the temple itself. Only a single wall remains from the second temple, the Western Wall (or Wailing Wall). What happened? A group of Jews revolted against Rome in AD 66, attempting to establish Jerusalem as an independent state. The revolt did not succeed. It took a few years for Rome to put it down; the suicide of Emperor Nero in AD 68 and the subsequent political intrigues regarding his successor (the Year of the Four Emperors) contributed to the delay, especially since that successor turned out to be Vespasian, who had been besieging Jerusalem when he learned of Nero's death. But eventually, in AD 70, Vespasian's son Titus, who had taken over the military campaign in Judah (and would also succeed his father as emperor in AD 79), crushed the revolt and destroyed the city and the temple. The Arch of Titus commemorating this victory still stands in Rome just outside the Colosseum. We have so much information about this revolt and its results because the Jewish historian Josephus, a general in the war, narrated the story in his *The Jewish War*.

In the days of Jesus, the second temple still stood, recently beautified by Herod. The early Christians regularly met in the temple and worshiped there (Acts 2:46; 3:1). But Jesus had a somewhat ambivalent attitude toward the temple, as did some other Jews, such as the Qumran group (i.e., the group that wrote the Dead Sea Scrolls). Jesus accused his contemporaries of corrupting the function of the temple, turning it into a den of robbers (Luke 19:45, quoting Jer 7:11). In the Gospel of John, he mysteriously indicated that he himself embodied the temple of God (John 2:18–21). And he also predicted that the Jerusalem temple would be destroyed. And all of this had implications for the nature of the movement that he was inaugurating. When asked by the Samaritan Woman about the proper place of worship, Jesus responded.

> Woman, believe me, the hour is coming when you will worship the Father neither on this mountain nor in Jerusalem. You worship what you do not know; we worship what we know, for salvation is from the Jews. But the hour is

coming, and is now here, when the true worshipers will worship the Father in spirit and truth, for the Father seeks such as these to worship him. (John 4:21–23)

The Olivet Discourse

The longest sustained block of teaching from Jesus in the Gospel of Mark comes near the end of the Gospel, in the narrative about Jesus's final week. Jesus emerges from the temple and stands on the Mount of Olives, and tells the disciples about coming events, particularly the temple's destruction. This "Olivet Discourse" appears in Mark 13, and also in expanded form in Matthew 24. Luke also records this same material, but here it is split in two different speeches, in 17:20–37 and 21:5–36. Luke does not bring up the location of Jesus when he makes these speeches, so it's not technically correct to talk about an Olivet Discourse in Luke, but almost all of the material in these two sections of Luke find parallels in the Olivet Discourses (explicitly so called) in Matthew and Mark.

Here are the parallels for Luke 17.

	Luke	Mark	Matthew
Kingdom is among you	17:20–21	--	--
You will long for the Son of Man	17:22	--	--

People will say, "look here"	17:23	13:21	24:23
Son of Man = lightening	17:24	--	24:27
3rd Passion Prediction	17:25	--	--
End is like Noah	17:26–27	--	24:37–39
End is like Lot	17:28–30	--	--
Don't go get your stuff	17:31	13:15–16	24:17–18
Remember Lot's wife	17:32	--	--
Saver of life will lose it	17:33 (cf. 9:24)	--	10:39
2 in bed, 1 taken	17:34	--	--
2 grinding, 1 taken	17:35	--	24:41
where the vultures gather	17:37	--	24:28

Why does Jesus say these things on the Mount of Olives? Well, it's across from the Temple Mount. The Mount of Olives is two miles east of Jerusalem, with the Kidron Valley running between the Mount of Olives and the Temple Mount. You can find modern photos online that give an impression of how Jesus and his disciples stood on the Mount of Olives and looked across the valley at the temple (though the golden Dome of the Rock has to stand in now for the temple). But also the Mount of Olives might have had theological significance. Zechariah prophesied a time when the nations would battle against Jerusalem (just as Jesus describes in the Olivet Discourse), and at that time the Lord's feet "shall stand on the Mount of Olives" (Zech 14:4).[1] In a sense, Jesus is now fulfilling Zechariah's depiction.

The Kingdom Is Among You

The first of Luke's passages containing material parallel to the Olivet Discourse begins with this chapter's epigraph, where Jesus says, "the kingdom of God is among you" (Luke 17:21), a saying that appears only in Luke. What does it mean? The KJV has that phrase as "the kingdom of God is within you," which sounds like Jesus is saying that the kingdom exists in people's hearts. One problem with that reading is that Jesus is talking to Pharisees, and it seems unlikely that he would say to them, "the kingdom exists in your hearts"—because ... probably it doesn't. The other problem with this way of thinking about Luke 17:21 (i.e., the kingdom is in your heart) is that Jesus never says anything like it elsewhere. Nowhere else does Jesus represent God's kingdom as something inside people. Rather, the kingdom is something that people themselves need to enter (e.g., Luke 18:24–25; John 3:5). So, probably "within you" is not the right translation for Luke

---

[1] For more, see N. T. Wright, *Jesus and the Victory of God* (Minneapolis: Fortress, 1996), 344–45.

17:21; probably Jesus means, "the kingdom of God is among you."[2] But what does that mean?

Fairly frequently Jesus represented the kingdom of God as something that was happening through his own ministry, inbreaking into ancient Jewish Palestine through his deeds of power, through his healings, through his teachings.

> Go and tell John what you have seen and heard: the blind receive their sight, the lame walk, the lepers are cleansed, the deaf hear, the dead are raised, the poor have good news brought to them. And blessed is anyone who takes no offense at me. (Luke 7:22–23)

> Blessed are the eyes that see what you see! For I tell you that many prophets and kings desired to see what you see, but did not see it, and to hear what you hear, but did not hear it. (Luke 10:23–24)

> But if it is by the finger of God that I cast out the demons, then the kingdom of God has come to you. (Luke 11:20)

Each of these passages (and others) suggests that God is beginning his long-awaited reign through the ministry of Jesus.

---

[2] See Graham Stanton, *The Gospels and Jesus*, 2d ed. (Oxford: Oxford University Press, 2002), 210–11, who stresses that the phrase in Greek is difficult to interpret.

To those Pharisees, Jesus could truly say, "the kingdom of God is among you."

TRIBULATION

What that does not mean is that all trouble is gone. Just because "the kingdom of God is among you" does not mean that everything is going to be easy from now on. In fact, just the opposite. The rest of Luke's chapter describes the coming tribulation. Things are going to get bad. The days of Noah were so bad (17:26–27), God destroyed the earth. The days of Lot were so bad (17:28–30), God rained down fire from heaven. The days Jesus is describing are going to be like those days. But what days is Jesus describing?

When he uses language like "as the lightning flashes … so will the Son of Man be in his day" (17:24), we tend to think he's talking about the Second Coming. But some of this passage is hard to interpret as pointing toward the end of time. For instance:

> On that day, anyone on the housetop who has belongings in the house must not come down to take them away; and likewise anyone in the field must not turn back. Remember Lot's wife. Those who try to make their life secure will lose it, but those who lose their life will keep it. I tell you, on that night there will be two in one bed; one will be taken and the other left. There will be two women grinding meal together; one will be taken and the other left. (Luke 17:31–35)

This hardly makes any sense as a description of the end of the world.[3] How would "one be left" in that case? Some people think Jesus is talking about the Rapture: at the secret coming of Jesus, he'll take the elect home and leave everybody else to suffer through the seven years of tribulation. If you've read the *Left Behind* books or seen the movies, you know what this idea is about, but it is doubtful Jesus is talking about that. After all, he's talking about destruction, and not a secret destruction. How else should we interpret the analogies to Noah and Lot? There was nothing secret about the flood, or about the destruction of Sodom and Gomorrah. According to Wright, this passage refers to troublesome times on this earth, when armies are invading and people are panicky. In such a situation, "being taken"— which we usually interpret positively (= being taken by Jesus)— is not a good thing. "It is a matter, rather, of secret police coming in the night, or of enemies sweeping through a village or city and seizing all they can."[4] In this context, you'd prefer to be the one left rather than being the one taken.

The last comment in this section is Jesus's response to the question, "Where, Lord?"

Where the corpse is, there the eagles/vultures will gather. (17:37)

---

[3] But for an attempt at this kind of reading, see Mark C. Black, *Luke*, The College Press NIV Commentary (Joplin, MO: College Press, 1996), 293.

[4] Wright, *Jesus and the Victory of God*, 366.

The eagle was a symbol for Rome.[5] Presumably, that's what Jesus means: the eagles (i.e., Romans) are going to gather at Jerusalem (cf. 19:43; 21:20), whether Jerusalem is itself the corpse mentioned by Jesus, or whether Jesus refers to his own corpse which will reside for a few days in Jerusalem.[6]

All of this looks to me like a description of the coming war with Rome, ending in the destruction of the temple. The main issue with that reading is that Jesus says he is describing a "day" when the Son of Man is going to be "revealed" (17:30). I think we can get a better handle on what Jesus means by those words if we take a look at his similar words in Luke 21.

Luke 21[7]

After commenting on the widow's mite (Luke 21:1–4; cf. Mark 12:41–44), Jesus exits the temple (Mark 13:1) with his disciples. When some people (Luke 21:5; a disciple, according to Mark 13:1; Matt 24:1) mention the temple's beauty, Jesus responds:

---

[5] Wikipedia: "Aquila (Roman)"; Warren Carter, "Are There Imperial Texts in the Class? Intertextual Eagles and Matthean Eschatology as 'Lights Out' Time for Imperial Rome," *Journal of Biblical Literature* 122 (2003): 467–87, esp. 473–76. See, e.g., Josephus, *Jewish War* 3.123.

[6] Wright, *Jesus and the Victory of God*, 360, who takes the corpse [lit. "body"] as a reference to Jerusalem; Ryan P. Juza, "One of the Days of the Son of Man: A Reconsideration of Luke 17:22," *Journal of Biblical Literature* 135 (2016): 575–95, at 593, who takes the corpse to be Jesus's body.

[7] See below for a chart with a verse-by-verse comparison of Luke 21 with Mark 13 and Matthew 24.

As for these things that you see, the days will come when not one stone will be left upon another; all will be thrown down. (Luke 21:6; cf. Matt 24:2; Mark 13:2).

The disciples are curious: "tell us more about that, Jesus." Here's their question in all three Synoptic Gospels.

Teacher, when will this be, and what will be the sign that this is about to take place? (Luke 21:7)

Tell us, when will this be, and what will be the sign of your coming and of the end of the age? (Matt 24:3)

Tell us, when will this be, and what will be the sign that all these things are about to be accomplished? (Mark 13:4)

In my experience, it is Matthew 24 that has been most discussed in church circles, and I have heard people try to separate the disciples' questions, as if they were asking two different things, leading to two different responses from Jesus.[8] First (according

---

[8] This is one of the interpretations of the Olivet Discourse mentioned as a possibility by Allen Black, *Mark*, The College Press NIV Commentary (Joplin, MO: College Press, 1995), 225–27. In this view, Jesus turns his attention to the Second Coming at Mark 13:32. For a different way of understanding the word "coming" in the disciple's question of Matthew 24:3 (παρουσία, *parousia*), see Wright, *Jesus and the Victory of God*, 345–46.

to this idea), the disciples ask about the destruction of the temple, and secondly they ask about the timing of the return of Jesus (the Second Coming). This division of the question into two is supposed to help explain why Jesus's response seems to go in two different directions, apparently describing the destruction of the temple in some verses and apparently describing his own return at the end of time in other verses. But this idea of the two questions doesn't really work too well, for two reasons. First, even in Matthew 24 (upon which the idea is based), Jesus doesn't address one question and then go to the other, but he seems to mix up his responses.[9] Second, the disciples' question in the other Gospels, Mark and Luke, do not divide so easily as in Matthew. The question in Luke doesn't say anything about the "coming" of Jesus but is focused solely on the temple's destruction. The same is true in Mark. Whatever the response of Jesus means, in Luke he is apparently giving more information about the destruction of the temple, since that's the question that is reported. Of course, not all interpreters agree. The traditional way of interpreting Luke 21 and its parallels involves Jesus's Second Coming,[10] a view that will be downplayed in the interpretation presented here.

---

[9] Two of the views mentioned by Black, *Mark*, 225–27, involve Jesus's interweaving (in Mark 13) comments about the destruction of Jerusalem with other comments on his Second Coming. It is one of these views that Black himself advocates.

[10] See, e.g., Black, *Luke*, 335–46.

According to Jesus, what is going to take place? When will the temple be destroyed? Here is what the Lord says.[11]

- First, false messiahs will arise "in my name" (21:8).
- Then there will be wars and rumors of wars (21:9–11). Think about the Jewish revolt against Rome in AD 66–70, which ended with the destruction of the temple.
- At this time, the apostles and other disciples will be persecuted (21:12–19). Jesus says, "not a hair of your head will perish" (21:18), a statement not paralleled in Mark (cf. Mark 13:13) or Matthew (cf. Matt 24:13). We can't really believe that the disciples were not harmed at all in a literal, physical sense. We have record of the deaths of disciples, even in volume two of Luke's history work when he narrates the murder of Stephen (Acts 7). So I think we're supposed to understand this promise from Jesus in some sort of more spiritual sense—that despite the physical trials that the disciples endure, God still has their hairs numbered (Luke 12:7) and guarantees their future, eternal security.
- Jerusalem will be surrounded by armies (21:20–24).[12] Jesus encourages his disciples to flee the destruction, to get out of the city. Of course, this time will be especially hard for pregnant women and families with young children. While it is normally considered a blessing to

---

[11] The following interpretation is heavily indebted to Wright, *Jesus and the Victory of God*, 339–67.

[12] For an in-depth treatment of these verses with extensive interaction with the Old Testament background to Jesus's words, see Wright, *Jesus and the Victory of God*, 348–60.

have children or to be expecting them, the usual rules don't apply during a time of desolation. Jesus says two especially interesting things in this paragraph, things not paralleled in the other Gospels. First, these predictions of destruction are "a fulfillment of all that is written" (21:22). And second, Jesus refers to the "times of the Gentiles." I imagine what he means by "Gentiles" here is foreigners that don't belong to God's people. In other words, I don't think he's using the term "Gentiles" in reference to non-Jews who come to accept Jesus as the Messiah (i.e., Gentile Christians). I think what he's getting at is that there is an appointed time for God's land to be dominated by people who do not belong to God (called here Gentiles), but their time will come to an end. As Caird notes, Jesus's words echo the book of Daniel, which prophesies the hegemony of Gentile kingdoms for a limited time (see Daniel 2 and 7).[13]

- Then Jesus says this:

There will be signs in the sun, the moon, and the stars, and on the earth distress among nations confused by the roaring of the sea and the waves. People will faint from fear and foreboding of what is coming upon the world, for the powers of the heavens will be shaken. Then they will see 'the Son of Man coming in a cloud' with power and great glory. Now when these things begin to take place, stand up and raise your heads,

---

[13] G. B. Caird, *Saint Luke* (Baltimore: Penguin, 1963), 231–32.

because your redemption is drawing near. (Luke
21:25–28)

Is Jesus still talking about the destruction of Jerusalem? It doesn't
sound like it, does it?[14] These are images we usually associate with
the end of time. I mean, he says that we will see "the Son of Man
coming in a cloud." What else could that refer to other than the
Second Coming of Jesus which will usher in the resurrection of
the dead and the final judgment?

But, I don't know …. Let me try to make a case that Jesus
is still, even here, talking about the destruction of Jerusalem. I'm
not fully convinced that he is, but if I had to pick an
interpretation, I would probably pick this one, that Jesus is not
talking about his Second Coming but is talking about something
that happened a long time ago, a few decades after his own death
and resurrection. (I admit, this is a difficult view to maintain, but,
really, so are all views of this passage. But this one is so difficult
that some scholars don't even consider it.)[15] For one thing, Jesus
goes on to say, "this generation will not pass away until all things
have taken place" (21:32; cf. Matt 24:34; Mark 13:30). And the
destruction of Jerusalem is what he has been talking about up to
this point.[16] I suspect that he's still talking about the destruction

---

[14] It is this passage at which Black, *Luke*, 337, sees Jesus turning his
attention from the destruction of Jerusalem to the Second Coming.

[15] Black, *Mark*, 225, rules out this interpretation of Mark 13 based on the
parallel with Matthew 24, which Black thinks more clearly contains
material about the Second Coming.

[16] Black, *Luke*, 344–45, thinks that Jesus means that the destruction of
Jerusalem and the signs of the Second Coming, but not the Second Coming
itself, will be accomplished in that generation.

of Jerusalem and he is describing it in cosmic language, or we might say figurative language. There are examples from the Old Testament.

Isaiah 13 is given the heading "an oracle concerning Babylon," and it is most certainly an oracle of doom, prophesying Babylon's destruction—not (let the reader understand) prophesying the earth's destruction. But the oracle reads in part:

> See, the day of YHWH comes,
>> cruel, with wrath and fierce anger,
> to make the earth a desolation,
>> and to destroy its sinners from it.
> For the stars of the heavens and their constellations
>> will not give their light;
> the sun will be dark at its rising,
>> and the moon will not shed its light. (Isa 13:9–10)

What do the stars and sun and moon have to do with Babylon? Well, not much, but these strange heavenly signs are an ill-omen for Babylon. Darkness is coming for Babylon—no, not literal darkness, but metaphorical darkness.

Or, how about this one, from later in Isaiah's book, where the subject is Edom.

> All the host of heaven shall rot away,
>> and the skies roll up like a scroll.
> All their host shall wither
>> like a leaf withering on a vine,
>> or fruit withering on a fig tree.
> When my sword has drunk its fill in the heavens,

> lo, it will descend upon Edom,
>
> upon the people I have doomed to judgment.
>
> YHWH has a sword; it is sated with blood,
>
> > it is gorged with fat,
> >
> > with the blood of lambs and goats,
> >
> > with the fat of the kidneys of rams.
>
> For YHWH has a sacrifice in Bozrah,
>
> > a great slaughter in the land of Edom. (Isa 34:4–6)

Here again we have this cosmic imagery, the skies being rolled up like a scroll, the heavenly host rotting away. Of course, none of that really, literally happened when Edom was destroyed, but for Edom it might as well have. Edom's world was coming to an end. So also, Isaiah says "YHWH has a sword" (v. 6), but of course he doesn't have a literal, physical sword. We get a graphic description of the Lord's sword, but it's all metaphorical.

There are other examples. A good one is Ezekiel 32, a prophecy against Egypt, in which the destruction of Egypt is described using the same cosmic imagery we've already encountered (32:7).

All that to say that there is precedent for talking about the destruction of a nation in terms of strange signs in the heavens, and the sun, moon, and stars going dark. So it's not too difficult to relate Jesus's words in Luke 21:25 to the destruction of Jerusalem.[17]

---

[17] For a good, brief discussion of the pros and cons of this type of reading, see Brant J. Pitre, "Apocalypticism and Apocalyptic Teaching," in *Dictionary of Jesus and the Gospels*, 2d ed., ed. Joel B. Green (Downers Grove, IL: IVP, 2013), 23–33, at 30. For a more detailed presentation of the

What about "the Son of Man coming in a cloud" (21:27)? Could that possibly refer to the destruction of Jerusalem? Certainly his disciples listening to him would not have thought that this language—which sounds so much like the Second Coming to us—indicated the way Jesus would come back at the end of time. After all, they didn't even realize that they were about to be separated from Jesus, that he was about to die with a resurrection to follow, no matter how many times Jesus had tried to tell them. So, the disciples would probably have understood Jesus to be talking in some way still about the destruction of the temple rather than his own return (which they were not yet ready to understand),[18] but what did Jesus mean by these words? Again, I think if you look at some Old Testament imagery, you'd come to the conclusion that Jesus might not be talking about his own Second Coming but something else. That is, the language of "coming" doesn't necessarily mean what we think of as coming. Just think for a moment about what the patriarch Joseph makes his brothers swear on his deathbed.

---

type of argument I'm advancing here, see Wright, *Jesus and the Victory of God*, 354–58.

[18] Even in the Gospel of John, in the Farewell Discourse (John 13–16), where Jesus is much more explicit (than he is anywhere in the Synoptic Gospels) about his imminent departure back to the Father, I'm not sure that the disciples ever really get the point (though see John 16:25–33). Note that even if in John's Gospel the disciples do finally understand something about the Second Coming, they would have done so only on the night of the Betrayal (= the setting of the Farewell Discourse), and therefore only after the Olivet Discourse.

> And Joseph took an oath of the children of
> Israel, saying, God will surely visit you, and ye
> shall carry up my bones from hence. (Gen 50:25)

"God will surely visit you." What does Joseph mean, or in what sense does God "visit" Israel. Exodus 13:19 quotes these words of Joseph as coming to fulfillment when the Israelites took up Joseph's bones at the time of the exodus. Ah, there it is—the exodus. The rescue of God's people from Egypt is the moment of God's "visiting" Israel. But it's not a "visit" (or a "coming") in the normal sense of the term; God visited Israel in the sense that he destroyed her enemies and rescued her from foreign oppression.

More to the point of what Jesus is getting at is Daniel 7, where "one like a son of man came with the clouds of heaven" (Dan 7:13) and "to him was given dominion and glory and kingship" (7:14). When the Son of Man comes on the clouds, that is the time that his kingship is confirmed. Not only that, but also this Son of Man is not coming to earth to reign as king but coming to the Ancient of Days, who is seated on his throne in heaven (see Dan 7:9–14). What people will see at the destruction of Jerusalem is the vindication of the Son of Man; this destruction will symbolize the ascent (not descent!) of the Son of Man to the Ancient of Days to be confirmed as king (see Eph 1:20–23; 1 Pet 3:22).[19]

If that's what "the Son of Man coming in a cloud" might mean, then I think it could also explain what Jesus meant that the

---

[19] For a strong insistence on this sort of reading the passage from Jesus's Olivet Discourse, see Wright, *Jesus and the Victory*, 360–65.

Son of Man would be revealed on a particular day (17:30).[20] Though the end of time might be something like what Jesus describes here, I suspect he is actually describing the destruction of Jerusalem, and his disciples would have understood him to be talking about the destruction of Jerusalem.

What Does It Matter?

Why do we care about the destruction of Jerusalem and the temple? This discussion will be painfully brief. First, there are warnings Jesus gave to his disciples that apply to disciples of Jesus throughout the ages. He warned his disciples to be watchful and to live in a state of preparation. This warning remains urgent for us. I appreciate how Allen Black put it in his commentary on Mark 13: "It is easy to understand these warnings. It is also easy to overlook them in the effort to sort out the exegetical conundrums of this chapter."[21] Black thinks that a good bit of the Olivet Discourse has reference to the Second Coming; I think maybe that it doesn't. But either way, both of us interpret Jesus's warnings in the same way. Be ready!

Second, the Bible talks a whole lot about the temple. And just as Jesus was ambivalent about the temple, so was God. God did not allow David to build a temple, partly because he never asked for such a thing (2 Sam 7). He does not inhabit a temple made by hands (Isa 66:1–2, quoted by Stephen in Acts 7:49–50). Too often, the temple became a symbol of God's protection, a

---

[20] For the interpretation offered here, see also Juza, "One of the Days of the Son of Man," 589–91.

[21] Black, *Mark*, 224.

false symbol, because God had little interest in protecting a sinful people. The people in Jeremiah's day knew that God would not allow the Babylonians to destroy Jerusalem because of "the temple of YHWH, the temple of YHWH, the temple of YHWH" (Jer 7:4). But Jeremiah warned them that the "robbers' den" (7:11) that the temple had become had no claim on God's affections or protection. We saw at the beginning of the chapter how Ezekiel depicted the "glory of the Lord" as departing the temple to reside on a mountain and watch the Babylonians destroy the city (Ezek 8–11).

Is the temple valuable as a symbol of God's presence among his people? Sure. Yes.

Is the temple dangerous as a symbol of God's presence among his people? Yes.

And for readers of the New Testament, looking at any building as the symbol of God's presence is just the wrong idea.

> So then you are no longer strangers and aliens, but you are citizens with the saints and also members of the household of God, built upon the foundation of the apostles and prophets, with Christ Jesus himself as the cornerstone. In him the whole structure is joined together and grows into a holy temple in the Lord; in whom you also are built together spiritually into a dwelling place for God. (Eph 2:19–22)

The church is the temple. The people of God are his dwelling place. His Spirit resides in human beings. Christians are the symbol of the presence of God.

Synopsis of the Olivet Discourse

Luke 21	Mark 13	Matthew 24
[8] And he said, "Beware that you are not led astray; for many will come in my name and say, 'I am he!' and, 'The time is near!' Do not go after them.	[5] Then Jesus began to say to them, "Beware that no one leads you astray. [6] Many will come in my name and say, 'I am he!' and they will lead many astray.	[4] Jesus answered them, "Beware that no one leads you astray. [5] For many will come in my name, saying, 'I am the Messiah!' and they will lead many astray.
[9] "When you hear of wars and insurrections, do not be terrified; for these things must take place first, but the end will not follow immediately."	[7] When you hear of wars and rumors of wars, do not be alarmed; this must take place, but the end is still to come.	[6] And you will hear of wars and rumors of wars; see that you are not alarmed; for this must take place, but the end is not yet.
[10] Then he said to them, "Nation will rise against nation, and kingdom	[8] For nation will rise against nation, and kingdom against	[7] For nation will rise against nation, and kingdom against kingdom,

against kingdom; [11] there will be great earthquakes, and in various places famines	kingdom; there will be earthquakes in various places; there will be famines.	and there will be famines and earthquakes in various places:
and plagues; and there will be dreadful portents and great signs from heaven.		
	This is but the beginning of the birthpangs.	[8] all this is but the beginning of the birthpangs.
[12] "But before all this occurs, they will arrest you and persecute you; they will hand you over to synagogues and prisons, and you will be brought before kings and governors because of my name. [13] This will give you an	[9] "As for yourselves, beware; for they will hand you over to councils; and you will be beaten in synagogues; and you will stand before governors and kings because of me, as a	

opportunity to testify.	testimony to them.	
		[9] "Then they will hand you over to be tortured and will put you to death, and you will be hated by all nations because of my name. [10] Then many will fall away, and they will betray one another and hate one another. [11] And many false prophets will arise and lead many astray. [12] And because of the increase of lawlessness, the love of many will grow cold.
	[10] And the good news must first be proclaimed to all nations.	[14] And this good news of the kingdom will be proclaimed

		throughout the world, as a testimony to all the nations; and then the end will come.
[14] So make up your minds not to prepare your defense in advance; [15] for I will give you words and a wisdom that none of your opponents will be able to withstand or contradict.	[11] When they bring you to trial and hand you over, do not worry beforehand about what you are to say; but say whatever is given you at that time, for it is not you who speak, but the Holy Spirit.	
[16] You will be betrayed even by parents and brothers, by relatives and friends; and they will put some of you to death.	[12] Brother will betray brother to death, and a father his child, and children will rise against parents and have them put to death;	

¹⁷ You will be hated by all because of my name.	¹³ and you will be hated by all because of my name.	
¹⁸ But not a hair of your head will perish.		
¹⁹ By your endurance you will gain your souls.	But the one who endures to the end will be saved.	¹³ But the one who endures to the end will be saved.
²⁰ "When you see Jerusalem surrounded by armies, then know that its desolation has come near.		
	¹⁴ "But when you see the desolating sacrilege set up where it ought not to be (let the reader understand),	¹⁵ "So when you see the desolating sacrilege standing in the holy place, as was spoken of by the prophet Daniel (let the reader understand),

21 Then those in Judea must flee to the mountains, and those inside the city must leave it, and those out in the country must not enter it;	then those in Judea must flee to the mountains; 15 the one on the housetop must not go down or enter the house to take anything away; 16 the one in the field must not turn back to get a coat.	16 then those in Judea must flee to the mountains; 17 the one on the housetop must not go down to take what is in the house; 18 the one in the field must not turn back to get a coat.
22 for these are days of vengeance, as a fulfillment of all that is written.		
23 Woe to those who are pregnant and to those who are nursing infants in those days!	17 Woe to those who are pregnant and to those who are nursing infants in those days!	19 Woe to those who are pregnant and to those who are nursing infants in those days!
	18 Pray that it may not be in winter.	20 Pray that your flight may not be in winter or on a sabbath.

For there will be great distress on the earth and wrath against this people; ²⁴ they will fall by the edge of the sword and be taken away as captives among all nations; and Jerusalem will be trampled on by the Gentiles, until the times of the Gentiles are fulfilled.		
	¹⁹ For in those days there will be suffering, such as has not been from the beginning of the creation that God created until now, no, and never will be.	²¹ For at that time there will be great suffering, such as has not been from the beginning of the world until now, no, and never will be.
	²⁰ And if the Lord had not cut short those days, no one would be	²² And if those days had not been cut short, no one would be saved;

	saved; but for the sake of the elect, whom he chose, he has cut short those days.	but for the sake of the elect those days will be cut short.
	²¹ And if anyone says to you at that time, 'Look! Here is the Messiah!' or 'Look! There he is!'—do not believe it.	²³ Then if anyone says to you, 'Look! Here is the Messiah!' or 'There he is!'—do not believe it.
	²² False messiahs and false prophets will appear and produce signs and omens, to lead astray, if possible, the elect.	²⁴ For false messiahs and false prophets will appear and produce great signs and omens, to lead astray, if possible, even the elect.
	²³ But be alert; I have already told you everything.	²⁵ Take note, I have told you beforehand.
		²⁶ So, if they say to you, 'Look! He is

		in the wilderness,' do not go out. If they say, 'Look! He is in the inner rooms,' do not believe it. ²⁷ For as the lightning comes from the east and flashes as far as the west, so will be the coming of the Son of Man. ²⁸ Wherever the corpse is, there the vultures will gather.
²⁵ "There will be signs in the sun, the moon, and the stars, and on the earth distress among nations confused by the roaring of the sea and the waves.	²⁴ "But in those days, after that suffering, the sun will be darkened, and the moon will not give its light, ²⁵ and the stars will be falling from heaven, and the powers in the heavens will be shaken.	²⁹ "Immediately after the suffering of those days the sun will be darkened, and the moon will not give its light; the stars will fall from heaven, and the powers of heaven will be shaken.

²⁶ People will faint from fear and foreboding of what is coming upon the world, for the powers of the heavens will be shaken.		
²⁷ Then they will see 'the Son of Man coming in a cloud' with power and great glory.	²⁶ Then they will see 'the Son of Man coming in clouds' with great power and glory.	³⁰ Then the sign of the Son of Man will appear in heaven, and then all the tribes of the earth will mourn, and they will see 'the Son of Man coming on the clouds of heaven' with power and great glory.
	²⁷ Then he will send out the angels, and gather his elect from the four winds, from the ends of the earth to the ends of heaven.	³¹ And he will send out his angels with a loud trumpet call, and they will gather his elect from the four winds, from one

		end of heaven to the other.
²⁸ Now when these things begin to take place, stand up and raise your heads, because your redemption is drawing near."		
²⁹ Then he told them a parable: "Look at the fig tree and all the trees; ³⁰ as soon as they sprout leaves you can see for yourselves and know that summer is already near.	²⁸ "From the fig tree learn its lesson: as soon as its branch becomes tender and puts forth its leaves, you know that summer is near.	³² "From the fig tree learn its lesson: as soon as its branch becomes tender and puts forth its leaves, you know that summer is near.
³¹ So also, when you see these things taking place, you know that the kingdom of God is near.	²⁹ So also, when you see these things taking place, you know that he is near, at the very gates.	³³ So also, when you see all these things, you know that he is near, at the very gates.

32 Truly I tell you, this generation will not pass away until all things have taken place. 33 Heaven and earth will pass away, but my words will not pass away.	30 Truly I tell you, this generation will not pass away until all these things have taken place. 31 Heaven and earth will pass away, but my words will not pass away.	34 Truly I tell you, this generation will not pass away until all these things have taken place. 35 Heaven and earth will pass away, but my words will not pass away.
	32 "But about that day or hour no one knows, neither the angels in heaven, nor the Son, but only the Father.	36 "But about that day and hour no one knows, neither the angels of heaven, nor the Son, but only the Father.
		37 For as the days of Noah were, so will be the coming of the Son of Man. 38 For as in those days before the flood they were eating and drinking, marrying and giving in marriage,

		until the day Noah entered the ark, [39] and they knew nothing until the flood came and swept them all away, so too will be the coming of the Son of Man. [40] Then two will be in the field; one will be taken and one will be left. [41] Two women will be grinding meal together; one will be taken and one will be left.
	[33] Beware, keep alert; for you do not know when the time will come.	[42] Keep awake therefore, for you do not know on what day your Lord is coming.
[34] "Be on guard so that your hearts are not weighed down with dissipation and drunkenness		

and the worries of this life, and that day catch you unexpectedly, 35 like a trap. For it will come upon all who live on the face of the whole earth. 36 Be alert at all times, praying that you may have the strength to escape all these things that will take place, and to stand before the Son of Man."		
	34 It is like a man going on a journey, when he leaves home and puts his slaves in charge, each with his work, and commands the doorkeeper to be on the watch. 35 Therefore, keep awake—for you	

| | do not know when the master of the house will come, in the evening, or at midnight, or at cockcrow, or at dawn, **36** or else he may find you asleep when he comes suddenly. ³⁷ And what I say to you I say to all: Keep awake." | |
| | | ⁴³ But understand this: if the owner of the house had known in what part of the night the thief was coming, he would have stayed awake and would not have let his house be broken into. ⁴⁴ Therefore you also must be ready, for the Son of Man is |

		coming at an unexpected hour. [45] Who then is the faithful and wise slave, whom his master has put in charge of his household, to give the other slaves their allowance of food at the proper time? [46] Blessed is that slave whom his master will find at work when he arrives. [47] Truly I tell you, he will put that one in charge of all his possessions. [48] But if that wicked slave says to himself, 'My master is delayed,' [49] and he begins to beat his fellow slaves, and eats and drinks with drunkards, [50] the master of that

		slave will come on a day when he does not expect him and at an hour that he does not know. [51] He will cut him in pieces and put him with the hypocrites, where there will be weeping and gnashing of teeth.

11

THE FINAL HOURS OF JESUS

LUKE 22

> But he said to them, "The kings of the Gentiles lord it over them; and those in authority over them are called benefactors. But not so with you; rather the greatest among you must become like the youngest, and the leader like one who serves. (Luke 22:25–26)

Jesus is in Jerusalem, which means it's the final week of his life. (You couldn't say that about the Gospel of John, which represents Jesus in Jerusalem several times during his ministry. But the Synoptic Gospels locate the adult Jesus in Jerusalem only once, leading up to his death.) Luke had narrated Jesus's arrival in Jerusalem in 19:28–40, after the long Travel Narrative (9:51–19:27). He had apparently come for the Passover, which is now near (22:1).[1] This is the festival that celebrates God's salvation of the enslaved Israelites from their Egyptian overlords. It formed

---

[1] On Passover in the first century, see E. P. Sanders, *Judaism, Practice and Belief, 63 BCE–66 CE* (Philadelphia: TPI, 1992), 132–38.

an appropriate backdrop to the salvation Jesus was about to perform, so much so that Jesus's actions have already been compared to the "exodus" while he was speaking with none other than Moses (and Elijah) on the mount of Transfiguration (9:31). Luke had said that Moses and Elijah were speaking with Jesus about his "departure," which in Greek is the word *exodos* (ἔξοδος). Other people were no doubt thinking that the Passover would provide an appropriate backdrop for the Messiah to liberate Israel in a different way—from the slavery they were then experiencing at the hands of their Roman overlords. Probably some of the disciples were also thinking along these lines. They expected Jesus to lead the armies of God in armed conflict against God's enemies, the Romans, and to destroy the pagan empire, just as God did at the Red Sea (Exod 14). They will be disappointed.

THE LAST SUPPER

Figure 5. Leonardo da Vinci's *The Last Supper* (1495–1498).
Public domain, via Wikimedia Commons.

Jesus wants to eat the Passover meal with his disciples (Luke 22:15), so he sends Peter and John to make preparations (22:7–13). They assemble in an unnamed person's guest room (v. 11), "a large room upstairs" (v. 12).[2]

It's Thursday evening. We know that because he dies on a Friday, and it takes all Thursday night and Friday morning to get through the trial and for him to arrive at Calvary.[3] It is not completely certain which day of the month it is. The Passover lamb is supposed to be slaughtered on the 14th day of the Jewish month Nisan (Exod 12:6), and then that evening there would be the Passover meal, after the date had turned over to Nisan 15. (Remember that the Jewish way of reckoning time has the day begin at sundown rather than midnight.) It seems like Luke (and the other Synoptic Gospels) mean to say that the Last Supper is the Passover meal, so that it is happening on Nisan 15. But the Gospel of John seems to date everything a day early. Of course, John does not include an account of the Last Supper, but he seems to have Jesus crucified on Nisan 14 (John 18:28), in which case the Last Supper would be at the beginning of Nisan 14 (i.e., in the evening just after it had turned over to Nisan 14, after sunset). I'm not sure what to do with all that; there are different

---

[2] Luke's account is very similar to Mark 14:12–16, but Matthew 26:17–19 offers a compressed narrative.

[3] Calvary or Golgotha? Golgotha was the Hebrew name for the place, as John 19:17 tells us, and it is used also at Matthew 27:33; Mark 15:22. These same passages also provide the translation for the Hebrew word, "skull." Luke does not use the word Golgotha; he merely provides the translation, "skull" (23:33). The Latin word for skull is Calvary, which appears in the KJV Luke 23:33 (and only here in the KJV).

ways of working out this apparent discrepancy.[4] It's only an issue when comparing the Synoptic Gospels to John; Luke does not comment on the difficulty, so for now we can leave it alone.

Much more important are the words Jesus says at the meal (22:14–22). He begins by saying how eager he has been to eat this Passover with his disciples "before I suffer" (v. 15).[5] That might seem like a strange thing to say; after all, the Passover meal is the beginning of the end, it's really the buildup to his own death, as Jesus well knew. From one angle, we might have expected that Jesus would want to put it off. But from a different angle, we can well imagine the eager anticipation of getting it over with. He had been predicting his own suffering and death for weeks or months now (9:22, 44; 13:33; 17:25; 18:31–33). His life may have seemed like one long tug of the band aid, and he may have been eager to just rip the thing off. Even during his early adult years, Jesus may have had his eye on this moment, and perhaps sometimes it seemed to him like it would never arrive. Finally, it's here. And from a third angle, Jesus may have been thinking that he would finally be able to go into full-fledged battle against the forces of darkness—suffer at their hands and thereby decisively defeat them and liberate his followers from the destructive power of sin. Jesus may have felt like a soldier waiting for the battle, not with dread but ready to engage, or like an athlete eager to start the game.

"I will not eat of it until it is fulfilled in the kingdom of God" (v. 16). What would his disciples have thought about this

---

[4] See Ed Gallagher, *The Book of Exodus: Explorations in Christian Theology* (Florence, AL: HCU Press, 2020), 96n15.

[5] This comment finds no parallel in the other Gospels.

statement? Well, his disciples were fully anticipating that Jesus the Messiah was about to start the war against the Romans in order to establish God's kingdom based in Jerusalem. (This misunderstanding on the part of the disciples helps to explain some of the subsequent confusion leading up to the arrest.) They would probably think that the Passover meal would be "fulfilled" in the kingdom of God when God had definitively liberated his people from the foreign oppressor and established them in security in their own kingdom. This liberation would fulfill the promise of Passover. In the kingdom of God—that is, God's kingdom based in Jerusalem—the disciples would join with the messianic king Jesus in frequent banqueting celebrating their victories (see Luke 13:28–29; cf. Matt 8:11).

That's not what Jesus meant, as even the first readers of Luke would know, because the history did not turn out that way. Honestly, I'm not exactly sure what Jesus meant, but I can think of a couple possibilities. One is that he expected that his followers would reenact this same meal frequently as they reminded each other of Jesus. He says "do this in remembrance of me" (v. 19).[6] Perhaps Jesus was thinking that in the context of Christian worship, when his disciples eat the bread and drink the cup in remembrance of their Lord, that Jesus himself also joins them in

---

[6] Note that in Luke Jesus makes this statement about repeated observance only in respect of the bread, and in Matthew and Mark he does not say these words at all. But Paul's account of the Lord's Supper, in a letter probably written before any of our Gospels, attached this statement to both the bread and the cup (1 Cor 11:23–25), and in respect of the cup Paul reports an expanded version of the statement: "Do this, as often as you drink it, in remembrance of me."

that meal. But a second possibility is that we are still looking forward to the fulfillment of this statement by Jesus. He does sometimes talk about what appears to be a future banquet that we will enjoy with him.

> There will be weeping and gnashing of teeth when you see Abraham and Isaac and Jacob and all the prophets in the kingdom of God, and you yourselves thrown out. And people will come from east and west, and from north and south, and recline at table in the kingdom of God. (Luke 13:28–29)

I don't guess that has happened yet. Maybe Jesus was looking forward to this banquet as the time when he will again eat the Passover meal with his disciples.

Cup-Bread-Cup

Another distinctive feature about the way that Luke presents the Last Supper is the order of the elements. Matthew, Mark, and Paul all have the order bread-cup, but Luke has an extra cup at the beginning.[7]

---

[7] There is a textual problem at this point in Luke's narrative; some manuscripts omit the second cup. Probably the unexpected sequence cup-bread-cup caused some scribes to try to fix the problem, but they ended up making the situation worse. For discussion of the textual problem, see the relevant note (note 49 of Luke 22) of the online NET Bible (netbible.org); see also Bruce M. Metzger, *A Textual Commentary on the Greek New Testament,* 2d ed. (New York: United Bible Societies, 1994), 148–50. For

Cup:
Then he took a cup, and after giving thanks he said, "Take this and divide it among yourselves; for I tell you that from now on I will not drink of the fruit of the vine until the kingdom of God comes." (22:17–18)

Bread:
Then he took a loaf of bread, and when he had given thanks, he broke it and gave it to them, saying, "This is my body, which is given for you. Do this in remembrance of me." (22:19)

Cup:
And he did the same with the cup after supper, saying, "This cup that is poured out for you is the new covenant in my blood. (22:20)

Notice how Jesus describes the two cups. Only the second cup is "for you" and is the cup of the covenant. That makes me think that the first cup is just a cup of wine during the Passover meal, not a "Lord's Supper cup." Matthew and Mark represent the institution of the Lord's Supper as taking place during a meal.[8]

---

an argument favoring the originality of a shorter form of the text, see Bart D. Ehrman, *The Orthodox Corruption of Scripture: The Effect of Early Christological Controversies on the Text of the New Testament*, 2d ed. (Oxford: Oxford University Press, 2011), 231–45.

[8] Paul does not make this point explicit (1 Cor 11:23–25).

> While they were eating, Jesus took a loaf of bread … (Matt 26:26)

> While they were eating, he took a loaf of bread … (Mark 14:22)

They drank more wine that night than merely the one sip to which we usually give attention. At least in later times (and perhaps also in the first century), it became customary to have four cups of wine during the Passover meal.[9] Unlike the other Gospel accounts, Luke reports the sharing of an earlier cup of wine. Just as he had said that he would not eat until he does so in the kingdom of God, so now with this first cup of wine he says that he will no longer drink except in the kingdom of God.

THE WORDS OF INSTITUTION

Let's compare the different accounts.
Bread:

> Take, eat; this is my body. (Matt 26:26)
> Take; this is my body. (Mark 14:22)
> This is my body, which is given for you. Do this in remembrance of me. (Luke 22:19)
> This is my body that is for you. Do this in remembrance of me. (1 Cor 11:23)

---

[9] For the significance of these four cups of wine, see Yosef Marcus, "What Is the Significance of the Four Cups of Wine?" *Chabad.org.*

Cup:

> Drink from it, all of you; for this is my blood of
> the covenant, which is poured out for many for
> the forgiveness of sins. I tell you, I will never
> again drink of this fruit of the vine until that day
> when I drink it new with you in my Father's
> kingdom. (Matt 26:27–29)

> This is my blood of the covenant, which is
> poured out for many. Truly I tell you, I will
> never again drink of the fruit of the vine until
> that day when I drink it new in the kingdom of
> God. (Mark 14:24–25)

> This cup that is poured out for you is the new
> covenant in my blood. (Luke 22:20)

> This cup is the new covenant in my blood. Do
> this, as often as you drink it, in remembrance of
> me. (1 Cor 11:25)

Luke has more in common with the tradition reported by
Paul than with Matthew and Mark at this point. The words about
the bread are expanded in the same way in Luke and Paul, and
the crucial wording about the cup also corresponds in Luke and
Paul and diverges from the account in Matthew and Mark.

First, let's think about the bread. Why does Jesus pick up
a loaf of bread and say, "this is my body"? Why doesn't he pick

up some lamb meat, which also should have been on the table?[10] Such an action would have spoken powerfully to Jesus's role as the lamb of God (cf. John 1:29). According to Paul, Jesus was understood to be "our Passover sacrifice" (1 Cor 5:7). And with the blood of the lamb providing protection to the Israelites against the death of the firstborn (Exod 12:7, 13), Jesus could have made a very obvious connection to his blood. On the other hand, the bread plays a relatively minor role in the story of Passover (Exod 12:39).

But the bread actually plays a major role in the remembrance of Passover. Immediately after the initial instructions regarding the Passover lamb and what to do with its blood (Exod 12:1–13), God institutes an annual celebration: "Seven days you shall eat unleavened bread" (Exod 12:15). Passover is just one day, but the festival of Unleavened Bread lasts a whole week. After the exodus from Egypt, God gives more instructions about this festival.

> Unleavened bread shall be eaten for seven days; no leavened bread shall be seen in your possession, and no leaven shall be seen among you in all your territory. You shall tell your child on that day, 'It is because of what the YHWH did for me when I came out of Egypt.' It shall serve for you as a sign on your hand and as a

---

[10] There is no lamb meat at a modern Passover seder, because there is no Passover sacrifice, because there is no temple. There is a lamb bone at a modern seder. Presumably, Jesus would have been eating lamb meat, though—if the Last Supper is indeed a Passover meal.

reminder on your forehead, so that the teaching of the YHWH may be on your lips; for with a strong hand the YHWH brought you out of Egypt. You shall keep this ordinance at its proper time from year to year. (Exod 13:7–10)

The child (v. 8) I suppose is going to ask why the family is eating unleavened bread, and a question that will offer an opportunity to teach about God and what he did for Israel. The bread is a reminder of God's goodness.

So, yes, the Passover lamb would have been—and is!—an appropriate way of thinking about the body of Jesus, but so also the bread. And the bread is also reminiscent of manna, a connection that Jesus makes in another context (his body = manna; cf. John 6:31–58). But there is at least one way in which bread is a better symbol of Jesus's body than the Passover lamb would have been. It is common. Especially in the ancient world, people did not eat meat everyday, and the Passover lamb itself was sacrificed only once a year. The Passover lamb made for a good annual memorial, but it wasn't going to be any more frequent than annual. Jesus wanted his disciples to have a more frequent memorial, and so the bread worked better than the lamb.

There is a lot to say about the significance of this memorial meal instituted by Jesus with his "do this in remembrance of me" (Luke 22:19), but here I'll only give a few, brief pointers toward what might be useful reflections on the Lord's Supper. This common, everyday bread represents the body of Jesus, which is just like all our bodies. The bread reminds us that Jesus was human just like all of us. It is a reminder of the

Incarnation. The fact that we eat the bread—we eat Jesus's body—suggests that we are granted the life that Jesus had within himself (that is the exact point Jesus makes in John 6:53–57)[11] and it is a symbol that our bodies are transformed so that we become more and more little "Christs" walking around on earth. Taking bread from Jesus makes us think of the other times that Jesus fed people (e.g., the feeding of the 5,000; the road to Emmaus), and we remember that all our provisions are from God. We cannot provide for ourselves. So also we think about the manna in the wilderness, and we know that this bread represents God's daily, loving provision for his people. We need God's grace daily. And of course we think about what would become of Jesus's body, hanging on the cross, and we recall why he did that, because of our sins. And eating this bread that is his crucified body reminds us that we too are called to take up our cross.[12]

Now let's get to the cup. In Matthew (and Mark is similar), the words are: "for this is my blood of the covenant, which is poured out for many for the forgiveness of sins." We've got two very clear Old Testament echoes here. First, "blood of

---

[11] On the interpretation of John 6, see Richard Bauckham, *Gospel of Glory: Major Themes in Johannine Theology* (Grand Rapids: Baker, 2015), 94–104. But Keith Stanglin is correct that whether or not Jesus himself was talking about the Lord's Supper (Bauckham argues that he was not), the language Jesus used does connect to the Lord's Supper; see Keith D. Stanglin, "Christ's Presence and the Thing Signified in the Lord's Supper," *Christian Studies* 30 (2018): 7–24, at 20.

[12] For further theological reflections on the Lord's Supper, urging a sacramental viewpoint consistent with Restorationist impulses, see Stanglin, "Christ's Presence."

the covenant" alludes to the ceremony in Exodus 24, when Moses ratified the Sinai covenant with Israel by making a sacrifice (Exod 24:5) and sprinkling some of the blood on the people (24:8) and saying, "See the blood of the covenant that the Lord has made with you in accordance with these words." Second, the phrase "for many for the forgiveness of sins" probably alludes to Isaiah 53:12, where the Servant of the Lord is described with these words: "he bore the sin of many, and made intercession for the transgressors." Both of those allusions could provide the basis for an extensive discussion about the meaning of Jesus's death. But we're studying Luke.

In Luke (and Paul is similar), the words over the cup go: "This cup that is poured out for you is the new covenant in my blood." The words "poured out" (which appear in all three Synoptic Gospels but not Paul) may allude to Old Testament sacrifice in general, in which the blood would be "poured out" (Exod 29:12; Lev 4:7, 18, 25; etc.).[13] But the main element that separates Luke's and Paul's version from the others is the presence of the word "new" attached to covenant. The idea of a "new covenant" certainly hearkens back to Jeremiah's prophecy:

> The days are surely coming, says YHWH, when
> I will make a new covenant with the house of
> Israel and the house of Judah. It will not be like
> the covenant that I made with their ancestors
> when I took them by the hand to bring them out

---

[13] The words are similar but not the same. The LXX uses the word ἐκχέω (ekcheō) in these passages, whereas the Gospel accounts of the words of Institution have ἐκχύννω (ekchunnō), which does not appear in the LXX.

of the land of Egypt—a covenant that they broke, though I was their husband, says YHWH. But this is the covenant that I will make with the house of Israel after those days, says YHWH: I will put my law within them, and I will write it on their hearts; and I will be their God, and they shall be my people. No longer shall they teach one another, or say to each other, "Know YHWH," for they shall all know me, from the least of them to the greatest, says YHWH; for I will forgive their iniquity, and remember their sin no more. (Jer 31:31–34)

This passage in Jeremiah does not use the word "blood," but it does explicitly mention the previous covenant "that I made with their ancestors when I took them by the hand to bring them out of the land of Egypt" (v. 32), which is of course the Sinai covenant. We have already seen that at Sinai, Moses sprinkled blood on the people and explained that it was the blood of the covenant. So Jesus, in Luke's version, is apparently alluding to both passages, Exodus 24:8 and Jeremiah 31:31–34, when he says "new covenant in my blood." The prophecy of Jeremiah that God would make a new covenant with his people is coming to fulfillment in Jesus through his blood. The writer of Hebrews understood these echoes (Heb 8:8–12).

OTHER EVENTS IN THE UPPER ROOM

In Matthew (26:30) and Mark (14:26), Jesus and the disciples head out to the Mount of Olives as soon as the Lord's Supper is over, but in Luke they stay a little while in the upper room and talk about other things. First of all, Jesus talks about his betrayal and tells his disciples yet again that he is about to die (Luke 22:21–22). He has already told his disciples several times about his impending death (9:22, 44; 13:33; 17:25; 18:31–33), and of course the words by which he has just now instituted the Lord's Supper include "my body, which is given for you" (22:19) and "new covenant in my blood" (22:20). For us, looking back, it is obvious that these words once again point to his death, but the disciples still don't understand. They certainly don't know what he means about being betrayed (22:23)—well, one of them does (22:3–6). This scene of the shock of the disciples at Jesus's announcement of betrayal—which comes up before the Lord's Supper institution in Matthew (26:20–25) and Mark (14:17–21)—forms the basis of Leonardo's famous painting.

What should occasion shock for us in this moment is that the disciples turn immediately from hearing about the betrayal and death of their Master to disputing about which one of them is the greatest (22:24). Or, maybe that shouldn't shock us. The disciples like to have this argument, just as much as sports radio hosts like to argue about LeBron vs. MJ. In fact, they have had this argument before as the immediate response to another one of the times Jesus announces his death (9:44–46). According to Matthew (20:17–21) and Mark (10:32–37), another time that Jesus announces his death elicits the response from James and John that they would like to get the chief seats in the kingdom. With such precedents, it probably shouldn't surprise us at all that when Jesus is talking about his sacrifice for our sins, the disciples are talking about their own greatness.

Jesus responds to this ridiculous argument among his disciples with some teaching very similar to teaching we encounter earlier within the Gospels of Matthew and Mark, both of which situate this teaching as a response to James and John's request for the best seats in the kingdom (a request that does not appear in Luke).

Luke 22:25–30	Mark 10:42–45	Matthew 20:25–28
[25]But he said to them, "The kings of the Gentiles lord it over them; and those in authority over them are called benefactors.	[42]So Jesus called them and said to them, "You know that among the Gentiles those whom they recognize as their rulers lord it over them, and their great ones are tyrants over them.	[25]But Jesus called them to him and said, "You know that the rulers of the Gentiles lord it over them, and their great ones are tyrants over them.
[26]But not so with you; rather the greatest among you must become like the youngest, and the leader like one who serves.	[43]But it is not so among you; but whoever wishes to become great among you must be your servant,	[26]It will not be so among you; but whoever wishes to be great among you must be your servant,

	⁴⁴and whoever wishes to be first among you must be slave of all.	²⁷and whoever wishes to be first among you must be your slave;
²⁷For who is greater, the one who is at the table or the one who serves? Is it not the one at the table? But I am among you as one who serves.		
	⁴⁵For the Son of Man came not to be served but to serve, and to give his life a ransom for many."	²⁸just as the Son of Man came not to be served but to serve, and to give his life a ransom for many."

Those comments from Jesus seem to me to be rather straightforward: if you're arguing about who is the greatest, you've got the wrong idea of what you've signed up for. Jesus has already taught his disciples to say about their own greatness: "We are worthless slaves; we have done only what we ought to have done" (Luke 17:10). Their discussion about greatness sounds a little too much like the prayer of the Pharisee (18:11–12). They need to strive for servanthood rather than greatness.

Twelve Thrones (vv. 28–30)

Jesus then tells them that they will receive a kingdom "so that you may eat and drink at my table in my kingdom, and you will sit on thrones judging the twelve tribes of Israel" (22:28–30). Matthew records a similar saying in the conclusion to his account of the Rich Young Ruler: "at the renewal of all things, when the Son of Man is seated on the throne of his glory, you who have followed me will also sit on twelve thrones, judging the twelve tribes of Israel" (19:28).

What is Jesus talking about? Clearly, the disciples' sitting on thrones is not something that happens within Luke's Gospel. Jesus says that it will happen "in my kingdom" (Luke 19:30) and "at the renewal of all things, when the Son of Man is seated on the throne of his glory" (Matt 19:28). I can think of two applications that might work: perhaps he's talking about the events narrated in the book of Acts (i.e., the beginnings of the church) or perhaps he's talking about the period following his Second Coming. Or perhaps both? I think the "my kingdom" description could apply to both. And the New Testament affirms that the Son of Man is now reigning in heaven, presumably on his own throne, but the New Testament usually represents him now as "at the right hand" of God.[14] So the idea that the Son of

---

[14] He is explicitly sitting at Colossians 3:1; Hebrews 1:3; 8:1; 10:12; 12:2. He is standing at Acts 7:55–56. He is at God's right hand also at Acts 2:33; Romans 8:34; 1 Peter 3:22.

Man is sitting on a throne could apply to the period of the church, or to the future. What about the phrase, "at the renewal of all things"? Hmm, can the church fit that description? Well, "if anyone is in Christ, there is a new creation" (2 Cor 5:17). So, maybe. Or it might work better to apply that "renewal" language to the time when all things are recreated (2 Pet 3:10–13). The bottom line is that I could imagine the apostles sitting on thrones around Jesus now judging Israel (with the understanding that the followers of Jesus constitute Israel)[15] in some sort of heavenly sense, and I can imagine it as a future activity. Part of the ambiguity here is what exactly is meant by the word "judging"? If it means something like "rendering a verdict," then probably we're talking about the final judgment, and it probably bears some connection to 1 Corinthians 6:2–3. But if "judging" means more like what we see in the book of Judges (essentially, leadership), then maybe the apostles are now seated on thrones "judging" Israel.[16]

The importance of this discussion for us is in our figuring out exactly what Jesus was up to. The fact that he chose precisely twelve apostles and here promises that they will judge the twelve tribes of Israel means that he sees his ministry as fulfilling the ancient promises of a reconstituted Israel (see esp. Ezek 37:15–28).[17] Jesus's followers are the revitalized twelve tribes of Israel led by twelve new patriarchs.

---

[15] Romans 9:6; Galatians 3:7; Revelation 7:1–10.

[16] See David H. Wenkel, "When the Apostles Became Kings: Ruling and Judging the Twelve Tribes of Israel in the Book of Acts," *Biblical Theology Bulletin* 42 (2012): 119–28.

[17] E. P. Sanders, *Jesus and Judaism* (Philadelphia: Fortress, 1985), 98–106.

250 / THE GOSPEL OF LUKE

Satan Sifting the Disciples (vv. 31–34)

Next, Jesus warns his disciples, and especially Peter, that Satan is at work. "Satan has demanded to sift you like wheat" (22:31). It is important to realize that the word "you" here is plural; Satan has demanded to sift all of the disciples. The NRSV is able to express this nuance by translating, "Satan has demanded to sift all of you like wheat." The image is similar to the first couple chapters of the book of Job, in which Satan (the heavenly accuser) is granted permission to afflict God's servant. Jesus says Satan has "demanded," and it must be from God that Satan has made this demand. We might think it presumptuous for Satan to make such a demand, but it also shows that Satan has no power in this relationship other than what God allows him. We remember from the book of Job that God allows Satan quite a bit of power over his servant, and here in Luke also apparently God granted Satan's demand; he would indeed be able to sift the disciples. "But I have prayed for you" (v. 32), Jesus says, speaking directly to Peter. Here the "you" is singular. Jesus has no doubt prayed for all his disciples, but in this context he is thinking specifically about his prayers for Peter, "that your own faith may not fail." Of course, Peter's faith will fail, momentarily, as Jesus is about to predict (v. 34). That's not what Jesus is talking about. Rather, Jesus has prayed that Peter's faith, once he has been sifted along with the rest of the disciples, will be strong again so that he might turn back and strengthen his brothers (v. 32).

FINAL INSTRUCTIONS (vv. 35–38)

Jesus now counsels his disciples to acquire a purse and a bag and a sword, even at the expense of their cloaks. This is in explicit contrast to his earlier instructions to carry none of these items on their journeys (9:3–5). I am not sure why Jesus is making these suggestions. Obviously, he doesn't want his disciples to use the swords to defend him, since he later forbids that very thing (22:50–51). In Matthew's account of the arrest, Jesus says, "Whoever lives by the sword will die by the sword" (26:52). We never see Paul carrying a sword in Acts to defend himself against persecution. So why does Jesus want his disciples to have swords here if he's not going to let them use them? I don't know, but let me make a suggestion.[18]

Notice that Jesus quotes the very end of Isaiah 53, "And he was counted among the lawless," and he says that this verse "must be fulfilled in me." Jesus needs to be counted among the lawless. Now, some scholars think that was accomplished at the Crucifixion when Jesus hung between two criminals (23:32).[19] But perhaps the "lawless ones" are the disciples themselves, who look like thugs walking around with purses and bags and swords. I'm not saying that the disciples were robbers, but I'm saying that they might look like robbers if they carry purses and bags and

---

[18] I first read this suggestion in Christopher R. Hutson, "Enough for What? Playacting Isaiah 53 in Luke 22:35–38," *Restoration Quarterly* 55 (2013): 36–43. For a critique of Hutson's article, see David Lertis Matson, "Double-Edged: The Meaning of the Two Swords in Luke 22:35–38," *Journal of Biblical Literature* 137 (2018): 463–80.

[19] This interpretation is favored by Matson, "Double-Edged."

swords. They might be reckoned as lawless people, and if Jesus is with them, he will be "counted among the lawless." In other words, on this interpretation, Jesus is telling his disciples to acquire such items in order that people will think they're a band of criminals, and thereby Isaiah 53:12 will be fulfilled. Why else would he tell them that two swords are enough (22:38)? Two swords are not enough for a battle, but they are enough to look like you're a lawless person.

When the arrest finally happens (22:47–53), Jesus says that they have come out against him as if he is a bandit (v. 52). Of course, he's completely innocent of that charge, but he does look the part. The appearance of his disciples as thugs helped to ensure that he would be arrested and charged with sedition and crucified.

MOUNT OF OLIVES

Finally Jesus arrives at the Mount of Olives (v. 39), where he has been accustomed to spending the nights during the past week that he has been based in Jerusalem (21:37). This time, he doesn't go to his sleeping quarters but he seeks out a place to pray. Luke does not name the place Gethsemane; that place name is in Matthew (26:36) and Mark (14:32), and they both locate Gethsemane somewhere on the Mount of Olives (Matt 26:30; Mark 14:26). John is apparently talking about Gethsemane when he says that Jesus entered with his disciples into a garden, where he was arrested (John 18:1–2). So we put all these things together and we talk about the Garden of Gethsemane on the Mount of Olives. Luke just says that Jesus is on the Mount of Olives.

Luke's account of Jesus's prayers is abbreviated in comparison with Matthew and Mark (whereas John completely omits the story). Luke doesn't inform his readers that Jesus separated Peter, James, and John from the others, as Matthew and Mark do; Luke does not tell us that Jesus prayed three times. If we just had Luke, we would think that Jesus prayed a single, simple prayer: "Father, if you are willing, remove this cup from me; yet, not my will but yours be done" (22:42).

Unfortunately, the most famous part about Luke's account probably was not written by Luke. In my NRSV, these words appear as verses 43–44.

> Then an angel from heaven appeared to him and gave him strength. In his anguish he prayed more earnestly, and his sweat became like great drops of blood falling down on the ground. (Luke 22:43–44)

But my NRSV puts brackets around these words, meaning that there is a problem with them. The common scholarly opinion is that Luke did not write these words, but they were added to certain manuscripts of his Gospel later than the first century. Our earliest manuscripts of Luke's Gospel do not contain these words, though they are present in the majority of later manuscripts, even in the fourth-century manuscript Codex Sinaiticus.[20]

---

[20] The issue is quite complex. For a brief presentation of the evidence, see the relevant note at the online Net Bible (netbible.org); see also Bruce M. Metzger, *A Textual Commentary on the Greek New Testament*, 2d ed. (New

At any rate, this episode on the Mount of Olives shows two main things, it seems to me. (1) Jesus did not want to die. (2) The disciples couldn't stay awake. Jesus rebukes them for falling asleep, but it's hard for us to blame them. It was late at night, and they hadn't yet understood what was about to happen. They still have no idea that Jesus is about to die. Jesus knows it, and that's why he's praying.

York: United Bible Societies, 1994), 151. Already in the mid-second century, Justin knew about copies of the "memoirs of the apostles" that recorded that Jesus sweated great drops of blood while praying before his arrest (*Dialogue* 103). A few decades later, Irenaeus recorded something similar (*Against Heresies* 3.22.2). But our two papyrus manuscripts of Luke's Gospel that contain this section both omit the passage (P[69vid], P[75]), as do Codex Vaticanus and Codex Alexandrinus and several others. The verse was an object of discussion in patristic times due to its problematic textual attestation, and some authors wanted to use the passage to affirm the humanity of Jesus; see the dissertation by Amy M. Donaldson, "Explicit References to New Testament Variant Readings among Greek and Latin Church Fathers" (2 vols., PhD diss., University of Notre Dame, 2009), 2.420–23 (available online: https://curate.nd.edu/show/5712m615k50). For a recent, brief argument favoring Lukan authorship of this disputed passage, see Dirk Jongkind, *An Introduction to the Greek New Testament Produced at Tyndale House, Cambridge* (Wheaton, IL: Crossway, 2019), 84.

12

The Death of Jesus

Luke 23

Then Jesus said, "Father, forgive them; for they
do not know what they are doing."
(Luke 23:34)

W hy did Jesus die? It's a question that might have a variety
of answers depending on the angle from which one
approaches it. Why did the Jewish religious leaders want Jesus
dead? Why did the Roman officials want Jesus dead? Why did
God want Jesus dead? All of these questions are contested and
have various answers. Like much in the Bible, if the answers seem
obvious at first, a little more prying reveals intriguing
complexities. Our focus here is on the Gospel of Luke, but we will
also bring in elements from the other Gospels (if for no other
reason than for the sake of comparison) and from other sources
of information for the first-century Roman world.

This chapter covers the arrest and execution of Jesus in
Luke, including the following episodes.

Arrest on the Mount of Olives (22:47–53)

Peter's denials (22:54–62)

> *Note:* distinctive element in Luke: "The Lord turned and looked at Peter" (22:61)
>
> *Note:* In Mark (= Matthew), Peter's denials (14:66–72) follow the trial before the Sanhedrin (14:53–65).

Captors abuse Jesus (22:63–65), mostly mocking, also beating

Trial before the Sanhedrin (22:66–71)

> *Note:* distinctive element in Luke: no theme of silence (cf. Mark 14:61; 15:4–5; Matt 26:63).

Accusations against Jesus before Pilate (23:1–2)

> *Note:* not reported by Mark or Matthew

Pilate questions Jesus (23:3–5)

Appearance before Herod (23:6–12)

> *Note:* not reported in Mark or Matthew
>
> *Note:* theme of silence (23:9)
>
> *Note:* mocking from Herod and soldiers (23:11)

Pilate maneuvers to release Jesus, fails (23:13–25)

On the way to Golgotha (23:26–31)

> *Note:* Jesus talks (not reported in Matthew or Mark)

Crucifixion (23:32–38) = Mark 15:22–32

> *Note:* distinctive element in Luke: "Father, forgive them" (23:34)

Criminal on the Cross (23:39–43)

> *Note:* conversation not reported in Mark or Matthew

The Death (23:44–49) = Mark 15:33–41

Note: distinctive element in Luke: "Father, into your hands" (23:46)

Burial of Jesus (23:50–56) = Mark 15:42–47

CRUCIFIXION IN THE ROMAN WORLD[1]

When Jesus challenged his followers to "carry the cross and follow me" (Luke 14:27), and even to do this "daily (Luke 9:23), they knew exactly what he was talking about. They had seen plenty of crucifixions.

The Romans (and other cultures) used crucifixion quite a bit. About seventy years before Jesus was born, the failed rebellion of Spartacus resulted in 6,000 crucifixions along the Appian Way.[2] A couple decades earlier, the Jewish leader Alexander Jannaeus crucified 800 Pharisees. After the death of Herod the Great, the Roman leader Varus crushed a Jewish rebellion and crucified 2,000 rebels.[3] Crucifixion was common.

---

[1] See the recent article by Felicity Harley, "Crucifixion in Roman Antiquity: The State of the Field," *Journal of Early Christian Studies* 27 (2019): 303–23, which reviews the following books: David W. Chapman, *Ancient Jewish and Christian Perceptions of Crucifixion* (Tübingen: Mohr Siebeck, 2008; Grand Rapids: Baker, 2010); David W. Chapman and Eckhard J. Schnabel, *The Trial and Crucifixion of Jesus* (Tübingen: Mohr Siebeck, 2015); John Granger Cook, *Crucifixion in the Mediterranean World* (Tübingen: Mohr Siebeck, 2014); Gunnar Samuelson, *Crucifixion in Antiquity: An Inquiry into the Background and Significance of the New Testament Terminology of Crucifixion* (Tübingen: Mohr Siebeck, 2011; rev. ed. 2013).

[2] As reported in Appian, *Civil Wars* 1.120.

[3] See Josephus, *Antiquities of the Jews* 17.286–98; *Jewish War* 2.66–79.

And it was horrible. The first-century Roman writer Seneca the Younger reflects on the horrors of crucifixion.

> Can anyone be found who would prefer wasting away in pain, dying limb by limb, or letting out his life drop by drop, rather than expiring once for all? Can any man be found willing to be fastened to the accursed tree, long sickly, already deformed, swelling with ugly tumours on chest and shoulders, and draw the breath of life amid long-drawn-out agony? I think he would have many excuses for dying even before mounting the cross! (Seneca, *Epistle* 101.14)[4]

Another well-known description of crucifixion is found in the previous century in the works of Cicero.

> But the executioner, the veiling of the head, and the very word "cross" should be far removed not only from the person of a Roman citizen but from his thoughts, his eyes and his ears. For it is not only the actual occurrence of these things or the endurance of them, but liability to them, the expectation, nay, the mere mention of them,

---

[4] Translation by Richard M. Gummere in Seneca, *Epistles 93–124*, Loeb Classical Library (Cambridge, MA: Harvard University Press, 1925), 167. This passage is quoted and discussed in Martin Hengel, *Crucifixion in the Ancient World and the Folly of the Message of the Cross* (London: SCM, 1977), 31–32.

that is unworthy of a Roman citizen and a free
man. (Cicero, *Pro Rabirio* 5.16)[5]

The third-century Christian writer Origen called it "the
most shameful death on a cross" (*mors turpissima crucis*).[6] New
Testament scholar Mark Goodacre finds that "many of us still
have very little grasp of just how appalling a death crucifixion
was. The remarkable thing about the Mel Gibson film was not so
much the magnitude of suffering depicted but its restraint in
showing many of the true horrors of crucifixion."[7]

Part of this terrible experience that we don't like to think
about and that is rarely depicted (for obvious reasons) in movies
and art is the nudity. Crucifixion victims were completely
exposed; they were naked. The Gospels do mention that some
soldiers divided up Jesus's clothing (John 19:23–24; cf. Mark
15:24). But perhaps Jesus retained some sort of undergarment?
"[T]here is some debate about whether he would have been

---

[5] Translation by H. Grose Hodge in Cicero, *Pro Lege Manilia; Pro Caecina;
Pro Cluentio; Pro Rabirio Perduellionis*, Loeb Classical Library
(Cambridge, MA: Harvard University Press, 1927), 467–69. This passage
is quoted and discussed in Hengel, *Crucifixion*, 42.

[6] This is in a comment on Matthew 27:22 in Origen's *Commentary on
Matthew*, series 124, translated in Ronald E. Heine, trans., *The
Commentary of Origen on the Gospel of St Matthew*, 2 vols. (Oxford:
Oxford University Press, 2018), 2.737; see also Celsus' comments in
Origen, *Against Celsus* 6.34.

[7] Mark Goodacre, "Scripturalization in Mark's Crucifixion Narrative," in
The Trial and Death of Jesus: Essays on the Passion Narrative in Mark, ed.
Geert van Oyen and Tom Shepherd (Leuven: Peeters, 2006), 33–47, at 33.
Of course, the "Mel Gibson film" is *The Passion of the Christ* (2004).

naked. Most ancient sources do not actually mention the naked (or clothed) status of the victim." Some ancient sources do mention or imply the nudity of the victim.[8]

The second-century Christian author Melito of Sardis mentions nudity in his reflections on Jesus's crucifixion:

> The Sovereign (ὁ δεσπότης) has been made unrecognizable by his naked body, and is not even allowed a garment to keep him from view. (*Peri Pascha*, §97)

Romans stripped their victims of clothing as a way of stripping them of dignity. We can understand this tactic. Think Abu Ghraib. From the victim's standpoint, think about the dream we've all had that we show up to school naked. Our instinctive reaction? Run away, or cover up our private parts—actions denied a crucifixion victim, whose arms are forcibly outspread.

Crucifixion was spectacle—and deterrent; others would see the humiliation of the victim and think twice about defying Rome.[9]

---

[8] See Chapman and Schnabel, *Trial and Crucifixion*, 673–74. As Chapman points out, the Palatino graffito (see p. 673) represents a figure that is naked, at least from the waist down, and the second-century AD Ephesian diviner Artemidorus (*Oneirocritica* 2.53) mentions the nudity of crucifixion victims, though there is some dispute as to whether "nude" (γυμνός) means completely nude.

[9] Josephus mentions the deterrent value of crucifixion at *Jewish War* 5.449–51. See also Chapman and Schnabel, *Trial and Crucifixion*, 673, citing Cicero, *In Verrem* 2.4.24 and other sources.

There are actually some remains of crucifixion victims from the ancient world, the most famous of which is the heel bone of Johanan, a crucifixion victim from the first century, whose ossuary containing his heel bone (with the nail still piercing it!) was discovered in Jerusalem in 1968.[10]

The Motivation of Pilate

It is easiest, I think, to understand the death of Jesus from the perspective of Rome. Though Pilate himself had misgivings about whether Jesus was guilty of the accusations leveled against him—and Luke makes these misgivings more prominent than do the other Gospels—he could have been in no doubt about the nature of the accusations and how seriously such accusations had to be taken. Jesus was accused of treason, and for that crime he was convicted.

By the way, we don't know a whole lot about Pilate.[11] Basically all we know about him is that he was the Roman prefect of Judea for about a decade, during the years AD 26–36. Josephus mentions him a few times, as does Philo, not in a positive light.[12]

---

[10] Wikipedia: "Jehohanan."

[11] Helen K. Bond, "Pontius Pilate," in *Dictionary of Jesus and the Gospels*, 2d ed., ed. Joel B. Green (Downers Grove, IL: IVP, 2013), 679–80.

[12] Josephus, *Jewish War* 2.169–77; *Antiquities of the Jews* 18.35, 55–62, 85–89; Philo, *Embassy to Gaius* 299–305. There is also a reference in Tacitus, *Annals* 15.44, but the relevant line may well be an interpolation; see Richard Carrier, "The Prospect of a Christian Interpolation in Tacitus, *Annals* 15.44," *Vigiliae Christianae* 68 (2014): 264–83.

There is also an inscription that mentions Pilate,[13] and some coins minted under him.[14] Without any doubt, the most famous thing Pilate ever did was oversee the crucifixion of a Jewish peasant from the village of Nazareth.

The accusations made against Jesus are summarized for us by Luke.

> They began to accuse him, saying, "We found this man perverting our nation, forbidding us to pay taxes to the emperor, and saying that he himself is the Messiah, a king." (Luke 23:2)

When Pilate expresses doubts about these accusations, Jesus's accusers double down.

> But they were insistent and said, "He stirs up the people by teaching throughout all Judea, from Galilee where he began even to this place." (Luke 23:5)

These accusations are much clearer, more detailed, than what we read in Mark (15:1–5) and Matthew (27:11–14), where the only accusation seems to be that Jesus is (or calls himself) the king of the Jews. The conversation between Jesus and Pilate is much longer in John's Gospel (18:28–19:16), but there's less information about the criminal charges than in Luke.

---

[13] Wikipedia: "Pilate Stone."
[14] Wikipedia: "Roman Procurator Coinage."

The Jewish leaders accuse Jesus of three separate activities that all amount to treason: (1) he's stirring up the people (23:2, 5), (2) he forbids taxes to Caesar, and (3) he calls himself a king. The last of these charges would surely be interpreted as a direct challenge to Caesar, and so certainly worthy of death from the Roman point of view. So would the charge that he forbids paying taxes and that he stirs up the crowd. In themselves, these charges are perfectly believable for the time period—there were Jewish rebels who hated the Roman government to the point that they considered it sacrilege to fund such a corrupt and pagan regime through taxes (see Luke 20:20–26), and they stirred up the crowd toward this purpose.

The problem in regard to Jesus was twofold: Jesus never did any of these things, and Pilate didn't believe that he did. As for the first point, Jesus actually shunned the title king (John 6:15); this reticence to proclaim himself king was almost certainly the reason he told people to be quiet about his works and he rarely or never called himself Messiah. His preferred title for himself was the ambiguous "Son of Man." He had basically nothing to say about taxes, except when asked, and then he gave an answer that was hard to interpret but might have meant that paying taxes was fine. As for stirring up the crowd, I guess that's in the eye of the beholder: he certainly made some people excited, but he wasn't about to lead a rebellion against Rome, no matter how much his own followers hoped he would. Probably two things made Pilate suspicious about the charges: Jesus's quiet manner, and the very fact that the Jewish leaders handed him over to the Romans. Pilate knew that the Jewish leaders rarely wanted to protect the power and dignity of Rome. Pilate may have reasoned that if Jesus really were guilty of sedition against

Rome, the Jewish leaders would be the last ones trying to capture him and bring him to justice. After all, they were the ones trying to get Barabbas released, a man already convicted of participating in an insurrection (Luke 23:19, 25).

Pilate insists Jesus isn't guilty (23:4, 14–15, 22). Of course, he's still going to have Jesus flogged (23:16, 22), just for wasting his time, I suppose. But he tries to make a deal to release Jesus, but the Jewish leaders aren't having it.

The Motivation of the Jewish Leaders

Who exactly are these Jewish leaders? We often think of the Pharisees as Jesus's opponents, but the Pharisees make their final appearance at Luke 19:39, at the time of the Triumphal Entry. They are not mentioned in regard to the trial of Jesus.[15] In Luke, the ones who arrest Jesus and try him are:

- Arrest: chief priests, temple police, elders (22:52)
- Jewish trial (sanhedrin): elders, chief priests, scribes (22:66)
- Before Herod: chief priests and scribes (23:10)
- Before Pilate: chief priests, leaders, people (23:13)

It was the temple authorities that seem to be most heavily involved in making sure that Jesus died. The problem is that Luke

---

[15] The same is true in Mark (final appearance of Pharisees at Mark 12:13), but in Matthew (27:62) and John (18:3) some Pharisees do participate in arresting Jesus and accusing Jesus before Pilate.

(or Matthew or Mark or John) never really tells us why they want Jesus dead. Oh, there are times when some people pick up stones to kill him during the course of his life, especially in John (5:18; 8:59; 10:39). In Luke, the hometown crowd got momentarily enraged and tried to throw him off a cliff (4:28–29), but these people were presumably not temple authorities, and the cause of their anger was probably not the same as what convinced the temple authorities that Jesus should die. What I'm saying is, we have to resort to guesswork.

Jesus had done various things that would probably make the temple authorities mad. The most obvious thing is Jesus's Temple Action (Luke 19:45–48). Since Jesus could not possibly hope to expel the moneychangers from the temple by overturning a couple tables, his action probably was less a "cleansing" of the temple and more a demonstration that God would soon bring judgment on the temple. At least, Jesus's action might have been interpreted in that way by the people in charge of the temple. And that interpretation would have been strengthened by some of the things Jesus said in the temple in the following week, especially the Parable of the Tenants (20:9–18). Luke records for us the reaction of the temple authorities to that parable.

> When the scribes and chief priests realized that
> he had told this parable against them, they
> wanted to lay hands on him at that very hour,
> but they feared the people. (Luke 20:19)

During that final week, Jesus would also predict the destruction of the temple (Luke 21), but it is doubtful whether Luke wants us to think that the temple authorities overheard these predictions. But another thing about Jesus that might have angered the temple authorities is that Jesus offered forgiveness of sins (5:20; 7:48). Forgiveness was the job of the temple. People may have interpreted this action by Jesus as a criticism of the temple, and Jesus may have so intended it.

The trial before the Sanhedrin is much shorter in Luke (22:66–71) than it is in Matthew (27:57–68) or Mark (14:53–65). (John omits the trial before the Sanhedrin, preferring instead to narrate an interrogation by Annas, the former high priest and the father-in-law of the current high priest, Caiaphas.; John 18:12–14, 19–24, 28.) Here is the trial according to Luke.

> When day came, the assembly of the elders of the people, both chief priests and scribes, gathered together, and they brought him to their council [= Sanhedrin]. They said, "If you are the Messiah, tell us." He replied, "If I tell you, you will not believe; and if I question you, you will not answer. But from now on the Son of Man will be seated at the right hand of the power of God." All of them asked, "Are you, then, the Son of God?" He said to them, "You say that I am." Then they said, "What further testimony do we need? We have heard it ourselves from his own lips!" (Luke 22:66–71)

Luke has compressed the narrative, omitting any reference to the false witnesses, or to Jesus's silence. Luke just gets to the point. Of course, these temple authorities already have determined that they want to kill Jesus; that's why they arrested him. The motivation was probably the criticisms of the temple that I've already mentioned. At the trial, they're looking for some sort of charge that they can bring to Pilate, who will care nothing about inter-Jewish religious squabbles regarding the temple. So they press the question about Jesus's identity as Messiah, because that is something Pilate ought to care about. Jesus gives them more than they bargained for. Instead of simply calling himself the Messiah—not a crime according to Jewish law but good enough for a treason charge in a Roman court—he identifies himself as the Son of Man from Daniel 7:13, the one who receives the kingdom and rides on a cloud next to God. In Mark (14:64) and Matthew (26:65), this same declaration by Jesus elicits the exclamation from the high priest, "blasphemy!" Apparently the high priest thinks that Jesus has called himself divine. Apparently he's right. Luke doesn't include the charge of blasphemy. Instead, he has the Sanhedrin ask whether Jesus is claiming to be the son of God (22:70), a traditional title for the Messiah (and for the Israelite king; i.e., not necessarily a divine title).[16] In other words, Luke does not mention the supposed blasphemy of Jesus, but rather focuses on the fact that the temple authorities got what they wanted out of this trial—a close-enough admission from Jesus that he is the Messiah.

---

[16] There is a brief discussion of the title "Son of God" in Chapter 1 above. See the extensive discussion in Adela Yarbro Collins and John J. Collins, *King and Messiah as Son of God: Divine, Human, and Angelic Messianic Figures in Biblical and Related Literature* (Grand Rapids: Eerdmans, 2008), 1–24.

THE MOTIVATION OF GOD

Many, many large books have been written on the significance of Jesus's death.[17] In fact, modern scholars routinely say that the four Gospels are basically reflections on Jesus's death. According to Martin Kähler's famous description, the Gospels are passion narratives with extended introductions.[18] This discussion will necessarily be painfully brief.

In Luke, Jesus predicts his death several times, but he doesn't really say what meaning his death will have (9:22, 44). It does become clear that his death is in accordance with Scripture (18:31–34), and that the death of Jesus conforms to the pattern of Israel's prophets (13:33–35). His death is the fulfillment of God's will; his "going" has been "determined" (22:22).

---

[17] For a survey of different views, see James Beilby and Paul R. Eddy, eds., *The Nature of the Atonement: Four Views* (Downers Grove, IL: IVP, 2006).

[18] Martin Kähler, *The So-Called Historical Jesus and the Historic, Biblical Christ* (Philadelphia: Fortress, 1964), 80n11. The original German work (p. 33 note 1; available at Hathi Trust: https://catalog.hathitrust.org/Record/008725787) was published in 1892 (second edition, 1896, from which the English translation was made—see p. 80 note 1; https://catalog.hathitrust.org/Record/008725678), and the relevant comment reads in German: "Etwas herausfordernd sönnte man die Evangelien Passionsgeschichten mit ausführlicher Einleitung nennen." This description of the Gospels has become ubiquitous, so that Kähler's footnote "must be one of the most-quoted footnotes in the history of the scholarly study of Jesus' death"; Joel B. Green, "'Was It Not Necessary for the Messiah to Suffer These Things and Enter into His Glory?' The Significance of Jesus' Death for Luke's Soteriology," in *The Spirit and Christ in the New Testament and Christian Theology: Essays in Honor of Max Turner*, ed. I. Howard Marshall, Volker Rabens, and Cornelis Bennema (Grand Rapids: Eerdmans, 2012), 71–85, at 82.

John's Gospel has a little more reflection on the meaning of Jesus's death, but Matthew and Mark, like Luke, tell us precious little about why God determined that Jesus ought to die. Matthew and Mark both have a single, very significant saying in this regard.

> The Son of Man came not to be served but to serve, and to give his life a ransom for many. (Mark 10:45; cf. Matt 20:28)

Despite the brevity of this statement, it is very suggestive. Jesus thought of his death as a ransom for others.

But this statement is not in Luke. How did Luke expect his readers to understand what Jesus had accomplished through his death? What does Luke stress about the death of Jesus? There are at least three points to consider:

(1) Luke has another volume, Acts, that contains further reflections on the death of Jesus. He doesn't have to fit everything into this first volume, the Gospel. Especially in some of the speeches in Acts, Luke is able to provide some theological reflections on the Crucifixion (esp. Acts 2, 3, 7, 13).

(2) Luke stresses the innocence of Jesus.[19]

> Pilate: "I find no basis for an accusation against this man" (23:4). "You brought me this man as one who was perverting the people; and here I have examined him in your presence and have

---

[19] This theme is also found in Acts 3:13–16; 13:27–28.

not found this man guilty of any of your charges against him. Neither has Herod, for he sent him back to us. Indeed, he has done nothing to deserve death" (23:14–15). "What evil has he done? I have found in him no ground for the sentence of death" (23:22).

Criminal: "This man has done nothing wrong" (23:41).

Centurion: "Certainly this man was innocent" (23:47).

This last statement is especially interesting, since in Mark (15:39) and Matthew (27:54), the centurion says, "truly this man was the son of God." Luke has apparently interpreted this statement for his readers as an indication of Jesus's innocence.

I think there is probably great significance to this theme in Luke, but before delving into it, we need to bring in the third point.

(3) Luke presents some material that suggests he interpreted the death of Jesus in terms of a sacrifice. There are primarily two passages favoring this idea: the Last Supper (Luke 22:14–23) and the quotation of Isaiah 53 (Luke 22:37). During the Last Supper, Jesus says that his body "is given for you" (22:19) and the cup "that is poured out for you is the new covenant in my blood" (22:20). This shows us that Jesus's death was on behalf of other people and that it established the new covenant

promised in Jeremiah 31:31. Moreover, the mention of blood (which does not come up in Jer 31:31–34) connects to sacrifice.[20]

The only time in the Gospels that Jesus quotes from Isaiah 53 is at Luke 22:37, after he tells the disciples to get some swords in order to fulfill the Scripture, "And he was counted among the lawless" (Isa 53:12). This verse suggests that Jesus saw himself as the fulfillment of the figure of the Servant of the Lord, who is described as a sacrifice on behalf of others (Isa 53:4–7).[21]

Taking together the second point (innocence) with the third (sacrifice), we could see Jesus's innocence in terms of a sacrifice without blemish. This idea is hinted at already in Isaiah 53, since it is "our sins" and not the Servant's own that he bears (vv. 4–9). Peter (1 Pet 2:22) actually quotes Isaiah 53:9 to the effect that "He committed no sin." Of course, other New Testament verses also declare that Jesus was without sin (Heb 4:15; 2 Cor 5:21). If we think about that idea with respect to the description of Jesus as a sacrifice, the "perfect, spotless" lambs of the Old Testament probably come to mind. And again, this may be part of the point, at least, for Luke to emphasize so prominently the innocence (spotless nature) of Jesus.

Why did God want Jesus to die? Luke provides nothing definite, only hints, but these hints point toward Jesus's dying as a sacrifice on behalf of others for the purpose of establishing the new covenant.

---

[20] We saw in the previous chapter that there is a textual difficulty in Luke's account of the Lord's Supper, but most scholars favor the authenticity of the longer reader with the two cups.

[21] For some additional nuance to the way Luke uses Isaiah 53 in reference to the death of Jesus, see Green, "Was It Not Necessary," esp. p. 84.

Other Elements

There is a lot more we could talk about in this section of Luke. What about the role of the evil spiritual forces in the death of Jesus? Clearly Satan was involved. "Then Satan entered into Judas called Iscariot, who was one of the twelve" (22:3). In fact, we had last encountered the devil during the Temptation Narrative (4:1-13).[22] At that time, we were told that the devil had left Jesus "until an opportune time" (4:13). Apparently Passover week is the opportune time. Satan reappears and prods Judas to betray his master. Throughout the Gospel Jesus has been battling evil spirits.[23] We could also explore ways in which the Crucifixion is part of this battle, Jesus vs. Satan.

There are also the unique elements to Luke's Passion Narrative. We have explored some of them (the theme of Jesus's innocence). Luke's is the only Gospel to narrate Jesus's conversation with women on his way to Golgotha (23:27-31). He again warns them of coming tribulation (as in Luke 17:22-37; and ch. 21).

Another unique element are the three sayings from the cross. In Mark (15:34) and Matthew (27:46), Jesus says only one thing on the cross: "Eli, Eli, lema sabachthani," a quotation of Psalm 22:1. Luke and John do not report this saying, but they

---

[22] There are other references to Satan throughout the Gospel (10:18; 13:16), but Satan does not appear as a character in the story between the Temptation Narrative and his entering into Judas.

[23] 4:31-37; 6:18; 7:21; 8:2, 26-39 (Legion); 9:37-43 (boy); 10:20; 11:14; 13:11.

each have three independent sayings. We won't look at the ones in John here (19:26–27, 28, 30), but the three sayings in Luke are the following.

> Father, forgive them; for they do not know what they are doing. (23:34)

> Truly I tell you, today you will be with me in Paradise. (23:43)

> Father, into your hands I commend my spirit. (23:46)

Each of these sayings is worthy of sustained reflection that we cannot give it here. The third saying in Luke is a quotation of Psalm 31:5. The second one comes as part of an interesting, surprising conversation between Jesus and one of the criminals crucified alongside him. The first one, one of the most famous sayings by Jesus, is debated as to whether it belongs in Luke. There is a textual problem with it, so that some Bibles print it in brackets. The saying is not present in some of our good, early Greek manuscripts of this Gospel. But, to keep it brief, I'll say that I think there are good reasons to think that this verse is original to Luke's Gospel.[24]

---

[24] For a brief presentation of the evidence, see the relevant note at the online NET Bible (netbible.org); see also Bruce M. Metzger, *A Textual Commentary on the Greek New Testament*, 2d ed. (New York: United Bible Societies, 1994), 154.

CONCLUSION

There are a lot of interesting elements in Luke's Passion Narrative. The main point is that all the major parties wanted Jesus dead: the temple authorities, the Roman authorities (with some hesitation from Pilate), and Jesus himself. The only group that did not want Jesus dead was his own disciples, because they had not yet figured out—despite Jesus's very direct statements—that his death was an essential part of God's plan to establish God's kingdom. But God did not intend for Jesus to stay dead.

13

ALL THINGS NEW[1]
LUKE 24

They said to each other, "Were not our hearts
burning within us while he was talking to us on
the road, while he was opening the scriptures to
us?" (Luke 24:32)

The Resurrection is an essential part of the gospel message.
We tend to focus more on the Death of Jesus, perhaps for
good reason, because Jesus's death was also necessary for us—
"he himself bore our sins in his body on the tree" (1 Peter 2:24)—
and the death shows more brilliantly the amazing love of God for
us miserable sinners (Rom 5:6–8). But the Resurrection is also

---

[1] On Luke 24, see the Bible Project video, "The Resurrection of Jesus: Luke
24." A major study of the Resurrection is N. T. Wright, *The Resurrection
of the Son of God* (Minneapolis: Fortress, 2003), who discusses Luke at pp.
435–39, 647–61. Also helpful is Kevin L. Anderson, "Resurrection," in
Dictionary of Jesus and the Gospels, 2d ed., ed. Joel B. Green (Downers
Grove, IL: IVP, 2013), 774–89.

amazing, not so much because it displays God's love for us (although, I guess you could make an argument for that), and maybe not even so much because it displays God's power (though it certainly does that), but more because it changes everything, it is the first fruits (Paul's term; 1 Cor 15:20) of making all things new. "Therefore if any man be in Christ, he is a new creature: old things are passed away; behold, all things are become new" (2 Cor 5:17). Just as Jesus, by virtue of his Resurrection, has become a new kind of person, so also we become new in Christ.

The Resurrection of Christ ought to be important to us, just as important as his Death, for several reasons. First of all, none of the Gospels end at Golgotha. They all spend at least some time talking about Sunday; all of them show the empty tomb, the body of Jesus no longer there. Secondly, the Resurrection is the demonstration that Jesus can take care of our sins. Even if those sins were born by Jesus on the cross, and even if his Death is a sign of God's great love for us, still, in a sense, the Crucifixion itself was no great feat. Many people were crucified by the Romans; there was nothing unusual in that. Even on that day at Golgotha, Jesus was not the only one crucified. But he was the only crucifixion victim who did not stay dead. He was the only one who rose from the dead a few days later, never again subject to death. The Resurrection demonstrates that Jesus is Lord, and he does have the power to save. Third, the human predicament isn't limited to sin. There is also the problem of death, a related problem, certainly (see Rom 5:12), but not the same thing. The Resurrection previews our own resurrection; Jesus's defeat of death assures us that through his power we too can participate in that victory over death (see Rom 8:11).

LUKE 24

There are three scenes in Luke 24, and the third scene itself has a threefold structure. The opening of Luke 24, the first twelve verses, tells the story of the women's discovery of the empty tomb, a story more-or-less equivalent to the opening of Matthew 28 and Mark 16. Luke then shifts to a road outside Jerusalem, and a couple of disciples on their way to a village called Emmaus (24:13–35). This story is not repeated in any other Gospel. Finally, Luke tells the story of Jesus meeting with his disciples (24:36–53). First in the gathering place (v. 33),[2] Jesus demonstrates the reality of his Resurrection (24:36–43) and commissions his disciples (24:44–49); then he leads them outside and ascends to heaven (24:50–53). Each of these elements in this final scene is more-or-less unique to Luke's Gospel, though there are, of course, stories somewhat parallel in other Gospels (e.g., the commissioning in Matt 28:18–20; the demonstration of the Resurrection in John 20:19–29).

This outline can more easily be displayed in this manner:

Empty Tomb (vv. 1–12)
To Emmaus (vv. 13–35)
    With the disciples (vv. 36–53)
        Proof of the Resurrection (vv. 36–43)

---

[2] Perhaps the upper room from the Last Supper (Luke 22:12)? The disciples are also meeting in an upper room at Acts 1:13 (though the Greek term for the room is different here). According to John (20:19, 26), on Resurrection Sunday the disciples were meeting behind locked doors.

Commission (vv. 44–49)
Ascension (vv. 50–53)

The way Luke tells the story here, it seems like all these things take place in a single day, as if the Ascension happens later on the same Sunday as the Resurrection. After all, the Emmaus road encounter happened "on that same day" (v. 13), and those two disciples ran to tell the apostles about it "that same hour" (v. 33), and "while they were talking about this, Jesus himself stood among them" (v. 36). But if you flip over to Acts, Luke tells his readers that there were actually forty days between the Resurrection and the Ascension (Acts 1:3).

For centuries—millennia, no doubt—readers of the Bible have noticed differences among the stories of the Resurrection. The Gospel writers all have the same basic story (empty tomb discovered by women, usually followed by Jesus's meeting with his disciples), but they each tell the story very differently from the others. John's Gospel is the most different from the other three (not surprisingly), but even the three Synoptic Gospels differ in some of the details. Was it one angel (Matthew, Mark), or two (Luke)? Was the angel sitting inside the tomb (Mark), or sitting on the stone (Matthew), or standing beside the women (Luke)? Did Jesus meet with his disciples in Galilee (Matthew, Mark) or Jerusalem (Luke, John)? And which women exactly were the ones who discovered the empty tomb?

Here are the passages, with differences highlighted, just for your convenience.

Matthew 28:1–10	Mark 16:1–8	Luke 24:1–12

After the sabbath, as the first day of the week was dawning, Mary Magdalene and the other Mary went to see the tomb. ²And suddenly there was a great earthquake; for an angel of the Lord, descending from heaven, came and rolled back the stone and sat on it. ³His appearance was like lightning, and his clothing white as snow. ⁴For fear of him the guards shook and became like dead men. ⁵But the angel said to the women, "Do not be afraid; I know that you are looking for Jesus who was crucified.

When the sabbath was over, Mary Magdalene, and Mary the mother of James, and Salome bought spices, so that they might go and anoint him. ²And very early on the first day of the week, when the sun had risen, they went to the tomb. ³They had been saying to one another, "Who will roll away the stone for us from the entrance to the tomb?" ⁴When they looked up, they saw that the stone, which was very large, had already been rolled back. ⁵As they entered the

But on the first day of the week, at early dawn, they came to the tomb, taking the spices that they had prepared. ²They found the stone rolled away from the tomb, ³but when they went in, they did not find the body. ⁴While they were perplexed about this, suddenly two men in dazzling clothes stood beside them. ⁵They were terrified and bowed their faces to the ground, but they said to them, "Why do you look for the living among the dead? He is not here, but has risen. ⁶Remember how he

⁶He is not here; for he has been raised, as he said. Come, see the place where he lay. ⁷Then go quickly and tell his disciples, 'He has been raised from the dead, and indeed he is going ahead of you to Galilee; there you will see him.' This is my message for you." ⁸So they left the tomb quickly with fear and great joy, and ran to tell his disciples. ⁹Suddenly Jesus met them and said, "Greetings!" And they came to him, took hold of his feet, and worshiped him. ¹⁰Then Jesus said to them, "Do not be afraid; go and

tomb, they saw a young man, dressed in a white robe, sitting on the right side; and they were alarmed. ⁶But he said to them, "Do not be alarmed; you are looking for Jesus of Nazareth, who was crucified. He has been raised; he is not here. Look, there is the place they laid him. ⁷But go, tell his disciples and Peter that he is going ahead of you to Galilee; there you will see him, just as he told you." ⁸So they went out and fled from the tomb, for terror and amazement

told you, while he was still in Galilee, ⁷that the Son of Man must be handed over to sinners, and be crucified, and on the third day rise again." ⁸Then they remembered his words, ⁹and returning from the tomb, they told all this to the eleven and to all the rest. ¹⁰Now it was Mary Magdalene, Joanna, Mary the mother of James, and the other women with them who told this to the apostles. ¹¹But these words seemed to them an idle tale, and they did not believe them. ¹²But Peter got up and ran to

tell my brothers to go to Galilee; there they will see me."	had seized them; and they said nothing to anyone, for they were afraid.	the tomb; stooping and looking in, he saw the linen cloths by themselves; then he went home, amazed at what had happened.

I don't have solutions to these issues. I recognize that it would be difficult to harmonize these accounts, though I don't think it would necessarily be impossible. At any rate, I don't particularly want to spend my time and energy thinking about these differences of detail (which, according to one view, actually increases the plausibility of the accounts)[3] rather than reflecting on the major points of common interest. The women discovered an empty tomb! Jesus was no longer dead! Jesus commissioned his followers to announce his victory!

THE EMPTY TOMB

I don't have much to say about the empty tomb. If we were trying to make an argument here about the reality of Jesus's Resurrection, about the historicity of the event, the empty tomb would probably play a large role. In such discussions, people often bring up the fact that in all four Gospels it is women who discover the empty tomb, which seems significant because female testimony was not accounted very highly in antiquity, and

---

[3] Wright, *Resurrection*, 648–49.

so someone inventing a story about an empty tomb probably would have had a group of trustworthy men discovering it.[4] But I don't want to argue about whether the Resurrection actually happened; I am starting with the presupposition that it did happen, and I just want to understand it. More than that, in the context of this chapter, I want to understand how Luke thinks about it.

There are a few things that I think are important about the way Luke tells this story of the empty tomb. First of all, something not unique to Luke: the tomb was empty. The body was gone. "Why do you look for the living among the dead? He is not here, but has risen" (v. 5). We could spend all of our time talking about the implications of this element. Many Christians today (and for many centuries now) have thought about the physical body as simply an "extra," as not a part of the real person, and so when we die, our soul goes to heaven and our body decomposes, never to imprison our soul again. But this is a misconception of the biblical idea of the human being, owing more to Plato than to Scripture. When Jesus rose from the dead, it's not that his soul floated up to heaven leaving his body to rot, but his soul/spirit reunited with his body, so that the tomb was empty. That's resurrection. Peter quoted Psalm 16:10 in this regard: "He was not abandoned to Hades nor did his flesh experience corruption" (Acts 2:31). Our hope is also for this same sort of resurrection: our bodies will be a part of our future,

---

[4] William Lane Craig is one prominent theologian who makes this kind of argument. You can find some online examples at his website, *Reasonable Faith* (https://www.reasonablefaith.org/). Go to his "Writings" section and click on "Historical Jesus."

though, as Paul explains (and as Luke's stories about Jesus's resurrected body already illustrate), our bodies will be transformed in some ways (1 Cor 15:35–57).

Second, the angels reminded the women that Jesus had predicted his Resurrection (vv. 6–7). Luke records several predictions of Jesus's death, some without mentioning the Resurrection (9:44; 13:33; 17:25; 22:14–22), but there are two predictions of the Resurrection.

> The Son of Man must undergo great suffering, and be rejected by the elders, chief priests, and scribes, and be killed, and on the third day be raised. (Luke 9:22)

> See, we are going up to Jerusalem, and everything that is written about the Son of Man by the prophets will be accomplished. For he will be handed over to the Gentiles; and he will be mocked and insulted and spat upon. After they have flogged him, they will kill him, and on the third day he will rise again. (Luke 18:31–33)

Remembering these words, seeing the empty tomb, and hearing from the "two men in dazzling clothes" (24:4) was apparently enough to remove all doubt from the women. They reported their experience to the disciples and others (v. 9).

Third, no one believed the women. "But these words seemed to them an idle tale, and they did not believe them" (v. 11). Perhaps in part that's because those telling the story were women (see above), but probably also—even though Jesus had told them beforehand—the idea of someone rising from the dead in the middle of history was so far out of left field that they couldn't make any sense out of it. (Luke 24:12 says that Peter ran to the tomb to confirm the story, as in John 20:1–10, and Luke says that he was amazed but doesn't say whether he believed.)

Let me explain what I mean that the disciples might not have been ready to believe that someone might rise from the dead in the middle of history.

Resurrection in Ancient Judaism

The Old Testament doesn't say a whole lot about what happens to people after they die. The place of the dead is called in Hebrew *Sheol*, and it's not that fun of a place: dark, dusty, no praise of God there (e.g., Ps 6:5; Job 17:13, 16). It is not really clear whether everyone goes to Sheol or only certain people.[5] But the only passage in the Old Testament that clearly speaks about the resurrection of the dead is Daniel 12.

> Many of those who sleep in the dust of the earth
> shall awake, some to everlasting life, and some
> to shame and everlasting contempt. (Dan 12:2)

---

[5] This has recently become a point of contention, especially due to the work of Jon D. Levenson, *Resurrection and the Restoration of Israel: The Ultimate Victory of the God of Life* (New Haven, CT: Yale University Press, 2006). The usual scholarly thought is that Sheol is the place to which everyone goes, but Levenson has challenged this notion.

In Second Temple Judaism, the idea became widespread that at the end of the age, there would be a general resurrection of the dead along the lines of Daniel 12. This is the belief expressed by the seven Maccabean martyrs who are killed, along with their mama, for their faith. They affirm that in the new age God will raise up their bodies and restore them to life (2 Maccabees 7). Since this belief is not common in the Old Testament, it became a point of contention among some groups. The Pharisees and most Jews looked forward to a resurrection, but the Sadducees denied the resurrection of the dead (Luke 20:27; Acts 23:8).

In the first century, as I said, many Jews looked forward to a general resurrection of the dead at the dawn of the new age. But they did not think that before the general resurrection, before the consummation of the new age, in the middle of the current, evil age, one person might rise from the dead. The resurrection was supposed to correspond to the end of the current world order, and the resurrection was supposed to involve everybody. No one really thought about the Messiah dying, much less rising from the dead. So when they heard about it, "these words seemed to them an idle tale, and they did not believe them."

THE ROAD TO EMMAUS

A couple disciples who had been with the apostles when the women made their strange report now left Jerusalem heading to Emmaus, a village whose whereabouts have been lost to history. One of these disciples is named Cleopas, perhaps the same as the Clopas mentioned in John 19:25, who had a wife named Mary. Early Christian tradition makes Mary and Cl(e)opas relatives of

Jesus,[6] though early Christian tradition does not necessarily identify Cleopas' companion as his wife Mary on the way to Emmaus.[7] At any rate, even if Cleopas was a relative of Jesus, Luke makes nothing of it in this story. He surely didn't expect his (Gentile?) readers to pick up on these obscure connections.

These two disciples are joined by a third person whom they do not recognize (v. 16), but whom Luke identifies for his readers as Jesus (v. 15). Why could Cleopas and his companion not recognize Jesus? Their eyes were prevented from doing so (v. 16). It seems to me that this story suggests some sort of divine action to prevent the disciples from recognizing Jesus until later. In a little bit we'll talk about why that might be.

Cleopas and his companion explain to the third traveler the events that have consumed their thoughts.

> The things about Jesus of Nazareth, who was a prophet mighty in deed and word before God and all the people, and how our chief priests and leaders handed him over to be condemned to death and crucified him. But we had hoped that he was the one to redeem Israel. Yes, and besides all this, it is now the third day since these things took place. Moreover, some women of our group astounded us. They were at the tomb early this morning, and when they did not find his

---

[6] You can find information on these early Christian traditions at Wikipedia: "Cleopas."

[7] Wikipedia: "Road to Emmaus Appearance," under the section "Unnamed Disciple."

body there, they came back and told us that they
had indeed seen a vision of angels who said that
he was alive. Some of those who were with us
went to the tomb and found it just as the women
had said; but they did not see him. (Luke 24:19–
24)

This speech is full of interesting elements. Why were
people attracted to Jesus and his message of the kingdom of God?
"We had hoped that he was the one to redeem Israel" (v. 21).
First of all, notice that the death of Jesus apparently dashed
whatever hopes they had entertained about his role in God's
plans. Their hopes for Jesus were valid only while he was alive,
but no longer. I point this out just to emphasize that people were
not anticipating a dying Messiah. There were passages in the Old
Testament that referred to a person as suffering (and dying?) on
behalf of others, such as Isaiah 53, but notice that Isaiah 53 is
about the Servant of the Lord, and not about the Messiah. What
I mean is that the word *messiah* does not appear in that chapter,
nor the term king, nor son of David, nor kingdom. There were
not many clues for people to connect Isaiah 53 to the Messiah,
and most people didn't. Most people thought whoever this
Servant of the Lord was, he wasn't the Messiah. "The servant was
not regarded as a messianic figure in pre-Christian Judaism."[8]

---

[8] John J. Collins, *The Scepter and the Star: Messianism in Light of the Dead
Sea Scrolls*, 2d ed. (Grand Rapids: Eerdmans, 2010), 147. On the Jewish
reception of Isaiah 53, see S. R. Driver and Ad. Neubauer, *The Fifty-Third
Chapter of Isaiah according to the Jewish Interpreters*, vol. 2: *Translations*
(Oxford: James Parker, 1877).

The Messiah would come and conquer Israel's enemies and establish God's kingdom. He wouldn't do that by dying.[9] To quote a famous (and cleaned-up version of a) speech from General Patton, "No one ever won a war by dying for his country; he won it by making the other guy die for his country."[10]

What had Cleopas and his companion hoped Jesus might do? Redeem Israel? What does that mean? The Greek word for redeem (λυτρόω, *lutróō*) is the same word used in some passages of the Septuagint in regard to God's redemption of Israel from Egypt (Exod 6:6; 15:13). I bet that's what was in people's minds in the first century, especially during the Passover, the celebration of that redemption from Egypt. I bet Cleopas and his companion were thinking that Jesus might be the one to liberate Israel from the foreign domination of the Romans, to establish Israel as a strong nation, to reign over Israel as the anointed king, the son of David, and to fulfill (their understanding of) those ancient prophecies that the Gentiles would stream into Jerusalem to learn the law (e.g., Isa 2:1–4).

But, no more. Jesus is dead.

Or, maybe? The tomb where he had been buried is apparently empty, judging not only from the report of some women but also some others of us who confirmed their story.

---

[9] For an evaluation of recent proposals that some Jews during the Second Temple period did imagine a suffering and dying Messiah, see Collins, *Scepter and the Star*, 141–48, 164–70, who insists, "There is still no evidence for a Jewish interpretation of Isaiah 53 in terms of a suffering messiah" (144).

[10] Wikipedia: "George S. Patton's Speech to the Third Army."

The women also say that some angels told them that Jesus was alive. So … weird. What can it all mean?

Now Jesus takes over.

> "Oh, how foolish you are, and how slow of heart to believe all that the prophets have declared! Was it not necessary that the Messiah should suffer these things and then enter into his glory?" Then beginning with Moses and all the prophets, he interpreted to them the things about himself in all the scriptures. (Luke 24:25–27)

Oh, how I wish Luke had recorded which Old Testament verses Jesus quoted—and his interpretation! No doubt we get some clue along these lines from the speeches in Acts, where the apostles are trying to prove the same thing: that the Messiah had to suffer and then rise from the dead. In Acts 2, Peter points to Psalm 16 (Acts 25–28) and Psalm 110 (Acts 2:34–35). In Acts 3, he points to Deuteronomy 18:15–19 (Acts 3:22–23). I think it is fair to say that none of these passages so obviously talk about the suffering of the Messiah that we are in a position to blame these first-century disciples for their dullness. I'm afraid we would be in the same boat. Speaking for myself, I would wonder how Psalm 16, for instance, has anything to do with the Messiah, or resurrection from the dead. Jesus can (and does!) blame these disciples for not getting it, but I don't think I better. Speck and log, you know.

This story is designed to illustrate the very thing these disciples are experiencing. They don't recognize Jesus because their eyes have been prevented from seeing clearly. They don't recognize the truth of Scripture because their minds have been closed to that reality. Jesus interprets for them, and their hearts start burning (v. 32). Jesus opened the Scriptures that had previously seemed locked—nay, previously been locked to these disciples though they had not realized it. Jesus gave them the key that they did not realize they needed. They had been waiting in an outer room of the Scriptures, under the impression that their room was the whole house, and now Jesus lets them out of the foyer into the living spaces of Scripture, rooms that the disciples had not realized existed.

And yet still they did not recognize Jesus. Not until they ate with him.

> When he was at the table with them, he took bread, blessed and broke it, and gave it to them. Then their eyes were opened and they recognized him; and he vanished from their sight. (Luke 24:30–31)

What does it take for these disciples to recognize Jesus in their presence? This story emphasizes two things: a proper understanding of Scripture, and then sharing a meal. Later these disciples will report both of these aspects to the apostles: "Then they told what had happened on the road, and how he had been made known to them in the breaking of the bread" (v. 35). N. T. Wright suggests a parallel with Genesis 3: just as a meal opened the eyes of Adam and Eve with very negative consequences, so also now a meal opens the eyes of these disciples with the most joyous consequences.[11]

Figure 6. Caravaggio's *Supper at Emmaus* c. 1601.
Public domain, via Wikimedia Commons.

This scene of the meal, often depicted by artists,[12] is reminiscent of the Lord's Supper. Luke seems to have intended that connection by the way he described the actions of Jesus: "he took bread, blessed and broke it, and gave it to them" (v. 30). While we cannot have the same experience as those two disciples

---

[11] Wright, *Resurrection*, 652.

[12] For some examples, see Wikipedia: "Road to Emmaus Appearance." The example I have included is Caravaggio, "Supper at Emmaus" (1601), image from Wikimedia Commons.

in Emmaus, their experience is a type of our own meal with Jesus, wherein we also hope to recognize him more perfectly.

This story also suggests that any such glimpse will only be fleeting. As soon as the disciples see Jesus clearly, he vanishes from their sight. Their experience is a model for what many believers routinely experience: fleeting glimpses of our Savior. Sometimes we glimpse him during a worship service, perhaps during the Lord's Supper in particular. Sometimes we recognize him while sharing a meal with friends. Sometimes we see him while serving others, or receiving service from others. Always, the vision passes, our eyes close, and we once again search for him. "For now we see in a mirror, dimly" and we long for that time when "we will see face to face" (1 Cor 13:12).

One more comment about this story: it corresponds in some ways to the story about the young Jesus in the temple at the end of Luke 2. In that story, Joseph and Mary journey away from Jerusalem thinking that Jesus is with them only to discover that he is not. At the end of the Gospel, Cleopas and his companion journey away from Jerusalem thinking that Jesus is dead only to discover that he is with them. Joseph and Mary hurry back to Jerusalem in a panic to find Jesus. Cleopas and his companion hurry back to Jerusalem anxious with joy to proclaim that Jesus is risen. Joseph and Mary are able to find Jesus only on the third day. What was lost has now been found (another Lukan theme).[13]

---

[13] See Wright, *Resurrection*, 650–51.

JESUS WITH THE DISCIPLES

Finally, Jesus meets with his apostles and others. This scene (in the upper room?) has two main elements apart from the Ascension which we will treat in a moment. First, Jesus seeks to demonstrate the reality of the Resurrection in terms of a physical body. This is of course consistent with the tomb being empty. The disciples think they might be seeing a ghost or a spirit (πνεῦμα, *pneuma*; v. 37). Jesus wants to prove that his body is physical. He presents three lines of evidence.

- Look at my hands and my feet (v. 39). The implication is that the nail holes would still be visible. Or, at least, that's what I think he's doing. Luke never mentions that Jesus was nailed to the cross, nor do any of the Gospels, actually.[14] But in the scene in John when the doubting Thomas doubts, he says, "Unless I see the mark of the nails in his hands, and put my finger in the mark of the nails, and my hand in his side, I will not believe" (John 20:25). This is the only verse in the New Testament that suggests that Jesus's hands had nail holes in them, but I guess everywhere else it's just assumed. Surely, in Luke, when Jesus shows his apostles his hands and his feet, he means that his hands and his feet bear the marks of crucifixion, not that his hands and his feet were so well

---

[14] Noted by Wright, *Resurrection*, 658n24.

known to his disciples as to be unmistakably those of Jesus. (It's not like his apostles would have spent a whole lot of time looking at Jesus's hands and feet before.)

- Touch me and see; for a ghost (*pneuma*) does not have flesh and bones as you see that I have (v. 39). Obviously, this test is just to establish that it's a real, physical body.

- He said to them, "Have you anything here to eat? They gave him a piece of broiled fish, and he took it and ate in their presence (vv. 41–43). The point here, again, is that his body works just like a normal, physical body. He can eat real, physical food. He's not faking it. Later, Peter will remember such times as a convincing proof of the Resurrection; he remembered being one of those "who ate and drank with him after he rose from the dead" (Acts 10:41).

These three lines of evidence are what Luke has in mind when he starts Acts with the description of Jesus: "After his suffering he presented himself alive to them by many convincing proofs" (Acts 1:3).

What kind of body does Jesus have? It does seem to be different in some ways from the body he had before his death. Not completely different. Again, the whole point of this scene of Jesus with his disciples is to convince them (and us!) that Jesus had the same body. And that's also the point of the empty tomb narrative. It is the same body that he had previously, but it seems to have undergone some sort of transformation. Now, that is not so obvious in Matthew and Mark, where this issue doesn't really come up. But there are certain features of the story in Luke and in John that suggest that Jesus's body is altered somehow. Jesus disappears (Luke 24:31). That hadn't happened before, not exactly. To be sure, Jesus previously had an uncanny knack for escaping trouble, almost as if he could disappear (Luke 4:30), but this seems different. He's right in front of Cleopas and the other one, they finally realize who he is, and then he's gone. Normal, physical bodies can't do that. It might also be this changed nature of Jesus's body that contributed to the Emmaus disciples not being able to recognize Jesus, though I also think God was preventing them from doing so (v. 16). Finally, in Luke, Jesus simply "appears" in the location where the disciples were meeting (v. 36). John says the doors were locked when Jesus showed up (John 20:19, 26), making it pretty clear that Jesus could float through walls, or at least apparate like Harry Potter.

These are hints that Jesus's body has undergone transformation. It's helpful to think about what Paul says regarding the nature of the resurrected body—he's thinking about us, not about Jesus, but he himself says that we're going to be raised just like Jesus, so it's relevant. Paul says that the resurrected body is a "spiritual body" (1 Cor 15:44), whatever that means. But Paul also makes it clear that it's the same body that we have now, it will die and then be raised up (vv. 42–44) and transformed into a body that can inherit the kingdom of God (v. 50).

N. T. Wright calls this aspect of the resurrected body "transphysicality" as a way of saying that it's the same physical body that we had, but now transformed.[15]

Then there's the commissioning (Luke 24:44–49). After doing for the apostles what he had done for the Emmaus disciples

---

[15] Wright, *Resurrection*, 661.

(v. 45), he explains the next moves: "repentance and forgiveness of sins is to be proclaimed in his name to all nations, beginning from Jerusalem" (v. 47). This commission is connected in thought to the Resurrection. Let me quote N. T. Wright again.

> Because Jesus is risen, he is demonstrated to be Israel's Messiah; because he is Israel's Messiah, he is the true lord of the world and will summon it to allegiance; to this end, he will commission his followers to act on his behalf, in the power of the Spirit which itself is a sign and means of covenant renewal and fresh life.[16]

Ascension

Luke is the only New Testament writer to narrate the Ascension.[17] Other writers assume it.[18] Paul, for instance:[19]

---

[16] Wright, *Resurrection*, 660.

[17] My assumption here is that Mark's Gospel originally ended at 16:8 and that the material now forming 16:9–20 is a later addition. This assumption is shared by the majority of scholars who have studied the issue; for a good explanation of this view, go to the online NET Bible (netbible.org) and see the relevant note on Mark 16.

[18] Aside from the passages quoted, see Hebrews 1:3; 4:14; 7:26; 8;4; 9:24; Revelation 5:6–14; 7:17; John 7:39; 8:54; 12:16; 14:13; 17:5.

[19] Besides these verses, see Philippians 2:9; 1 Thessalonians 1:10; 4:16; Ephesians 1:20; 4:7–13; 1 Timothy 3:16.

Who is to condemn? It is Christ Jesus, who died, yes, who was raised, who is at the right hand of God, who indeed intercedes for us. (Rom 8:34)

So if you have been raised with Christ, seek the things that are above, where Christ is, seated at the right hand of God. (Col 3:1)

And Peter:

And baptism, which this prefigured, now saves you—not as a removal of dirt from the body, but as an appeal to God for a good conscience, through the resurrection of Jesus Christ, who has gone into heaven and is at the right hand of God, with angels, authorities, and powers made subject to him. (1 Pet 3:21–22)

And John the Revelator, who quotes Jesus as follows:

To the one who conquers I will give a place with me on my throne, just as I myself conquered and sat down with my Father on his throne. (Rev 3:21)

The entire New Testament affirms that Jesus is now reigning in heaven, enthroned, at God's right hand. The entire New Testament assumes the Ascension; only Luke narrates it. Twice.

> Then he led them out as far as Bethany, and, lifting up his hands, he blessed them. While he was blessing them, he withdrew from them and was carried up into heaven. And they worshiped him, and returned to Jerusalem with great joy; and they were continually in the temple blessing God. (Luke 24:50–53)

> When he had said this, as they were watching, he was lifted up, and a cloud took him out of their sight. (Acts 1:9)

The whole Gospel has been aiming at this moment even more than that of the Resurrection. We could probably say that the entire Bible has been aiming at this moment, when the Messiah, the Son of David, would ascend to his throne to reign over a kingdom of disciples who would have the law of God written in their hearts and would proclaim to all nations the forgiveness that God offers on condition of repentance. The good news is not only that Jesus died for our sins, but that he rose from the dead and is now reigning in heaven, having been granted all authority in heaven and on earth (Matt 28:18).[20]

And our response? To follow the apostles' example: bless God with great joy!

---

[20] See Matthew W. Bates, *Gospel Allegiance: What Faith in Jesus Misses for Salvation in Christ* (Grand Rapids: Brazos, 2019).

Appendix A: Discussion Questions

1 Good News of Great Joy
Discussion Questions

- Angels make several announcements in Luke 1–2: to Zechariah, to Mary, to some shepherds. What do these angels say is about to happen?
- The widow Anna speaks about the child "to all who were looking for the redemption of Jerusalem" (Luke 2:38). What does the phrase "redemption of Jerusalem" mean, and what does that have to do with this child? Can you think of Old Testament prophecies about the redemption of Jerusalem? Do you think Anna might be thinking of something like Isaiah 2:1–4?
- Summarize Mary's song at Luke 1:46–55. What does she say that God has done? What does she mean by that?
- Zechariah's prophecy in Luke 1:67–79 has similar themes to Mary's song. How does Zechariah describe what God is about to do, and why he is about to do it?

- When Simeon sees the infant in the temple, what does he think is the significance of this child?

2 JOHN THE BAPTIST
DISCUSSION QUESTIONS

- As you read through the account of John's preaching in Luke 3:1–20, what are the main themes that you notice?
- At Luke 3:18, Luke describes John's preaching with a word related to "gospel" or "good news," as some translations make clear. What about John's preaching seems like "good news" to you? What about his preaching could seem like the opposite of "good news"?
- Jesus describes John's ministry at Luke 7:18–35. What does Jesus say about John?
- Luke is the single Gospel that narrates John's birth. How does the angelic announcement to Zechariah (Luke 1:5–25) describe John's purpose and mission?
- How does John's preaching (Luke 3:1–20) fulfill this purpose?

3 THE GENEALOGY OF JESUS
DISCUSSION QUESTIONS

- Why do you think Luke spends sixteen verses (Luke 3:23–38) giving the genealogy of Jesus? What is the point?

- What similarities do you see between the genealogy presented by Luke and the one presented by Matthew (Matt 1:1–17)?
- What are some of the differences between the two genealogies?
- Which of David's sons does Luke trace Jesus's ancestry through? Which of David's sons stands in the genealogy according to Matthew?
- Do you have any explanation for the differences? Have you heard any explanations?

4 Launching A Ministry
Discussion Questions

- In the synagogue at Nazareth, Jesus reads Isaiah 61:1–2. As you look at that passage in the Old Testament, what sorts of things does it prophesy?
- When Jesus says in the Nazareth synagogue "today this scripture has been fulfilled in your hearing" (Luke 4:21), what does he mean?
- Compare the response of the Nazareth crowd in Luke 4:22–30 to the way Mark tells the story (Mark 6:1–6). What similarities and differences do you see?
- What point is Jesus trying to make by mentioning Elijah (1 Kgs 17) and Elisha (2 Kgs 5)?
- Why do the people in Nazareth get so mad at Jesus? Does Jesus intentionally provoke them?

5 IN THE HOME OF A PHARISEE
DISCUSSION QUESTIONS

- Is it surprising that Jesus would eat with a Pharisee (Luke 7:36)? Is it surprising that a Pharisee would ask Jesus over for a meal? The same thing happens later in Luke (11:37; 14:1). Why do you think Simon the Pharisee wanted to have a meal with Jesus?

- A woman interrupts the meal. Who is she, and what does she do? Why do you think she does that?

- Imagine you were hosting this dinner party on your back porch. How would you respond to this woman's actions? How would your response compare to the response by Simon?

- What does Jesus's response to the woman and to Simon indicate about how he views these two people?

- Why do you think Luke includes this story in his Gospel? What does he want his readers to know about Jesus? What does he want his readers to know about discipleship?

6 THE GOOD SAMARITAN
DISCUSSION QUESTIONS

- Jesus gets the same question twice in Luke's Gospel, about inheriting eternal life, once from a lawyer (10:25) and once from the rich young ruler (18:18). How does Jesus respond each time?

- What do you think Luke means that the lawyer was "wanting to justify himself" (10:29)?

- In the parable told by Jesus, the priest and the Levite do not help the wounded man. Can you imagine some ways that they might "justify themselves" in not helping?
- How would you describe the actions of the Samaritan toward the wounded man? Is this the way religious people normally behave? Is that the way you would behave in a similar situation?
- What sorts of sacrifices did the Samaritan make on behalf of the wounded man? Which of these sacrifices do you find most difficult to replicate in your own life?

7 THE PRODIGAL SON
DISCUSSION QUESTIONS

- What do you think you would do if one of your children said to you what the prodigal son says to his father in Luke 15:12? What do you think about the father's response in this parable?
- This son becomes "prodigal" (= "wasteful," "reckless") when he goes to the Far Country (Luke 15:13). What do you think are the attractions of the Far Country? What are the dangers?
- What does the prodigal son teach us about repentance (Luke 15:17–21)?
- What is the false idea about his role within the family that the older brother has (Luke 15:25–30)?
- What do you think about the father's response to both brothers? What do those responses tell us about the father?

8 Two Parables about Money
Discussion questions

- In the Parable of the Dishonest Steward (Luke 16:1–9), what is the steward's problem and what is his plan to fix his problem?
- Do you think Jesus wants us to admire the dishonest steward? Are we supposed to imitate him? If so, how should we imitate him? If we are not supposed to imitate him, why does Jesus tell the parable?
- How does the teaching of Jesus in Luke 16:10–15 relate to the Parable of the Dishonest Steward?
- In the Parable of the Rich Man and Lazarus (Luke 16:19–31), what point is Jesus making about money?
- Why does the rich man want Lazarus to talk to his brothers? What does he want Lazarus to tell them?

9 Tow Tax Collectors
Discussion questions

- In the story of the Pharisee and Tax Collector (18:9–14), why does Jesus choose to talk about a Pharisee? What did people think about the Pharisees in the time of Jesus? What is the problem with the prayer that Jesus represents this Pharisee as praying?
- Why does Jesus choose a tax collector for his parable? What did people think about tax collectors? In what way is this particular tax collector an example for others?
- People grumble at Jesus in Luke 15:2 and 19:7. Why are they grumbling?

- What is similar about the example of Zacchaeus and that of the tax collector in 18:9–14?
- Zacchaeus, the "chief tax collector" (19:2), is obviously very rich. Compare his response to Jesus to that of the rich man in 18:18–23.

10 THE FUTURE ACCORDING TO JESUS
DISCUSSION QUESTIONS

- What do you think Jesus means that "the kingdom of God is among you" (Luke 17:21)?
- In Luke 13:28–29, Jesus speaks about the kingdom of God as something that people will experience in the future. Is the kingdom of God future or already present?
- In Luke 17:22–37, Jesus talks about "the day that the Son of Man is revealed" (verse 30). What day is he talking about?
- In Luke 21:5–38, Jesus talks about future signs. What will these signs indicate? How does this discourse relate to what Jesus was talking about in Luke 17:20–21?
- At Luke 21:27, Jesus says that the Son of Man will come in a cloud with power and great glory? Is he talking about his Second Coming or about something else?

11 THE FINAL HOURS OF JESUS
DISCUSSION QUESTIONS

- Luke's account of the Lord's Supper (22:14–23) is a bit different from that of Matthew (26:26–30) and Mark

(14:22–25). What differences do you notice? Why do you think Luke writes it up the way he does?

- Jesus tells his disciples that they're going to "eat and drink at my table in my kingdom" and "sit on thrones judging the twelve tribes of Israel" (Luke 22:30). What is he talking about? What do you think is going through the minds of the disciples?

- What does Satan "demand" (Luke 22:31)? From whom does he demand it? Is Satan granted his demand?

- Why does Jesus want the disciples to have swords (Luke 22:36)?

- Luke's account of Gethsemane (22:39–46) is a bit different from that of Matthew (26:36–46) and Mark (14:32–42). What differences do you notice? Why do you think Luke writes it up this way?

12 THE DEATH OF JESUS
DISCUSSION QUESTIONS

- When Jesus is arrested (Luke 22:47–53) and tried before the Sanhedrin (22:63–71), what charge against Jesus does the council find worthy of a death sentence?

- What ends up being the charge against Jesus for which Pilate crucified him? (Luke 23:1–25)

- While on the cross (Luke 23:32–49), Jesus says three things. What are these three sayings from the cross? Compare these sayings to what Jesus says from the cross in the other Gospels.

- How does the criminal on the cross (Luke 23:39–43) provide a better example of discipleship than some others that probably spent more time with Jesus? How do you think this criminal knew about Jesus?

- What strange things happen at the death of Jesus, as reported by Luke (23:44–49)

13 ALL THINGS NEW
DISCUSSION QUESTIONS

- As you read Luke 24, what do you make of Jesus's body? Is it the same body he had in the first 23 chapters of Luke? What's different about it?
- What had the travelers to Emmaus been hoping for prior to the Crucifixion?
- What does Jesus say in this chapter about the connection between the Old Testament and his own death and Resurrection? Why do you think his followers did not understand that connection?
- Do you think it is significant that it was at the breaking of the bread that the travelers recognized Jesus (Luke 24:30–31, 35)? Does Luke want his readers to grasp anything in particular from that occurrence?
- What are the final instructions Jesus gives to his disciples?

Appendix B: Discussion Guide

1: Good News of Great Joy

- Angels make several announcements in Luke 1-2: to Zechariah, to Mary, to some shepherds. What do these angels say is about to happen?

Gabriel announces to Zechariah the impending conception of his son, who should be named John (1:13–17). The most important part of the announcement is that this baby John will be the fulfillment of the prophecy about the coming of Elijah, which closes the last prophetic book (Mal 4:5). Since Elijah is coming, in the form of this baby John, then "the great and terrible day of the Lord," prophesied by Malachi, will be coming as well. And indeed, Gabriel announces that as "Elijah," Zechariah's son is going to be turning the people's hearts back to the Lord—just as Elijah had done (think Mt. Carmel; 1 Kings 18)—and thus preparing a people for the Lord (Luke 1:16–17).

Gabriel then goes to the virgin Mary to announce to her the impending conception of her own son, who should be named Jesus (1:30–38). As it turns out, this baby is the "Lord" whose way will be prepared by John in the role of Elijah. Notice that when Mary visits her relative Elizabeth, the older expectant mother realizes that her young relative is carrying in her womb "my Lord" (1:43). This baby Jesus is "Lord" because he is formed by a direct action of the Holy Spirit within the womb of Mary without the participation of a human father (1:35). All of this is rather unexpected and unusual. That is, Jews in the first century were not looking forward to the incarnation of God in the form of a baby. What they were looking forward to, in addition to the appearance of Elijah, was the coming of the son of David, long prophesied (cf. 2 Sam 7:12–16; Isa 11:1; Jer 23:4–5; Ezek 34:23; etc.). Gabriel informs Mary that her baby will fulfill this role.

After the birth of Jesus, an unnamed "angel of the Lord" (2:9) announces to some nearby shepherds the birth of "a Savior who is the Messiah, the Lord." This announcement again combines the two roles that Gabriel had earlier reported to Mary: Jesus is the fulfillment of the promises to David (i.e., the Messiah), and he is more exalted than being merely the Messiah, because he is Lord (= the most common way of referring to God in the Old Testament).

- The widow Anna speaks about the child "to all who were looking for the redemption of Jerusalem" (Luke 2:38). What does the phrase "redemption of Jerusalem" mean, and what does that have to do with this child? Can you think of Old Testament prophecies about the redemption of Jerusalem? Do you think Anna might be thinking of something like Isaiah 2:1–4?

I think that most people to whom Anna spoke would have thought about the phrase "redemption of Jerusalem" in very physical terms: the expulsion of the Roman overlords from Jerusalem and the establishment of a strong Jewish nation on their ancient homeland and ruled by a descendant of David. That is more-or-less the picture painted by Ezekiel 37:15-28, or Isaiah 11:1-10. The prophecy in Isaiah 2 also imagines Jerusalem becoming the chief city of the world, to which other nations stream in order to learn the law of the Lord.

I don't know whether Anna thought about redemption in physical terms, but clearly Luke did not. He knew how the story turned out, not with war against the Romans but with crucifixion of the Messiah, followed by his resurrection. No matter how Jesus' own contemporaries thought about the redemption of Jerusalem, Luke used this phrase to point to something deeper (and higher) than redemption from the Romans. The writer of this Third Gospel no doubt interpreted spiritually or metaphorically those ancient prophecies with images of physical redemption (such as Isa 2; Isa 11; Ezek 37; etc.) If Jerusalem stands for the people of God (as it does in Rev 21:2), then in the context of Luke's Gospel, "the redemption of Jerusalem" indicates the redemption of God's people from the spiritual forces of darkness and their tools, sin and death.

- Summarize Mary's song at Luke 1:46–55. What does she say that God has done? What does she mean by that?

Mary says that God has yanked rulers off their thrones and raised up the lowly; he has fed the hungry and sent away the full. At the same time, she is thinking about the ancient promises, especially to Abraham (1:55). I think what she means is that God's people are often the lowly, the powerless, who often seem to lack the blessings enjoyed by the wicked. But God is committed to justice, is committed to repaying the wicked for their deeds and rewarding the righteous, and that is evident in her own pregnancy, since she is carrying the long-awaited Messiah, who will execute God's justice. He is appointed (as Simeon will say) for the falling and rising of many in Israel. Of course, Mary is also thinking back to all the times God has brought justice before, whether by lowering Pharaoh through the plagues, or restoring the Jews after the exile, or many other times. Her own pregnancy is another example, the greatest example, of the character of God.

- Zechariah's prophecy in Luke 1:67–79 has similar themes to Mary's song. How does Zechariah describe what God is about to do, and why he is about to do it?

Even more than Mary, Zechariah describes God's actions through these children as judgment against God's enemies (1:71, 74). Again, I don't know exactly how Zechariah thought about this judgment, but Luke includes these words in his Gospel because he thought they accurately depicted something Jesus really did. The difference may be that Zechariah possibly thought God's enemies were the Romans and Jesus (and Luke) knew the enemies were Satan and his assistants.

- When Simeon sees the infant in the temple, what does he think is the significance of this child?

Simeon knows that he is holding the Messiah because the Holy Spirit revealed it to him (2:26), and so he knows that this child is God's salvation (2:30). We don't know what sort of salvation Simeon himself was actually imagining. His words perhaps carried more meaning than he realized. But Simeon also provides the first indication in the Gospel that Jesus would endure opposition, and "a sword will pierce even [Mary's] own soul too" (2:35). Simeon may have been thinking about such opposition in terms of a messiniac war, but the battle to be fought in the Gospel would actually be much different from any human warfare, and would involve crucifixion of the Messiah. As Mary looked on at the crucifixion (cf. John 19:26), no doubt she felt that sharp point of the sword.

Chapter 2: John the Baptist

- As you read through the account of John's preaching in Luke 3:1–20, what are the main themes that you notice?

What stands out to me is (1) hellfire and (2) repentance. John is a fiery preacher who has no interest in telling people about how much God loves them or that with a few changes to their life's routine they can make every day a Friday. John is in to telling people that they need to turn or burn. When you tell the people coming to you for baptism that they are a brood of vipers, you don't seem to be worried about making friends, or about reporting impressive baptism numbers to the sponsoring church back home. The way to avoid the coming judgment is to repent, and John provides some helpful examples (Luke 3:10–14).

- At Luke 3:18, Luke describes John's preaching with a word related to "gospel" or "good news," as some translations make clear. What about John's preaching seems like "good news" to you? What about his preaching could seem like the opposite of "good news"?

Well, that second question's easy: most of John's preaching seems like bad news—judgment is coming. But it's bad news in the same way that the Old Testament prophets brought bad news, warning Israel that God hated their behavior and so he was going to bring destruction. Such warnings from the prophets could actually be good news if the people believed the prophets and changed their behavior. Having the doctor tell you that you've caught the cancer early is good news in a way because you can do something about it, but it's not good news if you refuse to believe your doctor that you actually have cancer. John is the physician (like Jesus; Luke 5:31) warning the people about the cancer eating away at their souls. It's good news because now they can repent.

- Jesus describes John's ministry at Luke 7:18–35. What does Jesus say about John?

Jesus says that John is the long-promised messenger announced in Malachi 3:1, who would prepare the way before God (Luke 7:27). John is not just any prophet, but a special, eschatological prophet (Luke 7:26). But he will die before the establishment of the kingdom of God. Anyone in the kingdom of God is "greater" (Luke 7:28; probably: in a more fortunate position) than John.

- Luke is the single Gospel that narrates John's birth. How does the angelic announcement to Zechariah (Luke 1:5–25) describe John's purpose and mission?

Gabriel reveals that the baby's name should be John, and that he will bring great joy (Luke 1:13–14). John's avoidance of alcohol (Luke 1:15) sounds like the rules of the nazirite (Num 6:1–21; cf. Judg 13:4–5), though Gabriel says nothing here about John's haircut. Rather, he connects John's abstinence from alcohol to his being filled with the spirit (cf. Eph 5:18). Gabriel says that this baby will go "in the spirit and power of Elijah" (Luke 1:17), alluding to the prophecy of Malachi that Elijah's reappearance will precede the coming the Lord (Mal 4:5). In fact, Elijah's purpose, according to Malachi 4:6, is the same purpose that Gabriel ascribes to John (Luke 1:17): "to turn the hearts of parents to their children, and the disobedient to the wisdom of the righteous, to make ready a people prepared for the Lord."

- How does John's preaching (Luke 3:1–20) fulfill this purpose?

John prepares a people for the Lord by warning about coming judgment and offering a chance for repentance. In this same way, John attempts to turn the disobedient to the wisdom of the righteous, and he turns the hearts of parents to their children. That is, John's preaching is an attempt to get the disobedient to recognize their own folly and to follow the path of wisdom and righteousness outlined by John. Perhaps the way that John turns the hearts of parents to children is to get adults to think about the consequences of their sin on society and the future of their own people. This interpretation would be something like what we often say in modern America about the national debt, that we're burdening our children with repaying the trillions of dollars of loans, and that if we cared for our children, we would spend less money now, or try to balance the budget. Perhaps John's preaching about sin is helping people provide a secure future for their children. On the other hand, maybe John is really just telling parents that they need to take care of their kids. But John doesn't actually preach about parents in Luke 3, so I'm not sure whether that more straightforward approach is really the best interpretation.

Chapter 3: The Genealogy of Jesus

- Why do you think Luke used sixteen verses (Luke 3:23–38) giving the genealogy of Jesus? What is the point?

The genealogy in Luke is—at first glance—somewhat strange and harder to interpret than the genealogy in Matthew. The genealogy in Matthew 1 tells us how to interpret the genealogy: three sections of fourteen generations lead from Abraham through David to the messiah. Matthew makes clear who the important people in the genealogy are in the very first verse (Matt 1:1). There are no such explicit clues in Luke's genealogy. It goes in a straight line from Jesus all the way back to Adam and even to God. A simple reading of the genealogy simply reveals the ancestors of Jesus. You would have to know already who the important people in the genealogy are; Luke does not tell you.

There is much more going on in this genealogy than you can glean from a simple reading. In Chapter 3 above, I explore potential deeper meanings, leading to the conclusion that the generation of Jesus is the turning point, the decisive generation, in world history.

- What similarities do you see between the genealogy presented by Luke and the one presented by Matthew (Matthew 1:1–17)?

Similarities are not obvious. They amount to both genealogies sharing some names: Jesus, of course, and then most of the names between David and Abraham.

- What are some of the differences between the two genealogies?

The differences are easy to spot. First Luke's genealogy goes backwards (ending at the beginning, with Adam and then God), whereas Matthew's goes forwards (ending at the end, with Jesus). Matthew divided his genealogy into three sections of 14 generations each, whereas Luke makes no organization explicit. And a lot of the names are different. In Chapter 3 above, I offer some explanations for why there might be different names.

- Which of David's sons does Luke trace Jesus' ancestry through? Which of David's sons stands in the genealogy according to Matthew?

Luke: Nathan. Matthew: Solomon. This is a very interesting difference, and perhaps points toward the different purposes behind the two genealogies. I suggest in Chapter 3 above that perhaps Luke's genealogy is the biological genealogy of Jesus, whereas Matthew's genealogy is the "royal" genealogy. As a royal genealogy, Matthew's genealogy sticks with the kings and traces the royal descent through Solomon. As a biological genealogy, Luke's genealogy traces the descent of Jesus through one of David's non-royal sons, Nathan. This non-royal genealogy probably connects to the prophecy in Jeremiah 22:24–30, which says that none of the descendants of King Coniah (= Jeconiah = Jehoiachin) would ever be king of God's people.

- Do you have any explanation for the differences? Have you heard any explanations?

The most prominent explanation I've heard in churches is that Matthew presents the genealogy through the father of Jesus (Joseph) whereas Luke presents the genealogy through the mother of Jesus (Mary). Even if that were true, which I doubt, it would not solve all the problems. Actually, I don't think any explanation that I've heard or that I can think of solves all the problems, but I like best the explanation I offered under the previous question, that Matthew presents a royal genealogy whereas Luke presents a non-royal, biological genealogy.

Chapter 4: Launching a Ministry

- In the synagogue at Nazareth, Jesus reads Isaiah 61:1–2. As you look at that passage in the Old Testament, what sorts of things does it prophesy?

In its Old Testament context, Isaiah 61 seems to be spoken by the prophet, perhaps in the voice of the Servant of the Lord. The passage does not actually use the word "servant," but it does sound something like the "servant" passages of Isaiah 42 and 49. At any rate, the person speaking this oracle claims divine anointing by God's Spirit and that he has been sent by God to do several things that could all be read in terms of the Jubilee Year. Almost certainly, the first phrase of v. 2 references the Jubilee Year (cf. Lev 25:10), which brought with it a release from debt and slavery. So, in one sense, this passage from Isaiah is about the coming of God's Jubilee, which would entail the release of the Israelites from oppression.

- When Jesus says in the Nazareth synagogue "today this scripture has been fulfilled in your hearing" (Luke 4:21), what does he mean?

If Isaiah 61 is a prophecy about God's Jubilee, then Jesus would be saying that he himself has come to inaugurate that Jubilee. In other words, in his own ministry, he would be accomplishing the things that God's Jubilee entailed. Jesus would be setting people free, and preaching good news to the poor, and healing blind people. Now, some of this stuff Jesus actually did on a physical level—he actually, literally, healed some blind people. But I'm not aware that Jesus literally released anyone from captivity. That might be why John the Baptist thought he'd ask whether Jesus really was the one who was to come (Luke 7:18–19), since John himself had not been released from captivity. So I presume that we're supposed to understand some of these things spiritually or figuratively. It is interesting that Jesus describes one of his healings in terms of setting someone free from bondage to Satan (Luke 13:16). Ultimately the idea of God's Jubilee points toward the spiritual blessings available through the death of Jesus. Not all of that was fulfilled while Jesus was sitting in that Nazareth synagogue, but there was a beginning.

- Compare the response of the Nazareth crowd in Luke 4:22–30 to the way Mark tells the story (Mark 6:1–6). What similarities and differences do you see?

The story in Mark makes the crowd seem more uniformly negative. The crowd in Luke seems at first to be somewhat positive, or perhaps only passive aggressive, before they become straightforwardly aggressive. In both accounts, Jesus mentions the proverb about prophets in their hometown (Mark 6:4; Luke 4:24), in both the crowd mentions Jesus' family (Mark 6:3; Luke 4:22), in both Jesus does not perform any miracles (Mark 6:5; Luke 4:23). Mark actually says that the crowd took offense at Jesus (6:3) because of his teaching in the synagogue (6:2), and Mark attributes the lack of miracles in Nazareth to the unbelief of the people (6:5–6; cf. Matt 13:58). Mark does not tell us that the hometown folks tried to kill Jesus.

- What point is Jesus trying to make by mentioning Elijah (1 Kings 17) and Elisha (2 Kings 5)?

Jesus is talking about how the Old Testament scriptures attest to God's care for non-Israelites. Elijah cared for a widow in the gentile town of Zarephath, and Elisha healed Naaman, from the country of Aram. Jesus says there were plenty of widows in Israel that Elijah could have helped, and there were plenty of lepers in Israel that Elisha could have healed, but they both transmitted

God's grace to non-Israelites. The point is that God's grace does not come to people based on their bloodline but based on their faith.

- Why do the people in Nazareth get so mad at Jesus? Does Jesus intentionally provoke them?

I do think Jesus intentionally provoked them. Not that he was necessarily wanting them to reject him, but he didn't want a lukewarm reaction, because that wouldn't have done him or them any good. He wanted to provoke a clear choice: with me or against me. This isn't the only time Jesus did something like that: there's a similar thing in John 6 when Jesus was talking about eating his flesh and drinking his blood, and the people that were just hanging around looking for a meal didn't want to hear it anymore and left (John 6:60). It does seem a little strange that these synagogue-goers in Nazareth tried to kill Jesus, but since his ministry ends in death, it is appropriate that it begins with attempted murder.

Chapter 5: In the Home of a Pharisee

- Is it surprising that Jesus would eat with a Pharisee (Luke 7:36)? Is it surprising that a Pharisee would ask Jesus over for a meal? The same thing happens later in Luke (11:37; 14:1). Why do you think Simon the Pharisee wanted to have a meal with Jesus?

I discuss this in detail on p. 116–118. I think that for most readers today it is surprising that Jesus would have a meal with a Pharisee, and that a Pharisee would invite Jesus to a meal. We usually think of the Pharisees as altogether evil, forgetting that no group, and no person, is altogether evil. There are a couple of possibilities for why Simon might want to have a meal with Jesus.

Maybe he wanted to trap him in some way. That sometimes happens with Pharisees in the Gospels. But maybe Simon genuinely wanted to get to know Jesus, to see for himself whether he was a liar or a lunatic or Lord. We have the comparable example of Nicodemus (John 3) to show that sometimes Pharisees were not completely closed off to the message of Jesus.

- A woman interrupts the meal. Who is she, and what does she do? Why do you think she does that?

Luke does not tell us who this woman is, except that she is a sinner. As I discuss in the chapter, the reference to her being a "sinner" does not really narrow down the possibilities. Maybe she was a prostitute, maybe not. Most sinners in the Gospels are Gentiles or tax collectors or rich oppressors of the poor. Maybe she was one of those.

Anyway, what the woman did was start weeping at Jesus' feet, drying his feet with her hair, and anointing them with perfume of some kind. She says she was doing that to express her love because of her forgiveness. I interpret that to mean that Jesus has already encountered this lady before and pronounced forgiveness on her (in a story not narrated by Luke), and now she has found Jesus because she wants to express her appreciation again.

- Imagine you were hosting this dinner party on your back porch. How would you respond to this woman's actions? How would your response compare to the response by Simon?

People can answer this question for themselves, but I think most people I know would react something like the way Simon did, at least in expressing annoyance that this woman has come in, and perhaps surprise that Jesus would let this scene go on, as if he didn't care about the nice dinner party prepared for him. (See similarly Luke 10:38–42).

- What does Jesus' response to the woman and to Simon indicate about how he views these two people?

It seems to me that Jesus views them both equally, but that the woman has expressed greater love than Simon has. Jesus is unconcerned about any difference in social strata—and, again, we don't know whether the woman would be from a higher social stratum than Simon or not—or background, he's only concerned with how they respond to the call. This sinful woman has responded, and Simon is (at best) still thinking about it.

- Why do you think Luke includes this story in his Gospel? What does he want his readers to know about Jesus? What does he want his readers to know about discipleship?

Luke wants his readers to see themselves in this story, whether as the forgiven woman or as the doubtful Simon. Luke wants his readers to understand that Jesus welcomes sinners, and he expects people to recognize their own sinfulness, and to turn away from it. He wants people to live lives of faith (7:50). Discipleship involves expressing love and thankfulness to God, in assurance that he has granted forgiveness.

Chapter 6: The Good Samaritan

- Jesus gets the same question twice in Luke's Gospel, about inheriting eternal life, once from a lawyer (10:25) and once from the rich young ruler (18:18). How does Jesus respond each time?

Both times he refers to the Law of Moses as explaining the correct way to have life with God. Actually, the first time, he asks the lawyer what he read in the Law, and the lawyer provided the answer, which we know from elsewhere (Matt 22:34–40) as the two greatest commandments. The second time, Jesus started naming off to the Rich Young Ruler some of the Ten Commandments. The Rich Young Ruler said that he had kept these commandments, and he probably had, at least according to the bare letter of the commandment (he probably had not murdered anyone, or slept with another man's wife, etc.). But, of course, Jesus interprets the Ten Commandments as more all-encompassing than the bare letter would indicate. The command against murder also prohibits the anger that leads to murder; the commandment against adultery also prohibits the lust that precedes the adultery (cf. Matt 5:21–28). For Jesus, the Ten Commandments were not about discrete aspects of one's life, but about the entirety of life. And so he told the Rich Young Ruler that he still needed to do one more thing: give up his entire life for God. That is, essentially, what the two greatest commands also require. The way to inherit eternal life is to give up your life (cf. Luke 9:24).

- What do you think Luke means that the lawyer was "wanting to justify himself" (10:29)?

I think what that means is that the lawyer was hoping (and assuming) that Jesus would express an opinion that confirmed the lawyer's own bias. This idea implies that the lawyer thought of Jesus as some sort of authority. Perhaps the lawyer questioned Jesus because he wanted to "test" him (Luke 10:25), not that he wanted to trap Jesus, but he wanted to see if this reputed prophet knew anything about the Law. So he gave him a test: tell me how to inherit eternal life. Of course, Jesus turned it back around on him, but then Jesus ended up agreeing with the lawyer. Maybe at that point the lawyer's view of Jesus rose somewhat. And then he wanted Jesus to confirm that he also thinks like the lawyer that the commandment in Lev 19:18 does not really apply outside a select group of "neighbors." He wanted to justify his own practice.

- In the parable told by Jesus, the priest and the Levite do not help the wounded man. Can you imagine some ways that they might "justify themselves" in not helping?

Some people suggest that they might not have wanted to defile themselves with a dead body, if they thought the guy was dead. I guess that's possible. In the chapter above, I suggest that they just had too much to do and thought they didn't have time to stop and help someone they didn't know anyway. Shouldn't that be someone else's responsibility? Where is his family or friends? After all, the priest and Levite have really important jobs that not everyone can do, but anyone could stop and help this guy. Better someone do that who doesn't have the kind of burden that priests and Levites carry! Oh, there are all kinds of ways we can justify ignoring others.

- How would you describe the actions of the Samaritan toward the wounded man? Is this the way religious people normally behave? Is that the way you would behave in a similar situation?

I'll let you answer whether you would behave like the Samaritan. I will say that I think the Samaritan's actions are extravagant, not normal. I don't at all mean to say that we shouldn't imitate the Samaritan; I just mean that I don't typically see people imitating him.

- What sorts of sacrifices did the Samaritan make on behalf of the wounded man? Which of these sacrifices do you find most difficult to replicate in your own life?

The two main kinds of sacrifices I think of are time and money, both of which are very precious to most people. It is especially hard for me to sacrifice time. I'd much rather write a check to something than spend a day or more helping out with some project. I think we could say that the Samaritan also sacrificed in terms of culture or ethnicity or whatever. He was helping a man who under normal circumstances may very well hate this Samaritan or try to do him harm, and the Samaritan may have felt the same way. The Samaritan may even have suffered repercussions back home if word got out what he did for a Jew.

Chapter 7: The Prodigal Son

- What do you think you would do if one of your children said to you what the prodigal son says to his father in Luke 15:12? What do you think about the father's response in this parable?

I think what the prodigal says to his father in v. 12 is very disrespectful, and if I were the father, there is no way I'd give in to his request. I do believe that the father in this parable represents God (at least in some ways), but I don't think we have to take his response in v. 12—dividing up his estate so that his younger son could get an early inheritance—as the "godly" thing to do in that situation. In fact, I think it is a rather foolish thing to do. On the other hand, you could say it is generous (in a foolish kind of way), and our God is generous. But mostly I think this part of the parable is just the set-up for the main part of the parable, which is the repentance of the younger son, the joyful response of the father, and the final encounter between the father and the elder brother.

- This son becomes "prodigal" (= "wasteful," "reckless") when he goes to the Far Country (Luke 15:13). What do you think are the attractions of the Far Country? What are the dangers?

The Far Country is attractive precisely because it is far; it's nowhere close to your family, your church, anyone who knows you. And if you're wanting to engage in some riotous living, you want to do it in the Far Country where your family can't see you. The dangers of the Far Country are that you're nowhere near your family, that is, the dangers are the same as the attractions. If anything goes wrong in the Far Country—and, again, the whole reason you go to the Far Country is to do some wrong things—then you'll be nowhere near anyone who cares. And when you engage in riotous living in the Far Country, you're usually hanging out with people who are pretty shady characters. It's a recipe for disaster.

- What does the prodigal son teach us about repentance (Luke 15:17–21)?

There are two ways of looking at the repentance of the prodigal son: either it was genuine or it wasn't. Either way, it teaches what repentance ought to look like, and even the ambiguity about whether it was genuine repentance teaches us that often we can't really tell for sure whether someone else's repentance is genuine, and sometimes we can't even tell it about ourselves. But what he says to his father, or what he tries to say, is exactly what someone in that situation ought to say. You've got to get over your pride, over the fear of what everyone will say when you finally admit that you were wrong, that you blew all the money. You've got to know that people are going to be wondering what you were up to in the Far Country, or they'll already have a pretty good idea. And you've got to suck it up and do it. It's hard. Well, it's actually a lot easier than what you fear.

- What is the false idea about his role within the family that the older brother has (Luke 15:25–30)?

The older brother thinks he's a slave when he's actually a son. Or, at least, that's the way he feels. Or, at least, in this moment, that's the accusation he lobs at his father, since he's so upset that his father so quickly welcomed back this prodigal son. But the older son doesn't think he has access to the goods of the estate. He doesn't realize that he basically owns it all. There's a disconnect between the father and the older son, which results in the father being joyful and the son being angry.

- What do you think about the father's response to both brothers? What do those responses tell us about the father?

Jesus says that when the father saw his younger boy returning, he "was filled with compassion" (v. 20). That emotion characterizes the father's response to both sons. With the return of the younger son, the father's compassion leads also to joy. With the anger of the older son, the father's compassion prevents him from volleying insults in return for the insults he receives. Instead, he's just confused at why his son is so angry, and why he seems to think he can't eat whatever he wants, and why he thinks his life is so hard. In both situations, the father is fully ready to be reconciled to the estranged son.

Chapter 8: Two Parables about Money

- In the Parable of the Dishonest Steward (Luke 16:1–9), what is the steward's problem and what is his plan to fix his problem?

The steward's problem is that he was fired from his position for squandering his master's wealth. His plan to fix that problem is a little hard to work out. My guess is that he intended to use his position to do favors for some important clients of his master's so that these clients would then be in the debt of this steward. In that way, they would "welcome him into their homes," maybe meaning that they might offer him a job, or maybe welcome him into their social circles and introduce him to people who might give him a job.

- Do you think Jesus wants us to admire the dishonest steward? Are we supposed to imitate him? If so, how should we imitate him? If we are not supposed to imitate him, why does Jesus tell the parable?

It does seem to me that Jesus wants us to imitate—maybe not admire—the dishonest steward in some way. Jesus says we should make friends with the mammon of unrighteousness (v. 9), which is what the steward was doing. I think the steward is probably just a memorable example of someone who uses money to "make friends." I don't think that Jesus necessarily means that we should imitate the steward in the way he went about making friends, and certainly not in his dishonesty. The point, I think, is that we should use the money available to us to help others.

- How does the teaching of Jesus in Luke 16:10–15 relate to the Parable of the Dishonest Steward?

Jesus is teaching more explicitly in vv. 10–15 what the story was supposed to illustrate. People are stewards who are liable to be fired from their position if they don't use the money of their Master appropriately. Using this money that is not our own is a "very little thing" (v. 10), but it does show whether we are worthy to be given more responsibility (in the kingdom of God, I suppose).

- In the Parable of the Rich Man and Lazarus (Luke 16:19–31), what point is Jesus making about money?

Again, money should be used for others, such as Lazarus. The way Abraham words his rebuke of the rich man in v. 25, it sounds like his problem is simply that he had wealth. But reading the entire parable and putting it in the context of the entire Gospel suggests to me that the problem with the rich man's money is not so much that he had it but rather how he used it. He "was dressed in purple and fine linen and feasted sumptuously every day" (v. 19). He used his money—which (we have already seen) really belongs to Another—on himself, for his own enjoyment. Jesus thinks we ought to use our money for others.

- Why does the rich man want Lazarus to talk to his brothers? What does he want Lazarus to tell them?

The rich man wants Lazarus to go to his brothers "that he may warn them, so that they will not also come into this place of torment" (v. 28). He wants Lazarus to assure the brothers that there really is an afterlife, and your eternal destiny really is based on your behavior in your first life. And he wants them to repent (v. 30). He wants them not to act the way he did, spending all on himself and not on others. The idea is very reminiscent of Jacob Marley visiting Scrooge.

Chapter 9: Two Tax Collectors

- In the story of the Pharisee and Tax Collector (18:9–14), why does Jesus choose to talk about a Pharisee? What did people think about the Pharisees in the time of Jesus? What is the problem with the prayer that Jesus represents this Pharisee as praying?

Jesus chooses a Pharisee for his story because the Pharisees were known for their great piety. People had great respect for the Pharisees. The problem with the Pharisees' prayer (18:11–12) was that it demonstrated that this Pharisee "trusted in himself that he was righteous and regarded others with contempt" (v. 9). He exalted himself in his prayer (v. 14).

- Why does Jesus choose a tax collector for his parable? What did people think about tax collectors? In what way is this particular tax collector an example for others?

Jesus chooses a tax collector because tax collectors were well known for practicing a form of extortion, and for ignoring the Torah requirements about both charity and purity. People thought of tax collectors as big sinners (and they were pretty much right). This is especially clear in Matt 5:46; 18:17.

- People grumble at Jesus in Luke 15:2 and 19:7. Why are they grumbling?

It's the same reason both times: Jesus hangs out with sinners—specifically, tax collectors. Since tax collectors were known sinners, it makes sense that religious people would feel uneasy about associating with them, if that association would imply some sort of approval of their sin. (I say this line of thinking makes sense; I didn't say it was a good line of thinking.) But, of course, these people are wanting to hang out with Jesus, which implies that they're looking for something different in their lives, that they might be open to repentance. Certainly that is the case with Zacchaeus, whose story appears in Luke specifically to provide an example of a repentant sinner. The challenge for us is to open ourselves up to conversations with people who need to repent, to encourage their repentance without pressing too hard, and to avoid grumbling about others when they go about these things differently from the way we think appropriate.

- What is similar about the example of Zacchaeus and that of the tax collector in 18:9–14?

Both Zacchaeus and the tax collector in Jesus' parable needed to repent and did. They both provide examples of repentance. The tax collector in the parable prayed for God's mercy. That's not the whole of repentance, but it is a part. Zacchaeus shows us another aspect: restitution for wrongs done, and sacrifice on behalf of others, which is the lifestyle to which God calls all people.

- Zacchaeus, the "chief tax collector" (19:2), is obviously very rich. Compare his response to Jesus to that of the rich man in 18:18–23.

The Rich Young Ruler apparently did not change his life (though we actually don't know how his life turned out). He was righteous, like the Pharisee in 18:11–12, and so Jesus challenged him to increase in his faith even further. On the other hand, Zacchaeus had been a sinner, actively and willfully disregarding the commandments of God, and his encounter with Jesus led to a radical life change.

Chapter 10: The Future According to Jesus

- What do you think Jesus means that "the kingdom of God is among you" (Luke 17:21)?

I think he meant not that the kingdom of God is inside you, but that it is being revealed "among you," that Jesus himself is bringing about the kingdom of God within the world, through his ministry (his teaching, his healings, his miracles).

In Luke 13:28–29, Jesus speaks about the kingdom of God as something that people will experience in the future. Is the kingdom of God future or already present?

This is one of the great theological questions. The answer I prefer is "both." The kingdom is already inaugurated through the ministry of Jesus, but the kingdom is not yet consummated, not yet brought to completion. There are still enemies to defeat. We await the moment when every knee bows and every tongue confesses Jesus as Lord.

- In Luke 17:22–37, Jesus talks about "the day that the Son of Man is revealed" (verse 30). What day is he talking about?

As strange as it sounds, I think he's talking about AD 70 and the destruction of Jerusalem. In that destruction, the Son of Man is revealed, vindicated, since Jesus had predicted the temple's destruction and it was the temple leadership that had pushed for Jesus' execution.

- In Luke 21:5–38, Jesus talks about future signs. What will these signs indicate? How does this discourse relate to what Jesus was talking about in Luke 17:20–21?

Jesus uses the word "signs" at 21:11, 25. Again, I think Jesus is warning his disciples about the coming destruction of Jerusalem. It will be a time of vindication for Jesus (as I mentioned above, under the third question), and therefore it will show that in Jesus the kingdom of God truly was "among you."

- At Luke 21:27, Jesus says that the Son of Man will come in a cloud with power and great glory? Is he talking about his Second Coming or about something else?

If I had to guess, I would say he is not talking about his Second Coming but about something else, specifically the destruction of Jerusalem and of the temple. The case for this interpretation is made especially by looking at Dan 7:13–14 and noticing how the Son of Man receives the kingdom by "coming" to heaven, not from heaven. So, in other words, I think what Jesus means is that the destruction of the temple will be the visible manifestation of Jesus' invisible ascension to the throne in heaven. Once everyone sees the temple destroyed, that will show that Jesus was right and that he is now king, reigning in heaven.

Chapter 11: The Final Hours of Jesus

- Luke's account of the Lord's Supper (22:14–23) is a bit different from that of Matthew (26:26–30) and Mark (14:22–25). What differences do you notice? Why do you think Luke writes it up the way he does?

The biggest difference is that Luke has an extra cup. Matthew and Mark both have a very similar account, with the order being bread-cup. Luke's account has cup-bread-cup. But the first cup is not really a part of the Lord's Supper, apparently; at least, Jesus doesn't say "this is my blood" or anything like that. That kind of language only comes with the bread and the second cup. Why does Luke include this first cup, then? I don't know. I suppose it emphasizes that they are doing this in the context of a meal, the Passover meal. Traditionally there are four cups of wine at the Passover meal.

- Jesus tells his disciples that they're going to "eat and drink at my table in my kingdom" and "sit on thrones judging the twelve tribes of Israel" (Luke 22:30). What is he talking about? What do you think is going through the minds of the disciples?

To go to the second question first, I think the disciples assume that their hopes are about to be fulfilled. They're going to battle the Romans, and God is going to fight on their side, just like in the stories they heard about the ancient Israelites conquering Canaan and David winning his battles. When they drive the Romans out of their ancestral land, Jesus will reign as king on David's throne and the disciples themselves will assist Jesus in his rule. They also will sit on thrones. All the lost children of Israel will return to their homeland, as the ancient prophets foretold.

Of course, none of that happens, and that's not what Jesus is talking about. I do think he is referencing those prophecies, but he's interpreting them in a different way. Israel is reconstituted as his own followers; these followers represent the ingathering of the lost tribes. Feasting in the kingdom may refer metaphorically to the situation in the church, but it may also be something that we look forward to. Same thing for the twelve thrones. I'm not sure if we're supposed to understand that as something happening right now or something that will happen in the hereafter. Most likely, both.

- What does Satan "demand" (Luke 22:31)? From whom does he demand it? Is Satan granted his demand?

Satan demands to sift the apostles, just as he had earlier demanded to afflict Job. It must be God from whom Satan makes this demand, which shows Satan's subordinate position to God. But I think God grants Satan's request; Satan can sift the apostles like wheat. That might be a little disconcerting for us, to know that God sometimes allows Satan that kind of power over us. Then again, Jesus says that he prayed for Peter, and we also know that he intercedes on our behalf (Rom 8:34).

- Why does Jesus want the disciples to have swords (Luke 22:36)?

In the chapter, I suggest that he wanted the disciples to look like bandits in order to ensure that he would be arrested and suffer crucifixion, which was the plan of God. In this way, he would be counted among the lawless (Luke 22:37), thus fulfilling the role of the Servant of the Lord (Isa 53:12).

- Luke's account of Gethsemane (22:39–46) is a bit different from that of Matthew (26:36–46) and Mark (14:32–42). What differences do you notice? Why do you think Luke writes it up this way?

Luke compresses the narrative. He does not mention that Jesus separates Peter, James, and John from the other disciples (as Matthew and Mark do), and he does not report that Jesus said his prayer three times. Luke simply wants to say that Jesus did not look forward to his own death, wanted a way out, but was ultimately and completely obedient to the will of the Father, and Luke wanted to show that the disciples still were not aware of what would happen.

Chapter 12: The Death of Jesus

- When Jesus is arrested (Luke 22:47–53) and tried before the Sanhedrin (22:63–71), what charge against Jesus does the council find worthy of a death sentence?

The trial produces the charge that Jesus (sort of) claims to be "the Son of God" (22:70), which is a messianic title. That is the charge that they bring to Pilate: he says "that he himself is the Messiah, a king" (23:2). Such a charge, if proven true, would be considered treasonous and therefore worthy of execution according to Roman law.

- What ends up being the charge against Jesus for which Pilate crucified him? (Luke 23:1–25)

Pilate is not at all convinced that Jesus is guilty of treason, but that is the charge of which Jesus is convicted. The inscription over Jesus on the cross displayed his crime: "The King of the Jews" (23:38).[1] That mocking accusation was intended to show what happens to so-called kings who defy the power of Caesar.

- While on the cross (Luke 23:32–49), Jesus says three things. What are these three sayings from the cross? Compare these sayings to what Jesus says from the cross in the other Gospels.

We sometimes talk about the Seven Sayings from the Cross, which adds up all the sayings across the four Gospels. Matthew and Mark both report the single saying, "My God, My God, why have you forsaken me," a quotation of Psalm 22:1. That's the only thing Jesus says from the cross in Matthew and Mark. But Luke and John both report three different sayings each.

John's sayings are:

*Woman, here is your son ... here is your mother. (19:26–27)

*I am thirsty. (19:28)

*It is finished. (19:30)

---

[1] For ancient evidence for such inscriptions announcing the causes for the crucifixion, see Chapman and Schnabel, *Trial and Crucifixion*, 292–98.

Luke's sayings are:

*Father, forgive them for they do not know what they are doing. (23:34)

*Truly I tell you, today you will be with me in Paradise. (23:43)

*Father, into your hands I commend my spirit. (23:46)

- How does the criminal on the cross (Luke 23:39–43) provide a better example of discipleship than some others that probably spent more time with Jesus? How do you think this criminal knew about Jesus?

I have long been curious about this criminal on the cross. How does he know what no one else seems to know—that the cross does not spell the end of Jesus, but that Jesus will still be establishing a kingdom even though he is dying on a cross? I suspect that the criminal is himself dying on a cross because of his hope for the kingdom of God. That is, I suspect that he was convicted of treason himself, but—unlike Jesus—he was actually guilty, just like Barabbas (23:19). I imagine that this criminal was involved in some sort of armed revolt against Roman authority (probably the same revolt that Barabbas himself has participated in), and that this criminal participated in the revolt because he hoped that by such means God might establish his kingdom. That is, I think this criminal probably had the same sort of understanding of God's activity as did Peter, who also seemed to think that God's kingdom would be established through the violent overthrow of the Romans. But somehow the criminal, in his last moments, sees clearly that the kingdom is coming through the death of Jesus. Perhaps he had heard some of Jesus' predictions of his own death, and he now sees it coming true before his eyes? At any rate, his insight into the true activities of

God provides an example of discipleship superior to that of the disciples.

- What strange things happen at the death of Jesus, as reported by Luke (23:44–49)

There is darkness (v. 44), the curtain of the temple tears (v. 45), and a Roman centurion praises God and pronounces Jesus innocent (v. 47). These same elements are reported in Matthew (27:45, 51, 54) and Mark (15:33, 38–39). The interpretation of these things is disputed. I think we should probably interpret the darkness (not as God turning away from Jesus, as I have heard suggested, but) in light of Jesus' statement at his arrest that this is the time for the power of darkness (22:53). We could either say that the Crucifixion is the time when the darkness seemed to have won, or—if we want to say that God causes the darkness— that the darkness is a sign that God is going to bring judgment (think: ninth plague; Exod 10:21–29) upon those who have rejected the last and greatest prophet. Remember what Jesus said was the point of the Parable of the Tenants (20:9–18).

As for the tearing of the curtain in the temple, the curtain that marked the barrier between the Holy Place and the Most Holy Place, we have two options, and they might both be right: it might mean that God is not limited to the Most Holy Place (which was supposed to be his special habitation), or it might symbolize our own access to the Most Holy Place (which was supposed to be restricted to only the High Priest and only once per year). Of course, Jesus himself entered the Most Holy Place now with his own blood (Heb 9:12).

As for the centurion, his statement coheres with other statements about Jesus' innocence here in Luke's Gospel (23:4, 14–15, 22, 41). How did the centurion know? Luke says, "when he saw what had taken place," he pronounced Jesus innocent. In the immediate context, in terms of what Luke narrates, the only thing I think the centurion would have seen would be the darkness. He might very well interpret the darkness as a sign from God (or the gods?) that this particular crucifixion was a miscarriage of justice, because this man was not guilty of the crimes of which he was accused.

Chapter 13: All Things New

- As you read Luke 24, what do you make of Jesus' body? Is it the same body he had in the first 23 chapters of Luke? What's different about it?

It is the same body. That's the point of the empty tomb, and the scene with the disciples (vv. 36–43). But it also seems different. It can disappear (v. 31). The Emmaus disciples failed to recognize him (but see v. 16). And it seems he can appear in rooms (v. 36). It is the same body, but it seems altered somehow. It is a transformed body, a model for the kinds of bodies we will all someday have (1 Cor 15:35–57).

- What had the travelers to Emmaus been hoping for prior to the Crucifixion?

They tell us in v. 21—they had been anticipating the redemption of Israel. They probably have in mind a physical redemption, just like when God redeemed Israel form the power of Egypt. The Emmaus travelers probably wanted Jesus, as Messiah, the son of David, to redeem Israel from the oppression of Rome.

- What does Jesus say in this chapter about the connection between the Old Testament and his own death and Resurrection? Why do you think his followers did not understand that connection?

Jesus says that the Old Testament talks about the Messiah in terms of suffering, death, and resurrection (vv. 26–27, 44–46). Luke does not tell us the passages that Jesus explained, but probably he would have pointed to Psalm 16 (as did Peter in Acts 2) and maybe Psalm 110:1, as does much of the New Testament. I think the disciples had some trouble with this way of looking at the Old Testament because it does not seem very obvious. It almost takes a teacher to explain it to you (cf. Acts 8:30–31).

- Do you think it is significant that it was at the breaking of the bread that the travelers recognized Jesus (Luke 24:30–31, 35)? Does Luke want his readers to grasp anything in particular from that occurrence?

Yes, it must be significant. I do think Luke is telling this story not only because it happened but also because he thinks it provides a nice model for our own experiences. We also have trouble recognizing Jesus, but there are certain times that we gain a glimpse of him. The way Luke tells the story of the meal sounds like a description of the Lord's Supper, and Luke probably intends for his readers to understand that worship is one of those moments in which we are especially hoping for—and often receive—a fleeting glimpse of our Savior.

- What are the final instructions Jesus gives to his disciples?

Luke's version of the Great Commission is in 24:47–49 (the more familiar version is Matt 28:18–20). The apostles are supposed to announce to the Gentiles about God's offer of forgiveness on the condition of their repentance. And he tells them to expect "what my Father promised," when they will be "clothed with power from on high" (v. 49). These latter promises are fulfilled in Acts 2.

Appendix C: Color-Coded Synopsis

Material unique to Luke
Material shared among all three Synoptic Gospels
Material very similar to material found in Mark and Matthew
Material shared with Matthew
Material very similar to material in Matthew
Material shared with Mark

	Luke	Mark	Matthew
Preface	1:1–4	--	--
Birth announcement: John the Baptist	1:5–25	--	--
Birth announcement: Jesus	1:26–38	--	(1:18–25)

Mary visits Elizabeth	1:39–45	--	--
Magnificat	1:46–46	--	--
Birth and naming of John	1:57–66	--	--
Zechariah's prophecy	1:67–80	--	--
Birth of Jesus	2:1–7	--	--
Appearance to Shepherds	2:8–20	--	--
Purification at Temple	2:21–24	--	--
Simeon	2:25–35	--	--
Anna	2:36–38	--	--
Return to Nazareth	2:39–40	--	(2:19–23)
Lost at Passover	2:41–52	--	--
Time stamp	3:1–2	--	--
John the Baptist[1]	3:3–6	1:3–4	3:1–3
John's warning	3:7–9	--	3:7–10

[1] Luke fails to mention John's clothing and food.

John's advice	3:10–14	--	--
John on the Messiah	3:15–18	1:7–8	3:11–12
	Messiah's baptism, 3:16	1:7–8	3:11
	Messiah's shovel, 3:17	--	3:12
John jailed	3:19–20	(6:17)	(14:3)
Jesus baptized	3:21–22	1:9–11	3:13–17
Jesus' genealogy	3:23–38	--	(1:2–16)
Temptations	4:1–13	(1:12–13)	4:1–11
Teaching summary	4:14–15	(1:14–15)	(4:12–17 or 23–25)
Nazareth synagogue	4:16–30	(6:1–6)	(13:53–58)
	saying: prophet unwelcome, 4:24	6:4	13:57
Exorcism in Capernaum synagogue	4:31–37	1:21–28	(7:28–29)

Healing Simon's mother-in-law	4:38–39	1:29–31	8:14–15
many coming for healing	4:40–41	1:32–34	8:16–17
escape to be alone, tracked down	4:42–44	1:34–39	--
Call of first disciples	5:1–11	(1:16–20)	(4:18–22)
man with leprosy[2]	5:12–16	1:40–45	8:1–4
paralytic	5:17–26	2:1–12	9:1–8
call of Levi	5:27–28	2:13–14	9:9
eating with sinners	5:29–32	2:15–17	9:10–13
fasting question	5:33–39	2:18–22	9:14–17
Sabbath: heads of grain	6:1–5	2:23–28	12:1–8
Sabbath: withered hand	6:6–11	3:1–6	12:9–14
appointing twelve[3]	6:12–16	3:13–19	(10:1–4)

---

[2] Note how Luke inserts prayer at the end of the pericope.
[3] Luke inserts prayer.

summary: healing, exorcism	6:17–19	3:7–12	4:23–25
sermon on the plain	6:20–49	--	(chs. 5–7)
	beatitudes, 6:20–23	--	(5:3–12)
	woes, 6:24–26	--	--
	love your enemies, 6:27–30	--	(5:44, 39, 40, 42)
	Golden Rule, 6:31	--	7:12
	Be nice to mean people, 6:32–36	--	(5:46–47)
	Don't judge, 6:37	--	(7:1–2; 6:14–15)
	Give and you will receive, 6:38	--	--
	Blind guides, 6:39	--	15:14

	disciple not greater than teacher, 6:40	--	10:24
	log & splinter, 6:41–42	--	7:3–5
	trees & fruit, 6:43–45	--	(7:16–18)
	Two builders, 6:46–49	--	7:24–27
centurion's servant	7:1–10	--	8:5–13
widow of Nain	7:11–17	--	--
question from JB	7:18–23	--	11:2–6
Jesus praises JB	7:24–28	--	11:7–11
response of crowd	7:29–30	--	--
this fickle generation	7:31–35	--	11:16–19
at the home of Simon the Pharisee	7:36–50	(see Simon the leper, 14:3–9)	(see Simon the leper, 26:6–13)
women patrons	8:1–3	(15:40–41)	(27:55–56)

Parable of soils	8:4–15	4:1–20	13:1–23
lamp on a lampstand	8:16–17	4:21–23	(5:15; 10:26)
measure for measure	8:18	4:24–25	(13:12; 25:29)
my mother and my brothers	8:19–21	3:31–35	12:46–50
stilling the storm	8:22–25	4:35–41	8:23–27
Legion	8:26–39	5:1–20	8:28–34
Jairus' daughter/woman with hemorrhage	8:40–56	5:21–43	9:18–26
Limited commission	9:1–6	6:7–13	10
Herod's curiosity[4]	9:7–9	6:14–16	14:1–2
Feeding 5000	9:10–17	6:30–44	14:13–21
Peter's confession	9:18–21	8:27–30	16:13–20
1st Passion Prediction	9:22	8:31–33	16:21–23

[4] Luke does not tell the story of the death of John the Baptist; he merely alludes to it here. There is no Herodias or Salome.

Take your cross	9:23–27	8:34–9:1	16:24–28
Transfiguration	9:28–36	9:2–8	17:1–8
Demon-possessed boy	9:37–43	9:14–29	17:14–20
2nd Passion Prediction	9:43–45	9:30–32	17:22–23
Who is greatest?	9:46–48	9:33–37	18:1–5
non-disciple exorcist	9:49–50	9:38–40	--
Setting out for Jerusalem	9:51–56	--	--
discipleship is demanding	9:57–62	--	8:18–22
Sending 72	10:1	--	--
	Pray to the Lord of the harvest, 10:2	--	9:37–38
	lambs among wolves, 10:3	--	10:16
	no supplies, 10:4, cf. 9:3	--	--

	peace on the house, 10:5–6	--	10:12–13
	remain in the house, 10:7	--	--
	village welcomes you, 10:8	--	10:11
	heal, preach, 10:9	--	10:8
	village does not welcome you, 10:10–12	--	10:14–15
woe, Chorazin, Bethsaida	10:13–15	--	11:20–24
who welcomes you welcomes me	10:16 (cf. 9:48)	(9:37)	10:40
Return of the 72	10:17–20	--	--
Father reveals to babies	10:21–22	--	11:25–27
Happy your eyes	10:23–24	--	13:16–17
Question about Loving Neighbor	10:25–29	(12:28–34)	(22:34–40)

Good Samaritan	10:30–37	--	--
Mary & Martha	10:38–42	--	--
Lord's prayer	11:1–4	--	6:9–13
Parable: audacity in prayer	11:5–8	--	--
Ask and receive	11:9–10	--	7:7–8
Heavenly Father responds to requests	11:11–13	--	7:9–11
accusations of demon possession	11:14–18	3:22–26	12:22–26
your children are exorcists	11:19	--	12:27
power of God	11:20	--	12:28
strong man's house	11:21–22	3:27	12:29
who isn't with me is against me	11:23	--	12:30
wandering spirit returns home	11:23–26	--	12:43–45
Blessing on Jesus' mother	11:27–28	--	--

sign of Jonah	11:29–30	(8:11–13)	12:39–40
greater than Solomon/Jonah	11:31–32	--	12:41–42
eye important	11:33–36	--	6:22–23
meal with Pharisee	11:37	--	--
eating with unwashed hands	11:38–41	--	23:25–26
over-emphasis on tithing	11:42	--	23:23
Pharisees enjoy best seats	11:43	--	23:6–7
unmarked graves	11:44	--	(23:27)
scribes: loading men down	11:45–46	--	23:4
killing the prophets	11:47–51	--	23:29–36
key of knowledge	11:52	--	(23:13)
resentment by scribes & Pharisees	11:53–54	(12:13)	(22:15)
Yeast of Pharisees	12:1	8:15	16:6

secrets revealed	12:2–3 (cf. 8:16–18)	--	10:26–27
Fear not one able to kill body	12:4–5	--	10:28
value of sparrows	12:6–7	--	10:29–31
Confessing Son of Man	12:8–9	--	10:32–33
Blasphemy of H.S.	12:10	3:28–30	12:31–32
Apologia given by H.S.	12:11–12	(13:11)	10:19–20
Divide inheritance	12:13–14	--	--
Parable: Rich Fool	12:15–21	--	--
Don't worry	12:22–31	--	6:25–34
Don't fear, little flock	12:32	--	--
Sell all possessions	12:33	--	--
Where your treasure is	12:34	--	6:21
Master serves servants	12:35–38	--	--

anticipating a thief	12:39–40	--	24:43–44
lazy & wicked servants	12:41–46	--	24:45–51
degrees of punishment	12:47–48	--	--
Not peace but a sword	12:49–53	--	10:34–36
Signs of the times	12:54–56	--	16:2–3
Make peace w/ accuser	12:57–59	--	(5:25–26)
Repent or die	13:1–5	--	--
Parable: cut the fig tree down next year	13:6–9	--	--
Healing in synagogue on Sabbath: bent over woman	13:10–17	--	--
Parable: mustard seed	13:18–19	4:30–32	13:31–32
Parable: yeast	13:20–21	--	13:33

Question: who will be saved?	13:22–23	--	--
Narrow gate	13:24	--	7:13
Some will be shut out	13:25–27	--	(7:21–23)
Eating with Abraham, Isaac, and Jacob, others cast out	13:28–29	--	8:11–12
First = last	13:30	10:31	19:30; 20:16
Herod = fox	13:31–33	--	--
Weeping for Jerusalem	13:34–35	--	23:37–39
Meal with Pharisee on a Sabbath— healing a swollen man	14:1–6	--	--
	fall into a ditch, 14:5		12:11
taking a bad seat	14:7–11	--	--

invite the poor to your banquet	14:12–15	--	--
parable: dinner party	14:16–24	--	(22:1–14)
Hate your family	14:25–26	--	10:37
Take up cross	14:27	--	10:38
counting the cost	14:28–33	--	--
Tasteless salt	14:34–35	(9:50)	5:13
Parable: lost sheep	15:1–7	--	(18:12–14)
Parable: lost coin	15:8–10	--	--
Parable: Prodigal Son	15:11–32	--	--
Parable: Unrighteous Steward	16:1–9	--	--
Faithful with little, faithful with a lot	16:10–12	--	(25:21, 23)
Can't serve two masters	16:13	--	6:24
Greedy Pharisees	16:14–15	--	--

L&P until JB, then God's kingdom	16:16	--	(11:12–13)
Heaven and earth will pass away before the Law	16:17	--	(5:18)
Defining adultery	16:18	10:11	5:31–32; 19:9
Parable: Rich Man & Lazarus	16:19–32	--	--
causing others to sin	17:1–2	9:42	18:6–7
forgive repeatedly	17:3–4	--	(18:21–22)
apostles want more faith	17:5	--	--
power of small faith	17:6	--	17:20
We are unprofitable servants	17:7–10	--	--
Grateful Samaritan	17:11–19	--	--
Kingdom is among you	17:20–21	--	--
You will long for the Son of Man	17:22	--	--

People will say, "look here"	17:23	13:21	24:23
Son of Man = lightening	17:24	--	24:27
3rd Passion Prediction[5]	17:25	--	--
End is like Noah	17:26–27	--	24:37–39
End is like Lot	17:28–30	--	--
Don't go get your stuff	17:31	13:15–16	24:17–18
Remember Lot's wife	17:32	--	--
Saver of life will lose it	17:33 (cf. 9:24)	--	10:39
2 in bed, 1 taken	17:34	--	--
2 grinding, 1 taken	17:35	--	24:41
where the vultures gather	17:37	--	24:28

---

[5] But see also the earlier statement that Jesus is going to Jerusalem because a prophet can die nowhere else (13:33).

parable: Persistent Widow	18:1–8	--	--
parable: Pharisee and publican	18:9–14	--	--
Allow the children	18:15–17	10:13–16	19:13–15
RYR	18:18–30	10:17–31	19:16–30
4th Passion Prediction	18:31–34	10:32–34	20:17–19
Blind man healed (Bartimaeus)[6]	18:35–43	10:46–52	20:29–34
Zacchaeus	19:1–10	--	--
Parable: minas	19:11–27	--	(25:14–30)
Triumphal Entry	19:28–40	11:1–11	21:1–11
Brief prediction of Jerusalem's destruction	19:41–44	--	--
Cleansing temple	19:45–46	11:15–19	21:12–17
Jesus vs. Leaders	19:47–48	--	--

---

[6] Named only in Mark.

Question: Authority	20:1–8	11:27–33	21:23–27
Parable: Tenants	20:9–19	12:1–12	21:33–46
Question: Taxes	20:20–26	12:13–17	22:15–22
Question: Resurrection	20:27–40	12:18–27	22:23–33
David's son?	20:41–44	12:35–37	22:41–46
Beware the scribes	20:45–47	12:38–40	(ch. 23)
Widow's mite	21:1–4	12:41–44	--
Temple destruction	21:5–33	13:1–31	24:1–35
Stay alert	21:34–36	--	--
Summary of Jesus' activities	21:37–38	--	--
Update on the plot against Jesus	22:1–2	14:1–2	26:3–5
Judas plot	22:3–6	14:10–12	26:14–16
Preparing for Passover	22:7–13	14:12–16	26:17–19
Lord's Supper	22:14–20	14:22–26	26:26–30

Prediction of Betrayal	22:21–23	14:17–21	26:20–25
Who is greatest?	22:24 (cf. 9:46)	--	--
Servant is greatest	22:25–27	10:42–45	20:25–28
Disciples granted royal power	22:28–29	--	--
Twelve thrones	22:30	--	19:28
Satan sifting Peter	22:31–32	--	--
Peter proclaims steadfastness	22:33–34	14:29–31	26:33–35
Get ready, and buy swords	22:35–38	--	--
Mount of Olives (Gethsemane)	22:39–46	14:32–42	26:36–46
Arrest	22:47–53	14:43–50	26:47–56
Peter's denials	22:54–62	14:66–72	26:69–75
Taunting Jesus	22:63–65	14:65	26:67–68
Trial before High Priest	22:66–71	14:53–64	26:57–66

Trial before Pilate	23:1–5	15:1–5	27:1–2, 11–14
Jesus sent to Herod	23:6–12	--	--
Barabbas chosen	23:13–25	15:6–15	27:15–26
Simon of Cyrene	23:26	15:21	27:32
Don't cry for me	23:27–31	--	--
Crucifixion	23:32–33	15:22, 27	27:33, 38
Father, forgive them	23:34a	--	--
Dividing his clothes	23:34b	15:24	27:35
Taunting Jesus	23:35–37	15:29–32	27:39–44
Inscription of charge	23:38	15:26	27:37
Thief on the cross	23:39–43	--	--
Darkness	23:44	15:33	27:45
Curtain torn	23:45	15:38	27:51
Into your hands….	23:46a	--	--
Death	23:46b	15:37	27:50
Centurion confession	23:47	15:39	27:54

Crowds beat chests	23:48	--	--
Women watching	23:49	15:40–41	27:55–56
Burial	23:50–56	15:42–47	27:57–61
Empty Tomb	24:1–8	16:1–8	28:1–8
Women report to apostles	24:9–11	16:9–11	
Peter investigates	24:12	--	
Road to Emmaus	24:13–32	16:12	
Comparing notes	24:33–35	16:13	
Appearance to the XII	24:36–49	16:14–18	28:16–20
Ascension	24:50–51	16:19	
Christian community	24:52–53	16:20	

GLOSSARY

Apocryphal. An ancient religious (Jewish or Christian) writing that is not a part of the Hebrew Bible or the traditional (27-book) New Testament.

Benedictus. A Latin word meaning "blessed" and the traditional title of Zechariah's prayer of praise in Luke 1:68–79, based on the first word of the prayer in Latin.

Codex. Referring to a book format such as a modern book, where the reader advances through the book by turning pages—as opposed to a scroll (= book roll).

Dead Sea Scrolls. These scrolls were discovered in the 1940s and 1950s in caves near a settlement called Qumran, on the northwest shore of the Dead Sea, about 20 miles east of Jerusalem.

Euangelion. A Greek word basically meaning "good news." This Greek word gives us the English word "evangelism" (and related words).

Haftarah. A Jewish synagogue service features a reading from the Torah and a reading from the Prophets. This second reading, the one of the prophets, is called the Haftarah, a Hebrew word meaning "taking leave."

Hebrew Scripture. The Hebrew Bible. The Old Testament.

LXX. This is an abbreviation for Septuagint, the Greek translation of the Old Testament. The word "Septuagint" comes from the Latin septuaginta, "seventy," and refers to the legend of the translation of the Old Testament into Greek by seventy(-two) Jewish sages. The abbreviation LXX is the Roman numeral for seventy.

Magnificat. A Latin word meaning "magnifies," and the traditional title for Mary's song in Luke 1:46–55, named for the first word of the song in Latin.

Marcan Priority. A theory that Mark was the first Gospel written.

Metanoia. A Greek word meaning "repentance."

Mishnah. This rabbinic document is usually dated to around AD 200, though it contains some traditions going back long before that time, some perhaps from the time of Jesus or before. It is arranged as a group of sixty-three tractates. To find something in the Mishnah, you first have to open it to the right tractate, just like when you want to find something in the Bible you first have to open to the right book. Each tractate is divided into chapters and small paragraphs (called mishnahs, but you can also think of each paragraph as like a verse).

Pentateuch. See Torah.

Q-Hypothesis. Educated guesswork that states that there might have been an early collection of sayings of Jesus that Matthew and Mark might have used in writing their gospels.

Qumran community. This is the community responsible for the Dead Sea Scrolls.

Septuagint. See LXX above.

Shema. This Hebrew word meaning "hear" is the traditional Jewish name for a series of biblical passages, the first of which is Deut 6:4–9, which begins: "Hear [shema], O Israel, YHWH your God is one YHWH." Jews traditionally recite the Shema every day, morning and evening.

Synoptic gospels. The gospels of Matthew, Mark, and Luke are referred to as the synoptic Gospels because they include many of the same stories, often in a similar sequence and in similar or sometimes identical wording.

Synoptic Problem. Most scholars who have studied the Synoptic Gospels have concluded that they must be dependent on each other somehow, since they often tell the same stories in the very same words. The "Problem" is—how to explain their similarities? Is it because Matthew used Mark as a source, and Luke used Matthew and Mark as sources? Or is it because Matthew and Luke both independently used Mark as a source alongside another source, now lost, that we can all Q? Or is there some other explanation?

Talmud. The Talmud is the chief work of rabbinic literature. It is a commentary on the Mishnah. Whereas the Mishnah is written in Hebrew, the commentary is written in Aramaic. There are actually two Talmuds, one from Jerusalem, completed perhaps in the early fifth century AD, and one from Babylon, completed perhaps around the sixth century AD. Whenever someone simply mentions "the Talmud," they are invariably referring to the Babylonian Talmud, which is much larger than the Jerusalem Talmud and traditionally much more authoritative. The Talmud is referenced according to the tractate name (like the Mishnah) and the page number and page side (e.g., 18a = page 18, side a) of the "Vilna Shas," i.e., the edition of the Talmud printed in Vilna, Lithuania in the 1870s and 1880s and still commonly reprinted.

Tax Collector. In the ancient world, tax collectors were assigned a quota and could pocket whatever amount they collected above their quota. The system easily led to corruption.

Torah. This Hebrew term meaning "instruction" or, sometimes, "law," is the traditional Jewish designation for the first five books of the Bible, the Torah of Moses (i.e., the Pentateuch).

Yahweh. This is the probable pronunciation for the name of the God of Israel, which appears six thousand times in the Hebrew Bible. But the Hebrew Bible spells this name with consonants only (YHWH).

YHWH. This is an English rendering of God's name as revealed to Moses at the burning bush (Exod 3:14). Hebrew has traditionally not been written with vowels, so that is why people often leave the vowels out of this word.

BIBLIOGRAPHY

Allison, Dale C. Jr. "Mark 12.28–31 and the Decalogue." Pages 270–78 in *The Gospels and the Scriptures of Israel*. Edited by Craig A. Evans and W. Richard Stegner. Sheffield: Sheffield Academic, 1994.

Anderson, Kevin L. "Resurrection," Pages 774-89 in *Dictionary of Jesus and the Gospels*. 2nd ed. Edited by Joel B. Green. Downers Grove, IL: IVP, 2013.

Bates, Matthew W. *Gospel Allegiance: What Faith in Jesus Misses for Salvation in Christ*. Grand Rapids: Brazos, 2019.

Bauckham, Richard. *Gospel of Glory: Major Themes in Johannine Theology*. Grand Rapids: Baker, 2015.

_____. *Gospel Women: Studies of the Named Women in the Gospels*. Grand Rapids: Eerdmans, 2002.

_____. "The Lukan Genealogy of Jesus." Pages 315–73 in *Jude and the Relatives of Jesus in the Early Church*. London: T&T Clark, 1990.

Beasley-Murray, G. R. *Baptism in the New Testament.*
    Paternoster, 1972; Repr. Eugene, OR: Wipf and Stock,
    2006.

Beilby, James, and Paul R. Eddy, eds. *The Nature of the
    Atonement: Four Views.* Downers Grove, IL: IVP, 2006.

Bird, Michael F. "Sin, Sinner." Pages 863–69 in *Dictionary of
    Jesus and the Gospels.* 2nd ed. Edited by Joel B. Green.
    Downers Grove, IL: IVP, 2013.

Black, Allen. *Mark.* The College Press NIV Commentary.
    Joplin, MO: College Press, 1995.

Black, Mark C. *Luke.* The College Press NIV Commentary.
    Joplin, MO: College Press, 1996.

Bond, Helen K. "Pontius Pilate." Pages 679–80 in *Dictionary of
    Jesus and the Gospels.* 2nd ed. Edited by Joel B. Green.
    Downers Grove, IL: IVP, 2013.

Brand, Miryam T. "1 Enoch." Translated by Michaeld Knibb.
    Pages 1359–1452 in *Outside the Bible: Ancient Jewish
    Writings Related to Scripture.* 3 vols. Edited by L.H.
    Feldman et al. Philadelphia: JPS, 2013.

Burridge, Richard. *What Are the Gospels? A Comparison with
    Graeco-Roman Biography.* 25th Anniversary Edition.
    Waco, TX: Baylor University Press, 2018.

Buttrick, David. *Speaking Parables: A Homiletic Guide.*
    Louisville: WJK, 2000.

Cadbury, Henry J. *The Making of Luke-Acts.* 2nd ed. London: SPCK, 1958.

Caird, G. B. *Saint Luke.* Baltimore: Penguin, 1963.

Carey, Greg. *Luke: All Flesh Shall See God's Salvation: An Introduction and Study Guide.* T&T Clark Study Guides to the New Testament. London: Bloomsbury, 2017.

Chapman, David W. *Ancient Jewish and Christian Perceptions of Crucifixion.* Tübingen: Mohr Siebeck, 2008; Grand Rapids: Baker, 2010.

Chapman, David W., and Eckhard J. Schnabel. *The Trial and Crucifixion of Jesus.* Tübingen: Mohr Siebeck, 2015.

Cicero. *Pro Lege Manilia; Pro Caecina; Pro Cluentio; Pro Rabirio Perduellionis.* Translation by H. Grose Hodge. Loeb Classical Library. Cambridge, MA: Harvard University Press, 1927.

Cohan, Shaye J. D. "Is 'Proselyte Baptism' Mentioned in the Mishnah? The Interpretation of *M. Pesahim* 8.8 (= *M. Eduyot* 5.2)" Pages 278–92 in *Pursuing the Text: Studies in Honor of Ben Zion Wacholder on the Occasion of His Seventieth Birthday.* Edited by John C. Reeves and John Kampen. Sheffield: Sheffield Academic, 1994.

Cohen, Shaye J. D. *The Beginnings of Jewishness: Boundaries, Varieties, Uncertainties.* Berkeley: University of California Press, 1999.

Collins, Adela Yarbro, and John J. Collins. *King and Messiah as Son of God: Divine, Human, and Angelic Messianic*

Figures in Biblical and Related Literature. Grand Rapids: Eerdmans, 2008.

Collins, John J. *The Scepter and the Star: Messianism in Light of the Dead Sea Scrolls*, 2nd ed. Grand Rapids: Eerdmans, 2010.

Cook, John Granger. *Crucifixion in the Mediterranean World.* Tübingen: Mohr Siebeck, 2014.

Danker, Frederick William, ed., *A Greek-English Lexicon of the New Testament and Other Early Christian Literature.* 3rd ed. Chicago: University of Chicago Press, 2000.

Davies, W. D., and D. C. Allison. *The Gospel according to Saint Matthew.* 3 vols. International Critical Commentary. London: T&T Clark, 1988–1997.

de Jonge, M., ed. *The Testaments of the Twelve Patriarchs: A Critical Edition of the Greek Text.* Leiden: Brill, 1978.

_____. "The Two Great Commandments in the Testaments of the Twelve Patriarchs." Pages 141–59 in *Pseudepigrapha of the Old Testament as Part of Christian Literature: The case of The* Testaments of the Twelve Patriarchs *and the Greek* Life of Adam and Eve. Leiden: Brill, 2003.

Donaldson, Amy M. "Explicit References to New Testament Variant Readings among Greek and Latin Church Fathers." 2 vols., PhD diss., University of Notre Dame, 2009. (available online: https://curate.nd.edu/show/5712m615k50).

Downs, David J. "Economics." Pages 219-26 in *Dictionary of Jesus and the Gospels*. 2nd ed. Edited by Joel B. Green. Downers Grove, IL: IVP, 2013.

Driver, S. R., and Ad. Neubauer. *The Fifty-Third Chapter of Isaiah according to the Jewish Interpreters*. vol. 2: *Translations*. Oxford: James Parker, 1877.

Ehrman, Bart D. *The Orthodox Corruption of Scripture: The Effect of Early Christological Controversies on the Text of the New Testament*. 2nd ed. Oxford: Oxford University Press, 2011.

Evans, C. F. *Saint Luke*. TPI New Testament Commentaries. Philadelphia: Trinity Press International, 1990.

Feldman, Louis H. *Flavius Josephus: Judean Antiquities 1–4*. Leiden: Brill, 2000.

Ferguson, Everett. *Baptism in the Early Church: History, Theology, and Liturgy in the First Five Centuries*. Grand Rapids: Eerdmans, 2009.

Foakes Jackson, F. J. and Kirsopp Lake, eds., *The Beginnings of Christianity*. Part 1: *The Acts of the Apostles*. Vol. 2: *Prolegomena II: Criticism*. London: Macmillan, 1922.

Gallagher, Edmon L., and John D. Meade. *The Biblical Canon Lists from Early Christianity: Texts and Analysis*. Oxford: Oxford University Press, 2017.

_____. *The Book of Exodus: Explorations in Christian Theology*. Florence, AL: HCU Press, 2020.

_____. *The Sermon on the Mount: Explorations in Christian Practice.* Cypress Bible Study Series. Florence, AL: HCU Press, 2021.

_____. *The Translation of the Seventy: History, Reception, and Contemporary Use of the Septuagint.* Abilene, TX: ACU Press, 2021.

Gibson, Mel, and Benedict Fitzgerald, directors. *The Passion of the Christ.* Icon Productions, 2004.

Graves, Michael. "Languages of Palestine." Pages 484–92 in *Dictionary of Jesus and the Gospels.* 2nd ed. Edited by Joel B. Green. Downers Grove, IL: IVP, 2013.

Green, Joel B. *The Theology of the Gospel of Luke.* Cambridge: Cambridge University Press, 1995.

_____. "'Was It Not Necessary for the Messiah to Suffer These Things and Enter into His Glory?' The Significance of Jesus' Death for Luke's Soteriology." Pages 71–85 in *The Spirit and Christ in the New Testament and Christian Theology: Essays in Honor of Max Turner.* Edited by I. Howard Marshall, Volker Rabens, and Cornelis Bennema. Grand Rapids: Eerdmans, 2012.

Gregory, Andrew. *The Reception of Luke and Acts in the Period before Irenaeus: Looking for Luke in the Second Century.* WUNT; Tübingen: Mohr Siebeck, 2003.

Gregory, Andrew F., and C. Kavin Rowe, eds. *Rethinking the Unity and Reception of Luke and Acts.* Columbia, SC: University of South Carolina Press, 2010.

Goodacre, Mark. "Scripturalization in Mark's Crucifixion Narrative." Pages 33–47 in *The Trial and Death of Jesus: Essays on the Passion Narrative in Mark*. Edited by Geert van Oyen and Tom Shepherd. Leuven: Peeters, 2006.

Harrison, George. "Taxman." (1966).

Hays, Richard B. *Echoes of Scripture in the Gospels*. Waco, TX: Baylor University Press, 2016.

Hengel, Martin. *Crucifixion in the Ancient World and the Folly of the Message of the Cross*. London: SCM, 1977.

_____. *The Four Gospels and the One Gospel of Jesus Christ*. Harrisburg, PA: Trinity Press International, 2000.

Hollander, H. W., and M. de Jonge. *The Testaments of the Twelve Patriarchs: A Commentary*. Leiden: Brill, 1985.

Irenaeus. *Against Heresies*. Quoted from Henry J. Cadbury. "The Tradition." Pages 209–64 in *Beginnings of Christianity*. Edited by F. J. Foakes Jackson and Kirsopp Lake. 5 vols. London: Macmillan, 1922.

Jongkind, Dirk. *An Introduction to the Greek New Testament Produced at Tyndale House, Cambridge*. Wheaton, IL: Crossway, 2019.

Josephus. *Jewish Antiquities, Books XVIII–XIX*. Translated by Louis H. Feldman. Loeb Classical Library. Cambridge, MA: Harvard University Press, 1965.

Josephus. *The Jewish War, Books I–II.* Translation by H. St. J. Thackeray. Loeb Classical Library. Cambridge, MA: Harvard University Press, 1927.

Josephus. Translated by Henry St. J. Thackeray et al. 10 vols. Loeb Classical Library. Cambridge: Harvard University Press, 1926-1965.

Kähler, Martin. *The So-Called Historical Jesus and the Historic, Biblical Christ.* Philadelphia: Fortress, 1964.

_____. *The So-Called Historical Jesus and the Historic, Biblical Christ.* Philadelphia: Fortress, 1964. The original German work (p. 33 note 1; available at Hathi Trust: https://catalog.hathitrust.org/Record/008725787) was published in 1892 (second edition, 1896, from which the English translation was made—see p. 80 note 1; https://catalog.hathitrust.org/Record/008725678).

Levenson, Jon D. *Resurrection and the Restoration of Israel: The Ultimate Victory of the God of Life.* New Haven, CT: Yale University Press, 2006.

Levine, Amy-Jill. *Short Stories by Jesus: The Enigmatic Parables of a Controversial Rabbi.* New York: Harper, 2014.

Levine, Lee I. *The Ancient Synagoague: The First Thousand Years.* New Haven, CT: Yale University Press, 2000.

Magness, Jodi. *The Archaeology of Qumran and the Dead Sea Scrolls.* 2nd ed. Grand Rapids: Eerdmans, 2021.

Marshall, I. Howard. *The Gospel of Luke: A Commentary on the Greek Text*. New International Greek Text Commentary. Grand Rapids: Eerdmans, 1978.

McGowan, Andrew B. *Ancient Christian Worship: Early Church Practices in Social, Historical, and Theological Perspective*. Grand Rapids: Baker, 2013.

Metzger, Bruce M. *A Textual Commentary on the Greek New Testament*. 2nd ed. New York: United Bible Societies, 1994.

Milik, J. T., ed. *Les Grottes de Murabba'ât*, Discoveries in the Judaean Desert 2. Oxford: Oxford University Press, 1961.

The Mishnah. Translated by Herbert Danby. Oxford: Oxford University Press, 1933.

New English Translation of the Septuagint

Origen. *The Commentary of Origen on the Gospel of St Matthew*. Translated by Ronald E. Heine. 2 vols. Oxford: Oxford University Press, 2018.

Philo. *On the Special Laws*. Translated by F. H. Colson. Loeb Classical Library. Cambridge, MA: Harvard University Press, 1937.

Phylactère C (4Q130). Edited by J. T. Milik. Page 55 in *Qumran Grotte 4, II*. Discoveries in the Judaean Desert 6. Oxford: Oxford University Press, 1977.

Pitre, Brant J. "Apocalypticism and Apocalyptic Teaching." Pages 23–33 in *Dictionary of Jesus and the Gospels*. 2nd ed. Edited by Joel B. Green. Downers Grove, IL: IVP, 2013.

Pummer, Reinhard. *The Samaritans: A Profile*. Grand Rapids: Eerdmans, 2016.

Rowe, C. Kavin. *Early Narrative Christology: The Lord in the Gospel of Luke*. Berlin: de Gruyter, 2006.

Samuelson, Gunnar. *Crucifixion in Antiquity: An Inquiry into the Background and Significance of the New Testament Terminology of Crucifixion*. Tübingen: Mohr Siebeck, 2011; rev. ed. 2013.

Sanders, E. P. *Jesus and Judaism*. Philadelphia: Fortress, 1985.

_____. *Judaism, Practice and Belief, 63 BCE–66 CE*. Philadelphia: TPI, 1992.

Schmidt, T. E. "Taxation: Jewish." Pages 1163–66 in *Dictionary of New Testament Background*. Edited by Craig A. Evans and Stanley E. Porter. Downers Grove, IL: IVP, 2000.

Schürer, Emil. *The History of the Jewish People in the Age of Jesus Christ*. Rev. ed. 4 vols. Edinburgh: T&T Clark, 1973–87.

Seneca. *Epistles 93–124*. Translation by Richard M. Gummere. Loeb Classical Library. Cambridge, MA: Harvard University Press, 1925.

Sommer, Benjamin D. *The Bodies of God and the World of Ancient Israel*. Cambridge: Cambridge University Press, 2009.

Stanton, Graham. *The Gospels and Jesus*. 2nd ed. Oxford: Oxford University Press, 2002.

_____. *Jesus and Gospel*. Cambridge: Cambridge University Press, 2004.

Tacitus. *The Histories and The Annals*. Translated by Clifford M. Moore and John Jackson. 4 vols. Loeb Classical Library. Cambridge: Harvard University Press, 1937.

Tsedaka, Benyamin. *The Israelite Samaritan Version of the Torah: First English Translation Compared with the Masoretic Version*. Grand Rapids: Eerdmans, 2013.

Tuckett, Christopher M. *Luke*. New Testament Guides. Sheffield: JSOT Press, 1996.

Udoh, Fabian E. *To Caesar What Is Caesar's: Tribute, Taxes, and Imperial Administration in Early Roman Palestine (63 B.C.E.–70 C.E.)*. Providence, RI: Brown Judaic Studies, 2005.

VanderKam, James C. *From Joshua to Caiaphas: High Priests after the Exile*. Minneapolis: Fortress, 2004.

Wise, Michael, Martin Abegg, Jr., and Edward Cook. *The Dead Sea Scrolls: A New Translation*. San Francisco: HarperSanFrancisco, 2005.

Wright, N. T. *Jesus and the Victory of God.* Minneapolis: Fortress, 1996.

_____. *The Resurrection of the Son of God.* Minneapolis: Fortress, 2003.

Journal Articles

Brown, Colin. "What Was John the Baptist Doing?" *Bulletin for Biblical Research* 7 (1997): 37–50.

Carlson, Stephen C. "The Accommodations of Joseph and Mary in Bethlehem: κατάλυμα in Luke 2.7." *New Testament Studies* 56 (2010): 326–42. http://www.hypotyposeis.org/papers/Carlson%202010%20NTS.pdf.

Carrier, Richard. "The Prospect of a Christian Interpolation in Tacitus, *Annals* 15.44." *Vigiliae Christianae* 68 (2014): 264–83.

Carter, Warren. "Are There Imperial Texts in the Class? Intertextual Eagles and Matthean Eschatology as 'Lights Out' Time for Imperial Rome." *Journal of Biblical Literature* 122 (2003): 467–87.

Cosgrove, Charles H. "A Woman's Unbound Hair in the Greco-Roman World, with Special Reference to the Story of the 'Sinful Woman' in Luke 7:36–50." *Journal of Biblical Literature* 124 (2005).

Donahue, John R. "Tax Collectors and Sinners: An Attempt at Identification." *Catholic Biblical Quarterly* 33 (1971): 39–61.

Friedman, Richard Elliott. "Love Your Neighbor: Only Israelites or Everyone?" *Biblical Archaeology Review* 40.5 (September/October 2014), 48–52.

Gathercole, Simon J. "The Titles of the Gospels in the Earliest New Testament Manuscripts." *Zeitschrift für die neutestamentliche Wissenschaft* 104 (2013): 33–76, available online: http://khazarzar.skeptik.net/books/titles.pdf.

Gignilliat, Mark S. "God Speaks Hebrew: The Hebrew Text and Septuagint in the Search for the Christian Bible." *Pro Ecclesia* 25 (2016): 154–72.

Harley, Felicity. "Crucifixion in Roman Antiquity: The State of the Field." *Journal of Early Christian Studies* 27 (2019): 303–23.

Hutson, Christopher R. "Enough for What? Playacting Isaiah 53 in Luke 22:35–38." *Restoration Quarterly* 55 (2013): 36–43.

Juza, Ryan P. "One of the Days of the Son of Man: A Reconsideration of Luke 17:22." *Journal of Biblical Literature* 135 (2016): 575–95.

Matson, David Lertis. "Double-Edged: The Meaning of the Two Swords in Luke 22:35–38." *Journal of Biblical Literature* 137 (2018): 463–80.

McNutt, Jennifer Powell, and Amy Beverage Peeler. "The First Christian." *Christianity Today* (Nov 22, 2019).

Peterson, Jeffrey. "The First and Second Tables of the Law in the New Testament." *Christian Studies* 23 (2009): 47–58.

Stanglin, Keith D. "Christ's Presence and the Thing Signified in the Lord's Supper." *Christian Studies* 30 (2018): 7–24.

Wenkel, David H. "When the Apostles Became Kings: Ruling and Judging the Twelve Tribes of Israel in the Book of Acts." *Biblical Theology Bulletin* 42 (2012): 119–28.

INTERNET SOURCES

Bible Project video.
"The Resurrection of Jesus: Luke 24."

"Shema/Listen."
(https://bibleproject.com/explore/video/shema-listen/).

Craddock, Fred. "When the Roll Is Called Down Here." YouTube.

Craig, William Lane. *Reasonable Faith.*
(https://www.reasonablefaith.org/).

Dudley, Chris. "Money Lessons Learned from Pro Atheletes' Financial Fouls." *CNBC.com* (May 14, 2018).

Goodacre, Mark. "Was Jesus Born in a Stable?" NTPod (https://podacre.blogspot.com/), episode 46. (Dec 15, 2010).

Google Images. "Reclining at table."

Levine, Amy-Jill. "The Jewish Origins of the Christmas Story." *TheTorah.com* (2019).

Marcus, Yosef. "What Is the Significance of the Four Cups of Wine?" *Chabad.org.*

NET Bible. (netbible.org)

Samaritan Update online. http://www.thesamaritanupdate.com/.

Sachs, Honor. "The Dark Side of Our Genealogy Craze." *Washington Post.* (Dec 13, 2019).

YouTube Videos

"Linus Christmas Speech."

"VeggieTales: Busy, Busy."

Zarephath. https://www.bibleplaces.com/zarephath/.

Wikipedia articles.

"Annio da Viterbo."

"Aquila (Roman)."

"Cleopas."

"11Q13."

"Eye of a Needle."

"4Q521."

"Farrer Hypothesis."

"George S. Patton's Speech to the Third Army."

"Golden Rule."

"Haftarah."

"Herodian Tetrarchy."

"Jehohanan."

"John (given name)."

"Marcan Priority."

"Pilate Stone."

"Ponce de León."

"Q Source."

"Road to Emmaus Appearance."

"Roman Procurator Coinage."

"Shema Yisrael."

"Spikenard."

"Tefillin."

"Ten Commandments."

"Theotokos."

"Two-Gospel Hypothesis."

"Vienne, Isère."

"Weekly Torah Portion."

"Yeshua."

Subject Index

Old Testament
Genesis

3	290	12:1–13	240
4:24	84	12:6	233
5:24	84	12:7	240
6:1–4	86	12:13	240
12:3	37	12:15	240
17:17	31	12:39	240
17:19	29	13:2	40
18	33	13:7–10	240–241
22:2	193	13:8	241
22:18	37	13:19	211
29:31	28	13:21–22	102
30:22–24	28	14	232
33:4	160	14:19–20	102
38:12	137	15:13	288
38:20	137	24	33, 243
39	154	24:5	243
50:25	211	24:8	243–244

Exodus

		24:10	33
3:14	367	29:12	243
6:6	288	**Leviticus**	
7:5	42	4:7	243
9:16	42	4:18	243
10:21–29	338	4:25	243
11:2	137	8:6	65

Credits

Also by Ed Gallagher

The Book of Exodus: Explorations in Christian Theology (Cypress Bible Studies Series) HCU Press 2019

The Sermon on the Mount: Explorations in Christian Practice (Cypress Bible Studies Series) HCU Press 2021

The Christian Life: Chapters for Bible Teachers Cypress Publications 2021

Jesus the Christ: Chapters for Bible Teachers Cypress Publications 2021

The Translation of the Seventy: History, Reception, and Contemporary Use of the Septuagint. Abilene, TX: ACU Press, 2021.

Gallagher, Edmon L., and John D. Meade. *The Biblical Canon Lists from Early Christianity: Texts and Analysis.* Oxford: Oxford University Press, 2017.